'Somewhere in Blood Soaked France'

Never More

On fame's eternal camping ground
Their silent tents are spread
And glory guards in Solemn sound
The bivouac of the dead

'Tis night far down our Northern Glens
The autumn breezes sigh
Afar the mountains echo back
The curlew's lonely cry
The river onwards flows the way
Of centuries before
But tonight the waters seem to sob and whisper 'Never More'

The drums of death are sounding across the Northern wave
And there's weeping 'mong the Highland Homes
For our beloved brave
For those who knew and loved those hills
In boyhood days of yore
For those who died for home and King
Amid the battles roar

Ah! Where are now our kilted lads
So handsome brave and grand
Who marched away for honour's sake
And love of this far land
'Tis o'er a strip of blue
Somewhere in blood soaked France
They sleep the ever lasting sleep
Behind the great advance

Elsie Spence Rae Banff, 7 November 1915
(Reproduced with permission of
Press and Journal Newspapers, Aberdeen)

'SOMEWHERE IN BLOOD SOAKED FRANCE'

The Diary of Corporal Angus Mackay, Royal Scots, Machine Gun Corps 1914–1917

Edited by Alasdair Sutherland

SPELLMOUNT

This book is dedicated to all soldiers killed at war fighting for their country.

The author wishes to thank the family of Angus Mackay for allowing him to write this book from the diaries which are now in the possession of Mrs Dorothy Johnson, St Andrews, Scotland.

First published 2011 by Spellmount, an imprint of
The History Press
The Mill, Brimscombe Port
Stroud, Gloucestershire, GL5 2QG
www.thehistorypress.co.uk

British Library Cataloguing in Publication Data.
A catalogue record for this book is available from the British Library.

ISBN 978 0 7524 6446 6

Typesetting and origination by The History Press
Printed in the EU for The History Press.

Contents

Introduction

In June 1992, I visited the First World War battlefields in Belgium and northern France with my family; we had gone in search of our relative, Private Angus Sutherland of the 8th Battalion Seaforth Highlanders, killed in action on 23 April 1917, during the Battle of Arras. His battalion was attacking the village of Guemappe when he was killed; he is buried in a war grave near where he fell in Guemappe British Cemetery, Plot 1, Row B, Grave 11 alongside many of his comrades who fell that day.

My first real encounter with the First World War was at Farr Junior Secondary School, as I sat in my History 'O' Level class. As I listened to our teacher Emily Campbell talk about the battles at Ypres, Passchendaele and the Somme, I looked at a picture of a soldier standing in a trench covered in mud with a smile on his face. I always looked at that photograph and wondered what he had to smile about; over the years I have learned more about the Great War and have found the answer to that question.

When I left school I became a soldier myself, and just like the one in that photograph I have stood, covered in mud in a muddy trench in the pouring rain with a smile on my face. The only difference between the soldier in the photograph and I was that no one was trying to kill me; he was involved in the most terrible war ever seen, when industrialised murder was inflicted by man on fellow man in the fields of France and Flanders.

Many times during my twelve years of service I wondered how I would survive during war, but I never found out, as those years were ones of peace and stability in Europe. My comrades and I were never called upon to fight because our enemies were held at bay by the nuclear threat. The Russian armoured columns we were trained to fight never came, the chemical and biological weapons we learned to combat were never used against us. I never found out what I would have done if I had been subjected to heavy shelling or walked into machine-gun fire, watching as my mates fell dead and wounded all around me. Would I have cracked under the strain of it all or would I have been a hero?

As I walked around the battlefields in 1992 those names from my school years returned, the city of Ypres, the hell of the Somme and the mud and misery of Passchendaele, I wondered if anyone from my home village of Tongue in the Highlands of Scotland had walked this way before me. I looked in the museums, at the huge war cemeteries, at all the names carved on the battlefield memorials. I did not realise I was following in the footsteps of the man who had kept a remarkable diary. I was given the diary to read by Mrs Dorothy Johnson, as I researched my first book *Never More*, and I was fascinated by the exploits of her relative Angus Mackay. It was a definite link to the past and a living document recording one of history's defining moments, an insight into the worst war ever fought.

Corporal Angus Mackay, who served in the 1st/5th Battalion of the Royal Scots and in the 88th Brigade, 29th Division Machine Gun Corps, was there over 70 years before me and had fought in the all the battles I had learned about in school, including the hellish first day of the Battle on the Somme at Beaumont-Hamel. This was a man who had experienced all the things I had thought about as a soldier and much much more. He was a Territorial Army volunteer, who fought in the broiling heat of the trenches in Gallipoli against the fierce Turkish Army and then served all over the Western Front in France. He served in the trenches from May 1915 until April 1917, when he was severely wounded and taken prisoner near Monchy le Preux in France. His diary entries stop the day before he entered the trenches for the final time, to take part in the attack that led to his fatal wounding and death in a prisoner of war camp in Germany.

Soldiers in the First World War were not allowed to keep diaries, in case they were captured and the enemy found secret information. They rarely kept a daily log of their activities, often just snippets written in journals, in letters home or on scraps of paper. Angus Mackay's diary is unique in that it gives an almost day-by-day account of his life from the time he enlisted until he was captured.

This book gives us an insight into the life of the soldiers had at the front lines during the First World War. It was not always a life of death and destruction but often one of boredom, comradeship and doing your duty alongside your mates until the war was won. The suffering of soldiers who are named on war memorials all over this country must never be forgotten, their deeds must live on in history to ensure future generations never have to suffer as they did.

This is the story of one soldier's life in the first truly global war ever fought; it is only one amongst the 9 million stories of men from every side who perished between 4 August 1914 and 11 November 1918. Of the over 70 million men mobilised in armies across the world, one man in eight was killed or died whilst on active service.

Glossary

Archies	heavy machine guns
brag	card game
bully	bully beef
C & R	Column of Route
C.O.	Commanding Officer
Ensign	Highland newspaper
F.M.O.	Field Marching Order
furlough	leave
Gold Flake	cigarette brand
G.P.	gun position
H.E.	high explosive
kilo	kilometre
MD	Medicine and Discharge
M.G.	machine gun
O.C.	Officer Commanding
P.C.	postcard
P.J.	*Press and Journal*
pom-pom	[anti aircraft] gun
tucker	food

1

The Road to War

Angus Mackay was born on 18 August 1895, the ninth child of Alexander and Isabella Mackay of 'Holding 162', Scullomie, Tongue, Sutherlandshire. Tongue is a small village in the Highlands of Scotland, about 100 miles north of Inverness; the small hamlet of Scullomie lies about three miles to the east of Tongue on the Thurso road. Angus's father Alexander was born in Scullomie on 21 January 1847, the second son of crofter John Mackay and his wife Margaret. Alexander came from a large family of five boys and two girls, all born in the middle of the nineteenth century. He went on to became an agricultural labourer in Tongue, before he married Isabella on 23 January 1880 at Strathtongue Free Church. Their first son John was born on 23 January 1881, and was followed by five more sons before Angus was born: Donald (June 1885); William (July 1888); George (July 1890); Hugh (July 1891); and Robert (May 1893). After Angus came Magnus (February 1898) and Sandy (April 1901). Their two daughters Dolina (March 1883) and Margaret (1886), both died in infancy.

The family lived in the small community of Scullomie on a small croft or farm, run by Alexander to supplement the wage he earned as a farm labourer in the Tongue area. Alexander was known around Tongue as Alex 'Bolt' due to his upright posture. Isabella worked in Tongue as a domestic servant, which helped with the small family income. Their home was a small cottage built beside the dirt road leading down from the Thurso road to Scullomie pier; half the building was given up for use as a 'byre' or stable, holding the family's livestock. Many crofters kept cows for milk and made their own cheese, in the form of sour crowdie, in a scullery at the side of the house. The crofters also kept a small flock of sheep and some chickens for eggs, to add to the family's meagre diet.

In the fields below the cottage Alex and his sons grew potatoes and root vegetables, both for the family's consumption and to sell on to other families or local shops in the area. The fields around the house were used to grow hay as feed for the family's livestock and their horse, their only means of transport. The family horse was once nearly lost when Alex took some rubbish and stones from the old byre beside the house, down to the rocks to dump them in the sea. As he prepared to dump the debris over the cliff onto the beach below, his horse and cart fell over the edge and disappeared from view. Believing his horse to have been killed in the accident, Alex returned home to inform his wife what had happened. When he finished telling her of his misfortune, he came out of his house to find the horse standing waiting for him, with the shafts of the cart still attached to its harness. Somehow the horse had survived the fall and made its way back home, having had a very lucky escape.

The family home had fine views out over the blue-green water of the Kyle of Tongue, towards the Rabbit Islands and the village of Melness beyond. The front of the Mackay house faced the small village of Coldbackie and the heather-covered Watch Hill, so called from the days when local men kept look out for marauding bands of Vikings approaching from the north. If any were sighted then warning beacons were lit to alert local people. Below the house the golden sands at Coldbackie beach nestled in the lee of the land beside the 'Rean' burn, where Angus and his brothers played as children, fishing for small trout and sticklebacks.

Out beyond the Kyle of Tongue the rocky cliffs of Island Rhoan can be seen jutting out into the Pentland Firth. The island had a thriving community of herring fishermen in the days before the First World War; Alex 'Bolt 'must have purchased some of their catch when the small herring boats docked at Scullomie Pier. The nearest school for Angus and his brothers was at the small community of Rhi-Tongue, about halfway to Tongue village. This involved a daily walk from Scullomie of about two miles each way.

The scenery and landscapes in and around Scullomie today are much the same as when Angus was a child, the houses are still spread out alongside the road leading down towards the pier, only there are fewer occupied houses today; many lie in ruins. Today there are modern roads, telephone poles and television aerials beside the houses, but the problems faced by young people then are faced by the young people of today. There was and still is, little employment in Tongue and its surrounding area; if you couldn't get a job in Burr's new shop or at Tongue Hotel, then crofting or fishing were the only ways to earn a living.

As Alex's sons grew and matured, they moved away from the family home in Scullomie to seek employment elsewhere, as there was precious little work beyond the small crofts. Many local men moved south into the Central Belt of Scotland seeking employment in ship building and other heavy industry, others travelled to take the Queen's shilling in the Army or became civil servants. The two eldest sons John and William moved to Leith, near Edinburgh, where they joined the Police; John finished his service with the rank of Detective Inspector. George joined the British Army, serving in Sierra Leone, West Africa and in the trenches of the Western Front. Whilst he was serving with the 83rd Siege Battery of the Royal Garrison Artillery in France, he won the Distinguished Conduct Medal for bravery. He was badly gassed in 1918 and this affected his health for many years after the war. He married Catherine Bell Macleod from Invernaver on 30 December 1919, and lived with his wife and eight children at The Manse, 4 Claremont Park, Leith. He died in 1955.

Hugh also joined the army and served in Serbia and India during the First World War. At the end of his military service he also moved to Leith, where he lived with his wife Ina and three children. Robert similarly moved to Leith, where he became a worker in the docks, dying in Windygates in Fife. Donald moved to New Zealand and joined the New Zealand Armed Forces at the outbreak of war.

Angus had two younger brothers: Magnus joined the army in 1914 aged sixteen, lying about his age to enlist in the Argyll and Sutherland Highlanders. Alexander (Sandy) left Scullomie in 1926 to work on a sheep station in the Australia outback; he died in Australia in 1952.

Some time prior to the outbreak of the First World War, Angus travelled from Scullomie to join his brothers John and William in Leith. He stayed at 61 Restalrig Road with John and managed to gain employment in Leith's huge dockyard; he also enlisted in the 1st/5th Battalion (Queens Edinburgh Rifles), Royal Scots. The 1st/5th Royal Scots was a Territorial Force (T/F) battalion with its drill hall close to Leith, where the battalion spent its time drilling and practising for its home defence role.

In early 1914 the threat of war hung over Europe. It was clear that war was coming and that all it would take was a spark, after a decade of tension. Many politicians anticipated the inevitable conflict with enthusiasm. Others knew the suffering it would bring. That spark was the death of a man in Sarajevo, one that would lead to the deaths of nine million others. The assassination of Archduke Franz Ferdinand by Gavrilo Principal on 28 June 1914, echoed around Europe. The Austrians threatened to invade Serbia; on 28 July Russia told Austria that any attempt to invade Serbia would mean war between the two countries. Germany then entered the war of words, saying that any war declared on Austria was a war on the German Empire.

On 31 July 1914 France came in on Russia's side and mobilised her army against Germany on 1 August. The stage for war was now set as both sides formed up their armies ready to fight. Great Britain promised to defend the neutrality of Belgium and any attack by Germany. When the Germans failed to accept these proposals, Britain had no option but to declare war and deploy her troops overseas.

The British War Office knew war was coming and had prepared for it well; the 1st/5th Battalion Royal Scots were mobilised by telephone at 5.30pm on 4 August 1914. Men began to arrive in the battalion drill hall at Forest Road at 7.30am on 5 August, other men reporting to the battalion war station in the

Maltings, at Moray Park in Lochend Road. The soldiers were issued with all their equipment including rifles, and stood to ready to join the British Expeditionary Force bound for France and Belgium.

Germany had declared war on Belgium on 4 August at 6.00am and invaded the country at 8.00am that day, quickly moving through Belgium towards Luxembourg and France. On 3 August the British Army had been officially ordered to mobilise, British Army unit commanders receiving detailed embarkation orders on 5 August with advance parties of the BEF secretly crossing to France to prepare assembly sites for the main body of the army on 7 August. The main BEF (80,000 men) then crossed to France on 12 August and began to march east from Amiens towards Belgium to meet the German attacks, making contact with the Germans at Mons in Belgium on 23 August.

The 1st/4th Royal Scots battalion remained in Forest Road and Lochend Road. They had a strength of 1250 men, made up of 800 on standby to move, the remainder being held in reserve. On 28 September 1914, the main battalion moved to the cavalry stables at Redford Barracks to join the Lothian Brigade, tasked with coastal defence east of Edinburgh.

As the BEF fought the German Army at Mons, Le Cateau and then at Battle of the Marne from 5–12 September, the 1st/5th Royal Scots deployed along the coast near Edinburgh. Battalion Headquarters was set up at Marine Gardens in Portobello; the remainder of the battalion was deployed on the coast east towards the town of Dunbar. Private Angus Mackay was deployed with part of 'W' Company to a blockhouse at Eskmouth near Musselburgh, where he remained for the whole of November and December 1914. The Scots Territorial units had been deployed on the coast in case of enemy invasion of the homeland. The soldiers in their blockhouses, bunkers and trenches would have also guarded against spies and Fifth Columnists coming ashore from enemy submarines, but their main enemy was the biting cold wind blowing in off the North Sea.

Over on the continent the regular soldiers of the BEF fought the enemy with their backs to the wall, around the city of Ypres in Belgium. In October, the Germans had began to move north from the river Marne in a race to the sea with the British; as the two armies moved the trench systems of the Western Front began to form.

The BEF fought desperate battles in the 'race to the sea', as they tried to stop the Germans taking the channel ports and the French coast. There were no reserves left by this time, and the BEF fought a frantic battle against massed German infantry attack; somehow the line was held and the British soldiers became known as the 'Old Contemptibles'. The nickname came from the German Kaiser's statement to his troops before the battle: he told his soldiers to attack and 'walk all over General French [the BEF Commander] and his contemptible little army.'

2

Gallipoli

The 1st/5th Royal Scots remained along the coast east of Edinburgh for the next five months, as the war in Belgium and France bogged down into the stalemate of trench warfare. The war plans of both sides had not been effective and lay in tatters. The Germans had failed to capture France with their Shlieffen Plan but had captured a large part of French territory. The British Army had virtually ceased to exist, losing over 50,000 men blocking the German Army from reaching the channel ports. Meanwhile the French Army was in primitive trenches stretching from the river Aisne south to the Swiss border.

In March 1915, as the British prepared to attack the Germans at Neuve Chapelle in France, the Commanding Officer of the 1st/5th Royal Scots received orders from the War Office to prepare for embarkation. The battalion was ordered to join the 29th Infantry Division 88th Brigade in Leamington, England and prepare to go overseas to fight in the Middle East.

The 1st/5th Royal Scots left Portobello and marched to Waverley Station in Edinburgh on 8 March 1915, through crowds of people cheering them on their way. The pipes and drums led the battalion; the baggage train followed on at the rear. On 10 March the battalion arrived by troop train at Leamington Spa in Warwickshire and was billeted with the local population; Angus Mackay was placed with a local family at 4 Knebworth Street. The placing of soldiers in civilian houses was common practice in the early days of the war as there were insufficient barracks to accommodate all the troops under training.

The 1st/5th Battalion's Territorial soldiers now began to train alongside their regular army counterparts in the 29th Division and soon attained a highly level of competency, putting them on a par with their highly trained opposite numbers. The days were spent carrying out route marches in full kit, improving rifle drill on the square and shooting on the firing range. The 29th Division was already very experienced, with most of its units drawn from the regular army stationed overseas; the division was under the command of Major-General A.J. Hunter-Weston and consisted of the following battalions arranged into brigades.

86th Brigade
2nd Royal Fusiliers
1st Lancashire Fusiliers
1st Royal Munster Fusiliers
1st Royal Dublin Fusiliers

87th Brigade
2nd South Wales Borderers
1st King's Own Scottish Borderers
1st Royal Inniskilling Fusiliers
1st Border

88th Brigade
2nd Hampshires
4th Worcester
1st Essex
1st/5th Royal Scots

As a division of the regular army the men of the 29th were not used to a battalion of territorial soldiers in their midst and it would have taken some time for Angus and his fellow Royal Scots to settle in. The regular battalions had all served abroad before the outbreak of war, mainly in India and the Far East: the Royal Munster Fusiliers had been in Lahore, the Dublin Fusiliers in Bangalore, the Inniskilling's at Secunderabad and the 4th Worcester in Malta.

Private Angus Mackay contracted measles in Leamington and spent the next twelve days in Heathcote Hospital; on his discharge he was found to be unfit for duty and was given leave. He spent his leave with his family in Scullomie and then visited his brothers in Edinburgh. He was not to be reunited with his battalion until 26 May, and they would go on to Gallipoli without him.

While Angus was on leave, his Divisional Commander received orders to proceed overseas. The British High Command had decided to attack Germany's ally Turkey, in an effort to protect the Suez Canal and break the deadlock of trench warfare in France. Lord Kitchener and the First Lord of the Admiralty, Winston Churchill, also wanted to open a supply route to Russia through the Dardanelles from the Mediterranean. The task was initially to be carried out by the Royal Navy and French Navy with no army support; there would be no need to draw troops away from the Western Front.

On 18 March 1915 a Franco-British naval force tried to force its way up the Dardanelles and into the Sea of Marmora, in an attempt to shell the Turkish capital

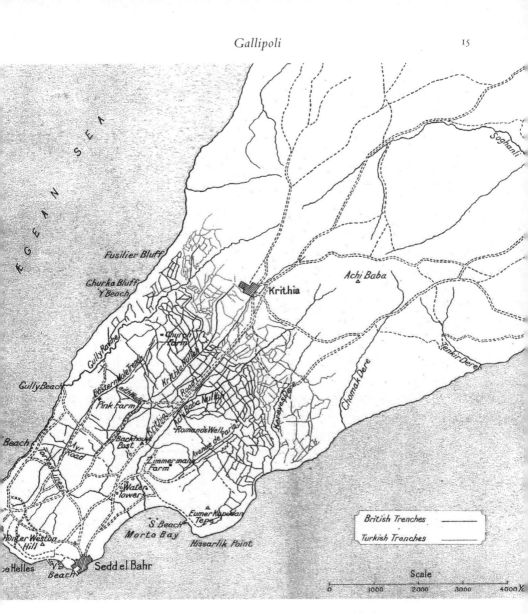

Constantinople. The attack failed resulting in the loss of two British and one French warships. Three other ships were also severely damaged by the mines laid along the strait by the Turkish defenders. When the War Office in London heard what had happened, the conclusion was reached that troops would be required to take the Gallipoli Peninsula, helping the naval force push on up the Dardanelle Strait. Australian and New Zealand troops in Egypt were put on standby to move to the Island of Lemnos in the Aegean, and a Mediterranean Expeditionary Force (MEF) was sent from England to assist with the task.

The 29th Division was reviewed near Dunchurch by the King, then left Leamington Spa on 20 March; the 1st/5th Royal Scots travelled to Avonmouth and were issued and fitted with Foreign Service helmets before boarding the troopships SS *Caledonia* and SS *Melville*. The battalion travelled to Egypt via Malta, joining up with the Australian and New Zealand Army Corps (ANZAC) as they trained near Suez. This made a force of over 70,000 men who were training for an attack which it was hoped would knock Turkey out of the war.

Once the battalion landed at Alexandria on 2 April 1915 it spent a few days recovering from the journey before embarking on seven small ships. It travelled to Mudros Bay on Lemnos Island, about 12 miles east of Gallipoli, to train in full kit for the forthcoming attack. For the next week the battalion practised descending rope ladders from ships into small boats.

On 25 April 1915 the British forces landed at the tip of the Gallipoli Peninsula; advance units of the 29th Infantry Division landed on Cape Helles in an attempt to capture the Kilid Bahr Plateau. Heavy casualties were sustained on 'V' Beach, as the first battalions ashore met withering fire from the Turkish defenders on the hills beyond the beach. 'V' Beach, east of the town of Sedd el Bahr, was very sandy and led up to an embankment below an old fort, which dominated the approaches from the sea.

The 1st/5th Royal Scots came ashore with the 88th Brigade, in the second wave of the attack formation. Soldiers found themselves going ashore in open boats, covered in the blood of men who had been hit as they tried to land on the beaches in the initial assault. As they landed on 'W' Beach, west of the main 29th Divisional landing area, the 88th Brigade found that they were totally unopposed by Turkish Forces.

The Royal Scots came ashore onto a beach of soft powdery sand about 350 yards wide, varying in width from 15 to 40 feet. The beach they stood on formed a perfect amphitheatre flanked by sheer inaccessible cliffs; the ground between ascended gradually up over sand dunes toward the lower levels of Achi Baba Ridge. Turkish troops had laid barbed wire on the beaches and were defending the area from trenches dug amongst the sand dunes. There were also redoubts built to the rear, so that Turkish snipers and riflemen could pick off the attackers as they scrambled through the wire.

The beaches were secure by the time the Royal Scots came ashore, so they were put to work unloading stores and ammunition. As the soldiers unloaded their transport ship, the SS *Dongola*, they did so in front of the gigantic battleship HMS *Queen Elizabeth*. Every discharge of the huge ship's guns made the transport ships dance and reel in the water, causing the men to stop work and watch as salvoes of shells crashed onto the Turkish positions up on the headland beyond.

On the first day of the Gallipoli campaign the 1st/5th Royal Scots came ashore without losing a man and dug in along the folds of land near the edge of the beach. Other units had not been so lucky and had suffered heavy casualties at the other landing sites. As the Scots lay in their trenches waiting for their orders to move, over 8,000 other soldiers came ashore on the beaches behind them. However, the force was without coherent command or objective; its commanders were still out on the ships in the bay.

The British, ANZAC and French forces fought stubbornly to get off the beaches and by nightfall on the first day, were trying to force their way up into the barren rocky scrubland beyond. A landing by Australian and New Zealand forces to the north of the British at Gaba Tepe was a brilliant success and the Allies now had a foothold on the Turkish mainland but were not yet secure.

Turkish forces now began to pour fire down onto the invaders in an attempt to drive the attacking force back into the sea. Only one mile of Turkish territory was secure by the end of the day, but the cost had been heavy with over a thousand men killed or wounded for each 100 yards of front line taken. A badly mauled British and ANZAC force now prepared to try and take the line forward.

On 26 April 1915 the Royal Scots were still in reserve trenches, viewing the ground they would have to attack over and then assault up to the Achi Baba Ridge high above. The slope in front of them rose steadily through numerous tree-filled hollows, where Turkish snipers and machine-gun teams lay waiting. Several dry watercourses, known as nullahs, furrowed the ground ahead, dominated by Turkish troops commanding the slope with their fields of fire.

The battalion was eventually moved into the front line on the afternoon of 27 April; W and X Companies made an advance of two miles and meeting no opposition dug in below the ridge. A brigade of French, who had landed on 'V' beach, came up into the front beside the British and swung the line right, halfway towards the village of Krithia. Turkish troops – badly demoralised by shattering naval gunfire – withdrew to new positions, just in front of the village.

At 8.00am the following morning, the 29th Division attacked an area to the right of Gully Ravine, straight into the heavily defended Turkish front line trench. The 1st/5th Royal Scots were deployed for the attack opposite Fir Tree Wood on Fir Tree Spur, just to the left of Krithia village, beneath the formidable Achi Baba Ridge.

As the attack was pressed home the battalion was quickly called forward and into the reserve trenches, then began to advance; they had only gone a short distance before the first casualties were taken. The adjutant Captain Hepburn was shot in the head and killed by a Turkish sniper; he died as he directed the battalion forwards one mile from Krithia village.

Combat in the front line trenches went on for four hours until the infantry, weighed down by their heavy equipment, were exhausted and could fight no more. The attack on the village of Krithia and Achi Baba Ridge had failed. The objectives were just beyond their grasp and the Allied forces were forced to pull back from ground they had taken with a heavy loss of life.

Supplies could not be brought up quickly enough to exploit the gains made, forcing the attacking troops to dig in until the beachhead was consolidated and a breakout achieved. The campaign was beginning to bog down into the stalemate of trench warfare, which would lead to heavy loss of life from both enemy action and disease.

The troops from both sides dug in amongst the hills, gullies and ravines of the peninsula; the trench lines were sometimes only yards apart. The conditions were horrendous as there was little food and less water; men were seen lying about in the dust gasping for a drink. It was only a matter of time before soldiers began to suffer from dysentery and disease, spread by the flies feeding off the dead from both sides that littered the no man's land between the trenches.

Turkish snipers, artillery fire and fanatical frontal attacks by enemy infantry battalions took a terrible toll on the Allied soldiers, as they tried to defend the narrow strip they held just inland from the beachhead. The Turks were proving to be tough fighters; in the hand-to-hand fighting as they defended their homeland from invasion, they died in their thousands as they bayonet charged the invader.

Two companies of the 1st/5th Royal Scots in the front line suffered heavy casualties; the battalion second in command Major Macdonald was wounded alongside many of the junior officers, the RSM F.J. Bailey was killed in action and the Commanding Officer Lieutenant-Colonel Wilson was wounded in the arm when the battalion was forced to withdraw. He then became detached from his men and was lucky not to be taken prisoner, rejoining the battalion later that night. Meanwhile the rest of the battalion, consisting of Y and Z companies, was engaged in unloading stores and ammunition from ships and onto the beaches. This backbreaking work was carried out under intermittent machine-gun and artillery fire, until the stores and ammunition dumps were established all along the shore area by early May.

At 10.00pm on 1 May, the Turks launched a surprise attack on the British line, and the Royal Scots – who were in reserve trenches astride the Achi Baba nullah (gully) and the Krithia road – came under heavy bombardment. An enemy infantry charge then broke through in several places; however one breakthrough in front of the Royal Scots position was repulsed by a brilliant counter-attack led by Captain McLagan. The Scots knew if they did not push the Turks back they may have broken the Allied line at that point managing to get into the British rear and cause havoc.

The 1st/5th Royal Scots counter-attacked the Turks with fixed bayonets and pushed the enemy back until only a few remained. Lieutenant Swinton Paterson's platoon managed to capture three German and one Turkish officer. Fighting raged all along the line until 3.00am the following morning, when orders came down from High Command for a general advance to be made, following the enemy as they retired. The Turks were now in some disarray as they fell back but unfortunately the weary Allied troops were unable to exploit the advantage and the attack had to be cancelled. The Royal Scots however had been seen charging the enemy line by their Brigade General and had proved their worth; the Territorial soldiers were seen to be as good as their regular counterparts.

The 1st/5th Royal Scots became a whole battalion in the front lines on 2 May, when Y and Z companies came up from the beach to join W and X. On Monday 3 May a short truce fell on the line to bury the dead from the previous days of fighting; the newly arrived men from Z Company carried out this terrible task. The battalion then withdrew to rest trenches at Krithia Nullah on 4 May, to a place known as Clapham Junction, where they hoped to get some sleep and new equipment. However, at 8.00pm they had to rush forward and reinforce the Krithia road, digging in quickly for protection from heavy rifle and machine-gun fire pouring onto their positions.

At 8.00am on 5 May the battalion received orders to attack the enemy lines immediately to their front; this was the first time the Territorial Force soldiers from 1st/5th Royal Scots fought as a complete unit. A little over 600 men stood to that morning and fixed bayonets, preparing to attack Fir Tree Wood just in front of Krithia village. The attack went over the top at 10.00am and managed to penetrate the southern fringe of the wood, but the Royal Scots were unable to hold the ground. Shells howled into the wood all day, heavy machine-gun fire from the Turkish trench lines battered the battalion incessantly. Losses were heavy, including many of the surviving junior officers who were seen repeatedly leading charge after charge, in vain attempts to break the Turkish line.

The battered remains of Krithia remained outside the British grasp, enemy redoubts on the flanks poured heavy fire on the advancing Allied soldiers stalling any successful attack. At 5.00pm the Royal Scots attacked alongside the badly mauled South Wales Borderers; this attack was also a failure and the two battalions were forced to merge in the front line trench. X Company led by Lieutenant Swinton Paterson, managed to seize a slight ridge near Fir Tree Wood, but were too few in number to hold the ground. As the day went on the losses continued and Lieutenant Paterson was wounded alongside Captain F.W. Robertson as they crossed open ground swept by Turkish machine guns.

The attacks on Achi Baba Ridge had been another failure. 'Johnny Turk' fought hard over ever inch of land and would not give up his positions or retire, meaning that as the attacking Allied force could not break out from the beachheads they were forced to dig and await reinforcements. Fighting continued for the next few weeks; the 5th Royal Scots finally withdrew for a rest in reserve trenches on 16 and 17 May 1915. Whilst in reserve the battalion supplied a constant stream of men to the front, replacing the casualties as they fell from bullet, shellfire and disease. Finally a badly cut up 1st/5th Royal Scots withdrew to a relatively quiet rest area near a ruined house, which owing to the colour of its roof had been christened 'Pink Farm'.

While his comrades in 1st/5th Royal Scots were battling in the Turkish heat, Private Angus Mackay arrived at Euston Station in London at the end of his leave

British VIII Corps at Gallipoli

29th Division
86th Brigade
2nd Royal Fusiliers
1st Lancashire Fusiliers
1st Royal Munster Fusiliers
1st Royal Dublin Fusiliers

87th Brigade
2nd South Wales Borderers
1st King's Own Scottish Borderers
1st Royal Inniskilling Fusiliers
1st Borderers

88th Brigade
2nd Hampshires
4th Worcestershires
1st Essex
5th Royal Scots
The Newfoundland Battalion (joined in early September 1915)
London Regiments (joined on 24 September 1915)

42nd East Lancashire Division
125th Brigade
5th Lancashire Fusiliers
6th Lancashire Fusiliers
7th Lancashire Fusiliers
8th Lancashire Fusiliers

126th Brigade
4th East Lancashires
5th East Lancashires
9th Manchesters
10th Manchesters

127th Brigade
5th Manchesters
6th Manchesters
7th Manchesters
8th Manchesters

52nd Lowland Division
155th Brigade
4th Royal Scots Fusiliers
5th Royal Scots Fusiliers
4th King's Own Scottish Borderers
5th King's Own Scottish Borderers

156th Brigade
4th Royal Scots
7th Royal Scots
7th Scottish Rifles
8th Scottish Rifles

157th Brigade
5th Highland Light Infantry
6th Highland Light Infantry
7th Highland Light Infantry
5th Argyll and Sutherland Highlanders

Royal Naval Division
1st Naval Brigade
Drake Battalion
Nelson Battalion
Hawke Battalion
Hood Battalion

2nd Naval Brigade
1st Battalion Royal Marine Light Infantry
2nd Battalion Royal Marine Light Infantry
Howe Battalion
Anson Battalion

on 10 May 1915; he reported to the military authority on the station and was then marched to Waterloo railway station. From there he travelled to Plymouth, where he was billeted in Raglan Barracks at Devonport.

On 11 May Angus boarded the P&O shipping lines troopship SS *Osarera*, sailing in a convoy bound for Egypt; he was finally on his way to join his battalion on the beaches at Gallipoli. The ship sailed to Gibraltar, then Malta before finally docking in the Egyptian port of Alexandria on 24 May. He then boarded the minelayer HMS *Reindeer* and proceeded to the island of Lemnos in Greece, about 12 miles from the Gallipoli Peninsula, used by the attacking force as a forward base and re-supply point. The island had huge stores depots and a military barracks located on it, there were also a number of large military hospitals and rest camps for the wounded.

On 26 May, Angus came ashore at 'W' Beach Gallipoli in a party of three officers and 97 soldiers under command of Lieutenant Wetherall. On the 28th they rejoined the remnants of the 1st/5th Royal Scots battalion in reserve trenches at Pink Farm. The battalion spent the next five days in the rest camp under heavy shrapnel fire, with 400 men building a mule track from 'Clapham Junction' supply track into the support trenches.

The reserve trenches were only just behind the lines and there was no real rest from the constant shellfire from Turkish artillery. Enemy observers could see into the Allied rear area from their positions high up on Achi Baba ridge, and the only respite the British soldiers could get was if they were badly wounded enough to be taken onto one of the hospital shops in the bay.

The battalion was then detailed to dig a track from the beachhead to the front line, spending the next two days on the task. On 3 June, the Royal Scots returned to the front line to make ready for a general advance on the morning of the next day. As the men took up their positions on the firing lines they were told that the line must be held at all cost. They were once again in position near Fir Tree Wood, and watched as the Allies laid down heavy artillery bombardment from 8.00am. The Allied artillery spotters concentrated the bombardment on identified Turkish positions and they also hit support trenches to the rear. Just before 11.40am the bombardment ceased and the British infantry watched as the Turks rushed fresh troops into their front line trenches. The artillery bombardment was then resumed, their ruse had worked; Turkish troops sent up to reinforce the front line were destroyed by the second wave of artillery fire.

At noon, the British troops hurled themselves forward as their artillery switched target from the Turkish front line to the rear, in order to prevent reinforcements moving up. The British took heavy casualties as they crossed no man's land; some units were almost destroyed by the devastating Turkish machine-gun fire.

The 1st Battalion King's Own Scottish Borderers and Worcester Regiment managed to reach the Turkish lines but had to fall back, finding no support units available on their flanks. The 1st/5th Royal Scots managed to advance well, although the right flank of the battalion did have some difficulty keeping in touch with the units on their right. Lieutenant Wetherall and his men found them themselves about 300 yards from and 50 yards in front of the support elements. The linking up of the two units was secured by the use of sentry posts, strung out along the trench line.

The Turks counter-attacked on 6 June, regaining all the ground they had lost and forcing the British to withdraw to their original lines. There was heavy fighting in the gullies and ravines on the Helles front, as British and Australian troops fought the Turks for control of the maze of trenches and dugouts. Further attacks on the Turkish lines were a failure, as over 6500 men became casualties; about 4500 of these were British. Frontal bayonet charges had been costly in the face of the heavily armed and well dug in Turkish defenders.

Angus Mackay was slightly wounded on 7 June during a Turkish counter-attack and taken to the battalion first aid post behind the lines; he was then evacuated to a casualty clearing station on the beach. He remained there until the 9th, before being taken off the beach and onto the hospital ship, *Grantully Castle*. The ship sailed to Alexandria in Egypt, where Angus was taken to the 15th General Hospital (Ward S11B), to recover from his wounds. He remained in hospital until 6 July when he was transferred to Cyprus, aboard the cruise ship SS *Surada*.

Angus remained in a rest camp on Mount Troodos in Cyprus recovering from his wounds until 3 August, then returned to Mustapha in Egypt. On 13 August he boarded the troopship SS *Tunisia* bound for Lemnos Island and Gallipoli to rejoin his unit; however the ship developed engine problems on the way and was forced to return to port. He then boarded another ship, the SS *Deirflinger*, and proceeded to Lemnos at 7.00pm on 20 August; Angus spent his time on ship performing guard duties.

On 24 August, he was transferred to the warship HMS *Prince Edward* and completed his journey back to Gallipoli, landing on the Peninsula at 4.00am on 26 August; he was with 27 other men under the command of Captain Radcliffe. The party rejoined the battalion in reserve trenches at Suvla Bay on the morning of 27 August 1915, the day on which he began his diary.

His battalion had been badly mauled in his absence and he found only a skeleton of the contingent which had left Edinburgh six months before. The reinforcements from Edinburgh had failed to bring the battalion up to full strength; casualties from the fighting, disease and deprivation had taken a terrible toll on the Lothian soldiers. The 1st/4th and 1st/7th Battalions of Royal Scots had both arrived on the Peninsula and immediately joined the fighting, however only two companies of the 1st/7th had made it to Gallipoli from Edinburgh; the remainder of the battalion had been on a troop train that ran into a local train at Gretna Green (Quintinshill Junction) on 22 May 1915. Signalmen then allowed the London to Glasgow express through the junction and it slammed into the wreckage of the first two trains. 227 people were killed, including 3 officers, 29 NCOs and 182 men of the Royal Scots. Few train crashes in Scotland can have had more of an impact upon one small community than the Gretna rail disaster. The special troop train carried the 7th Battalion, Royal Scots, Territorial Force bound for Liverpool on their way to Gallipoli as part of 156th Brigade of the 52nd (Lowland) Division.

The 7th Battalion, Royal Scots was made up of eight companies of local men with A to G Companies based in the drill hut at Dalmeny Street with H Company in Musselburgh. The Battalion had been mobilised at the outbreak of the First World War and had served on coastal defences. Bound for war and in high spirits they left Larbert near Stirling in two trains and headed south. It was the second of these trains that was involved in the crash. Of the 500 troops on the train, only 53 answered the roll call after the accident. On this one day the battalion lost 42 per cent of its total casualties for the whole of the war.

The 1st/5th battalion had also been back into the front lines at Helles on more than one occasion, repulsing heavy Turkish counter-attacks. On 28 June Lieutenant Steel had led Y Company up a sap on the left into the front line, while Lieutenant Wetherall had led W Company on the right. The sap ended in no man's land near a ridge and it was from this point they assaulted the enemy trench. The attack was a failure; the Turks shot the Scots down when they topped the ridge.

The British had landed at Suvla Bay during the night of 6 August, in an attempt to take the Turkish flank by landing troops behind the enemy lines and breaking the stalemate. The landing was another disaster, even though the Turks only had a small detachment of troops on the beach with sentry posts at Nibrunesi Point and only a small force of men near Suvla Bay its self. At 2.00am the first of the Allied troops came ashore in force and began to cross the dried up salt lake behind the beaches, heading for the hill at Lala Baba. The 32nd Brigade quickly carried the hill from B Beach, but a Turkish outpost on Hill 10 checked the Yorkshire battalions, to the north of the lake.

Hard fighting took place as the British came ashore and began to fan out, attacking the Turks entrenched behind the landing beaches. The 31st Brigade took the largest share of the fighting with its battalions well to the fore; the 6th Royal Inniskilling Fusiliers, 6th Royal Irish Fusiliers and 6th Royal Dublin Fusiliers were forced to fight hand-to-hand with the enemy, as they pushed forward.

The British High Command dithered about what to do next, as chaos ensued when the reinforcement units began to land in the wrong place and became mixed up with the initial landing force. If the British and French forces had been issued with clear and precise orders at this time and pushed on into the hills, the plan might have succeeded. In the event, the attacking force only took the beach area and the foothills beyond, failing to carry on and take the hills at Teke Tepe, Anfarta Ridge and Chunuk Bair near the Australians at Anzac Cove.

The Turks quickly reinforced their forces at Suvla Bay and began to launch fanatical attacks towards the beaches; the British attack stalled and they had to dig in. Trench warfare returned to the front as the soldiers began to dig trench lines just a few miles inland from the beach; the British plan to break out at Suvla had failed.

On 20 August, the 29th Division landed at Suvla Bay from the Helles front, in an attempt to reinforce the line and give the attacking forces some momentum. The Division landed in the morning and after spending some time on the beach, were eventually sent to relieve units in the front line trenches on Chocolate Hill.

Chocolate Hill was on the right flank near Anzac Cove, an area of ground first captured on the night of 7 August. The 29th Division took over the front line trenches on the hill and began to dig in, preparing their defences for the advance they knew that they would have to make.

Angus Mackay rejoined his battalion sometime after the initial fighting at Suvla Bay was over and the fighting had bogged down into trench warfare. The first dated entry in his diary reads

27 August
Digging in. Water very scarce, went up to firing line at 11pm and improved the trenches for four hours. I then returned to camp and received letters from home. Wrote letter to Robert.

A little later that day Angus wrote in his diary

Memo
Lay about in reserve trenches fairly gasping for water, received half water bottle per man for all day. Officers however managed to get buckets of perfect drinking water for bathing purposes. Men get fatigues for four hours carrying sandbags, ammo, digging trenches and only got about two spoonfuls each when done. Cannot understand how officers could waste such precious stuff for washing purposes when men were in such a state.

The water was in short supply because it was coming ashore as part of the re-supply system and had to be carried into the front lines. Water cans were also in short supply as were carrying parties to take them into the lines. Ammunition was prioritised but without water the men could not function.

On 29 August the Royal Scots Commanding Officer received orders from Divisional Headquarters to withdraw his battalion to the beach, then wait in a gully for embarkation from the Peninsula. Angus spent this period on guard in a dug out and did not embark from the beach until 9.00pm the next day. The battalion boarded the steamship *Osmanieh* and was taken to a rest camp on the island of Imbros, close to Lemnos. The battalion spent the next eight days on the island resting and recovering from their ordeal on the Gallipoli front.
Angus wrote in his diary,

30 August
Arrived on Imbros Island and fixed up blankets as shades. Lay about all day, it's very warm but water plentiful. Saw about six planes buzzing about overhead. I received two letters from Magnus he is still in Tain.

His younger brother Magus had joined the Argyll and Sutherland Highlanders and was undergoing military training in Tain, Ross-shire.

On 2 September 1915, Angus joined the machine-gun section of his battalion and began to receive instruction on the Vickers heavy machine gun. A Vickers gun crew consisted of six men: a gunner, ammunition loader, section commander (usually a Lance corporal), a runner/signaller and two men acting as ammunition carriers. The gun was a huge piece of equipment that could not be moved around the battlefield quickly; however once it was in action it was a very efficient killing machine.

The Vickers machine had been adopted by the British Army in 1912 and replaced the Maxim machine gun, in use since 1891. The Vickers was .303 inch calibre, the barrel weighed 40lbs, the tripod weighed 48.5lbs and the whole gun was 45.5 inches long. The gun was belt fed from canvas belts containing 250 rounds each, and once fed through the bullets left the barrel with a muzzle velocity of 2450 feet per second.

Such was the heat emitted while the gun was in use, that it needed a water jacket, that held seven pints. This boiled after 600 rounds had been fired, at a rate of 200 rounds per minute. The steam from the barrel was collected in a condensing can, and then reused to refill the water jacket; once 10,000 rounds had been fired the barrel had to be changed. The barrel change took a fully trained team two minutes to carry out, without loss of water from the cooling jacket.

Ammunition was supplied to the machine-gun sections in cardboard boxes of 100 rounds; the canvas belts were then filled by hand even though a mechanical loading device was available. Private Bill Hodges, a survivor of the 88th Battalion 29th Division Machine Gun Battalion, told the Machine Gun Corps Old Comrades Association that only ammunition marked 'Kynochs of Birmingham' was used, to minimise stoppages from faulty ammunition.

The 1st/5th Royal Scots remained on Imbros until 8 September, refitting and re-equipping for their return to the front. The men spent most of their days on the island with little to do but take part in parades and inspections, although some time was also spent carrying out military manoeuvres and practising attacks.

The main action at Suvla Bay had taken place on 29 August, when Australian troops took Hill 60, alongside Indian and the New Zealand troops from the Mounted Rifle Regiments. It was now secure and reinforcements were coming ashore to consolidate the small gains that had been achieved. The Turks had suffered heavy losses and had half their army spread out along the peninsula ready to resist further attacks. Even so, the British Generals began to wonder if the campaign could succeed and had to decide whether to hold the little ground gained, or abandon it all.

Their fellow commanders on the Western Front were doing little better. By early September 1915 the war in Europe had become deadlocked in the manner of a medieval siege; each side faced each other over a stretch of no man's land from heavily defended trench lines, which both sides found difficult to attack. The British and the French armies faced the Germans in France and Belgium; in Eastern Europe the Germans fought the vast Russian armies along a huge front line stretching from Memei (near Riga) on the Baltic coast, down through East Prussia (now Poland) to the Carpathian Mountains on the Romanian border.

In early 1915 the main focus of the fighting had been in the Champagne region of France, with the British attacking Neuve Chapelle in the north on 10 March and actually breaking through the heavily defended German lines. An attack on Aubers Ridge during the Battle of Festubert a few days later, failed to exploit the gains at Neuve Chapelle and the offensive was called off. In the east the Germans broke the Russian lines at Gorlice in Galicia on 2 May and forced an advance of 130 kilometres into Russian held territory.

As huge numbers of British volunteers – who had flocked to the colours in response to Lord Kitcheners recruitment campaign 'Your Country Needs You' – began to train, the remnants of the BEF and the territorial reinforcements planned a large scale attack on the enemy lines in northern France. The plan was to break through near the mining village of Loos, then push on to the Haut Duele Canal in the east. Once the first and second line enemy trenches had been taken a general breakout could occur into the German rear. General Haig, the British First Army Commander, wrote in his diary before the September attack 'this will be the greatest battle of the war so far, some 800,000 French and British troops will attack today.' The battle, entrusted to Haig's British First Army was doomed, but Haig had been against it from the start. He argued that it would fail because the supply of shells for the heavy guns was inadequate.

Having carried out a personal reconnaissance of the area to be attacked, just south of the La Bassee Canal, he concluded that, 'It is ground not favourable for attack.' It was bare of cover and could be easily swept by machine-gun fire from the German front line trenches in heavily fortified villages along the line.

Initially the British planned to attack with only two divisions in an attempt to avoid heavy loss of life, but when the French switched their attack from Artois to the less well-defended Champagne region, the British contribution was increased to six divisions. The attack was to be made in the south of the battlefield by the 1st, 15th (Scottish) and 47th Divisions; in the north the 2nd, 7th and 9th (Scottish) Divisions would attack the heavily defended Hohenzollern Redoubt.

General Haig urged that the British use poison chlorine gas for the first time. Generals French and Foch initially overruled this but Haig eventually received permission to reserve the use of gas until the last possible moment. If the weather conditions were favourable and a large-scale attack looked like it could be successful, then gas could be used. The British began to bombard the German lines on 5 September 1915; due to the ammunition shortage the artillery was limited to only 90 rounds of heavy gun ammunition and 150 rounds per field gun in a 24 hour period. The damage done was not extensive and the British hoped for a favourable wind so they could use gas. On the night before the battle the British

High Command watched the weather reports with some tension and anxiety. At 5.00am on 25 September, General Haig asked his aide-de-camp Major Fletcher to light a cigarette; as they stood together behind the lines, the cigarette smoke drifted away to the north-east. The wind direction was borderline but acceptable and the word was given to open the gas containers, codenamed 'Accessory'.

In the front line trenches the Royal Engineers Special Battalions released the gas. The gas valves were initially opened for twelve minutes, then smoke was sent over for eight minutes, followed by gas for twelve more minutes, eight minutes of smoke and then finally heavy smoke for two minutes. The first waves of troops were then to move off, hopefully camouflaged by the final screen of heavy smoke.

At first the gas cloud moved well over no man's land towards the Germans line but it was moving too slowly to have any real effect. On the left flank of the attack line the wind died away and the gas began to drift back over the British infantry battalions, waiting to throw themselves over the top. At 6.30am the British troops climbed out of their trenches, formed up as if they were on parade, then headed across no man's land into the haze of gas and smoke. Six divisions launched the initial attack, the 1st, 2nd, 9th (Scottish), 7th, 15th (Scottish) and 47th (London Territorial) formed the vanguard with two separate divisions, the 21st and the 24th, being kept well to the rear in reserve. The two reserve divisions were not under the command of General Haig but under the command General French, a fact that would have a direct bearing on the later stages of the battle.

On the southern edge of the Loos battlefield the speed of the attack was incredible; the first objectives on the enemy front line trenches were taken in fifteen minutes. The second objective, the enemy trenches near Loos Cemetery, was taken fifteen minutes later; this left only isolated pockets of resistance remaining in and around Loos village as the enemy fell back. Fierce hand-to-hand fighting took place in the streets, as the 'Jocks' cleared the houses and barricades one by one with rifles, bayonets and hand grenades. So fast was the penetration at Loos village the German High Command began to make preparations for an evacuation of the whole area. German troops as far back as the town of Douai, 27 kilometres away, began to prepare to fall back.

The fighting in Loos went on all night, beneath the mining machinery nicknamed 'Crystal Palace' and 'Tower Bridge' men from the 15th (Scottish) Division fought to carry the battle line forward. The 8th Seaforth Highlanders captured a battery of field guns, shooting dead its commander when he failed to surrender. Once the village had been taken the 15th (Scottish) Division moved on and attacked Hill 70 beyond, nearly 2000 yards from their start point. Little resistance was encountered as the infantry battalions advanced up the slopes of the hill, but with no orders the lead elements dug in and awaited further instructions.

In the centre the 1st Division was checked and had mixed fortunes; some units reached the village of Hulluch while others were forced to retreat under heavy

German artillery fire. The only place the gas had proved its worth was along the Hulluch to Vermelles road but even here the advantage gained had been lost; futile attacks in the face of heavy machine-gun fire were eventually stopped by General Horne after a protest from his Brigade commanders about the 'useless sacrifice of life'.

The 9th (Scottish) Division took heavy casualties in their attack but the 7th Division made good a gap on the left flank, using locally available reserves. However, the reserves were too far to the rear (16 miles) to be effective and were not in a position to exploit a breakthrough had it occurred as they had to march overnight to join the battle. Bad traffic arrangements hampered their move and to make matters worse they were not allowed to enter the town of Bethune, to the north of Loos, as they did not have the correct pass. It was not until dawn the next day that the reserve divisions arrived; exhausted after their all night march they prepared to attack. Over 8,000 men from this force of 10,000 men were killed and wounded in the fighting that followed; when asked later what had gone wrong one of the survivors said, 'we did not know what it was like [in action], we will do better next time.'

Haig now over estimated the success achieved and at 10.30am on 26 September ordered his 3rd Cavalry Division to advance. He then pushed forward on 21st and 24th Divisions to exploit gains he thought had been made, but the attack failed as there was no effective artillery support available. The tired and hungry attackers broke off their attack in front of the heavily reinforced German wire and began to stream back towards the British lines.

There was now a gap in the British line between Loos and Hulluch, and it was here that the newly formed Guards Division saw action for the first time. The Guards battalions came up into the gap and tried to regain a slagheap called Hill 70, losing many men as they did so. An observer later said, 'It was the most wonderful sight, the guards moving through open country under a curtain of fire. They marched as if they were on parade in Hyde Park and I was proud to think that some of them were friends of mine.'

The Germans now began to attack from the flanks on 28 September as French troops, under the command of General Foch, began to move into the front line around Loos. The French also attacked the German lines near Vimy Ridge, north of Arras, drawing the German Guards Corps away from the Loos/Lens battlefield and taking some of the pressure from the British.

Fighting around Loos went on until 13 October, with attack and counter-attack achieving nothing, and it was decided to continue the offensive was futile. The general situation on the Western Front had not been improved in any way, and there were 60,392 dead and wounded British soldiers and 20,000 Germans. The French lost 191,797 officers and men in their attacks in support of the British offensive. The failure at Loos cost General French the command of the British Forces in France, and he was replaced by General Haig.

3

Suvla Bay and Lemnos Island

On 8 September 1915, as the attack plans of the Loos offensive were being finalised, the 1st/5th Royal Scots returned to Suvla Bay in Gallipoli aboard the Steamship *Osmanieh*. The battalion disembarked onto the beach at 4.00am on 9 September 1915.

9 September
Proceeded towards the firing line. Lay about all day, then marched up to firing line at 1.00am.

The battalion then spent the night at the 29th Division's engineer dump, before entering the front line and relieving the Royal Munster Fusiliers at a point called area 118 in a salient. The battalion took over the line in good order with no casualties. Angus guarded a dugout until 2.00pm the following day, when he was relieved to help move a machine gun.

10 September
Machine gun section stood guard on the 10 and 11, then spent all day on the 12 digging a machine-gun emplacement. Nothing much doing but guard duty. Sunday spent in trenches improving line, I have received letters from home and from Robbie and John [his brothers] dated 12 August.

The stalemate of trench warfare had set in and soldiers spent their time trying to avoid artillery fire or a sniper's bullet. Water was in short supply, as the only way to get it to the men was to transport it in petrol cans carried up from the beachhead by mules. Disease spread, carried by the clouds of flies and mosquitoes that flourished in the Turkish heat.

The 1st/5th Royal Scots War Diary says that on 12 September 1915 'the battalion Machine Gun section dispersed Turkish troops at a range of 1800 yards.'

There is no mention of this incident in Angus Mackay's diary; he may not have been present.

14 September
Still improving trenches and carrying out guard duty.

15 September
A very quiet day in the trench.

16 September
There was some nasty shelling about tea-time.

17 September
Just the usual. More shelling on the 18.

It was around this time the battalion began to take heavy casualties; in the fierce fighting the peninsula became feared for.

18 September
Private Pierce was shot through the head at 4.30am by a stray bullet as the battalion stood to. He was the cook when we were on blockhouse duty in Musselburgh last November and December. Sergeant Beattie, an Edinburgh tramway man, also shot through the head at a well 50 yards behind our line.

19 September
Heavy shelling for about 15 minutes in forenoon, one man wounded in the forehead by shrapnel.

Gallipoli had become another holding action just like the Western Front. All along the front lines futile attacks were launched to try and break the stalemate and push on. The New Zealanders and Australians suffered heavy losses in the hills and gullies above Anzac Cove; the hills were given names that belied their bloody history: Baby 700, the Nek, Johnston's Jolly, Rhododendron Spur and Chunuk Bair.

The repeated failure of the Allies to capture Krithia or make any progress on the Helles front led General Hamilton, commander of the Mediterranean Expeditionary Force, to pursue a new plan for the campaign, which resulted in what is now called the Battle of Sari Bair. On the night of 6 August 1915 a fresh landing of two infantry divisions was to be made at Suvla, five miles north of Anzac Cove. Meanwhile at Anzac a strong assault would be made on the Sari Bair range by breaking out into the rough and thinly defended terrain north of the Anzac perimeter.

The landing at Suvla Bay by the British IX Corps was only lightly opposed but their commander, Lieutenant-General Sir Frederick Stopford, had so diluted his early objectives that little more than the beach was seized. Once again the Turks were able to win the race for the high ground of the Anafarta Hills, rendering the Suvla fronts another case of static trench warfare.

The landing had been preceded on the evening of the 6 August by a number of diversionary assaults at Helles and Anzac. At Helles, the diversion at Krithia Vineyard became another futile battle with no gains and heavy casualties on both sides. At Anzac, an attack on the Turkish trenches at Lone Pine by the infantry brigades of the Australian 1st Division won a rare victory. However, the main assault aimed at capturing and holding the peaks of Chunuk Bair and Hill 971 was less successful. The force striking for the nearer peak of Chunuk Bair comprised the New Zealand Infantry Brigade; it came within 500 metres of the peak by dawn on 7 August but was not able to seize the summit until the following morning. This delay had fatal consequences for another supporting attack on the morning of 7 August, that of the Australian 3rd Light Horse Brigade at the Nek which was to coincide with the New Zealanders attacking back down from Chunuk Bair against the rear of the Turkish defences. The New Zealanders held out on Chunuk Bair for two days before relief was provided by two of the New Army battalions from the Wiltshire and Loyal North Lancashire Regiments. A massive Turkish counter-attack, led in person by Mustafa Kemal, swept these two battalions from the heights. Of the 760 men of the New Zealanders' Wellington Battalion who reached the summit, 711 were casualties.

Another planned attack on Hill 971 never took place. The attacking force of the Australian 4th Infantry Brigade (General Monash), and an Indian brigade, were defeated by the terrain and became lost during the night. All subsequent attempts to resume the attack were easily repulsed by the Turkish defenders at great cost to the Allies.

By 21 September 1915, the Royal Scots were still in their trenches building dugouts and performing guard duties.

21 September
Joined by Newfoundlanders in the firing line for the first time, they are fine fellows. Still in firing line, quiet day so far.

22 September 22
We are busy making dugouts behind the line, naval monitors [small inshore gunboats] are shelling the enemy lines 100 yards in front of us.

The Turks however fought back tenaciously and returned the naval ships gunfire.

I can see the Turks working on their dugouts. Fleet still suffering gunfire.

26 September
Willie Kerr badly wounded in the back during night. We began to dig in front of the firing line.

Like many of his companions, Angus was laid low with a stomach complaint; the soldiers suffered from diarrhoea and dysentery, as well as trench foot, influenza and common colds made worse by a lack of food and water.

27 September
I still feel pretty bad with pains in the stomach. The Newfoundlanders are in beside us again, 5 men were wounded and 1 killed during the night.

28 September
R.S.M. Munro, C.S.M. Masterton, Sergeant MacGuinness and Corporal Balfour were all laid out by air torpedoes. Munro has been killed alongside Private Campbell who returned to the battalion from Mustapha, we have had a rough night. Three air torpedoes were discharged at us altogether, also some weird shells, which made a queer sound as they came over. We had rapid fire all along the line for three hours.

The battalions were periodically relieved in the front lines and sent to rest or get cleaned up.

29 September
Received welcome news that we are to pack up and await our reliefs who are to take our place in the firing line. We have been in the firing line now for 21 days continuously getting shelled, bombed etc all the time.

The battalion War Diary says the 'Hants' Regiment (possibly the 2nd Hampshire Regiment) carried out the relief. The 1st/5th Royal Scots were then moved to Worcester reserve bivouacs.

30 September
We have settled down in imitation dugouts about 2,000 yards behind the lines, which are in full view. Shelled during the morning.

Rest areas in Gallipoli were never far from the front lines and the battalions were always on call to go back into the line and shore up any weak spots that developed.

1 October
Received orders to move to firing line, took up positions just behind front. We then had a pretty hot time digging the reserve trench and dodging snipers.

2 October
Relieved by Newfoundlanders and returned to camp. Excellent dugouts.

Over the next few days the Royal Scots were in reserve billets behind the lines.

4 October
Lieutenant Simpson has been killed by a stray bullet. I attended sick parade and got off duty. Number 1 gun proceeded to our old position, devil of a racket kicked up by rapid fire and shelling for one hour.

5 October
We are remaining in same place, received uniforms etc.

6 October
Half hour bombardment of Turkish redoubt. Turks caught by machine-gun whilst running back.

7 October
Off duty, very quiet day.

8 October
Light duty, inspection then went up to firing line with ammunition.

As the fighting went on the battalion received drafts of men to replace the wounded and sick,; according to the War Diary, 'Lieutenant Ireland and forty men arrived from Edinburgh for duty.' The conditions on the peninsula continued to be bad.

11 October
We are still in our rest camp. Diet devilish.

12 October
Food a little better but still pretty light must get out of it. Better shot than starved any day.

Food varied little, mainly tinned meat, jam, tea and rock hard biscuits; vegetables and fresh food were in short supply. Flies swarmed everywhere, especially over uncovered food. On 16 October, Angus begins to complain of a sore throat, which was so bad he reported sick on 17 October.

17 October
Sunday shelled a lot during the morning, had my throat examined again and was sent to a clearing station. I was then sent on to the hospital ship, SS Galenka from the Union Castle Line. We sailed that night.

The hospital ship first took Angus to Mudros Bay on Lemnos Island, where he was placed in Number 3 Canadian Hospital.

19 October
First day in hospital received pyjamas and had a wash. Wrote letters.

He spent the next ten days recovering from his sore throat; the routine was always the same. He wrote that 'nothing was doing except doctors visits' and the food was 'better, in fact pretty decent'. He spent most of his time writing letters home.

29 October
Discharged from hospital and sent to convalescence camp, sent on fatigue party from 8–11am. Rest of the day spent buggering up and down. I'm longing for some letters from home. Sent postcard.

30 October
Still in convalescence camp doing fatigues etc. Wrote home then had a walk to detail camp where I heard the battalion is in Mudros having a rest.

The 5th Royal Scots had left Suvla Bay on the morning of 30 October aboard the steamship *Sarnia* and returned to Mudros Bay. The battalion, which had left Edinburgh with 800 men, now numbered less than 100, destroyed by fighting and disease. The battalion survivors would not see active service again until May 1916 and its arrival in France.

31 October
Sunday morning we are on fatigues as per usual. I think the Sunday observance has been ceased for the duration of the war.

Angus Mackay was a typical British soldier; good in battle and willing to do his duty for King and Country but in base camp it was a different story. Any chance to avoid a parade was taken gladly.

1 November
Began a new month by dogging early morning parade. It's very cold in the early morning, had some rain, fatigues lasted until 12 noon. I went over to the Greek village during the afternoon; everything is very dear and dirty. I think this is more like a convict prison than a convalescence camp, still rather sick than out among the Turks.

5 November
Rumour gone round that the King of Bulgaria, King Ferdinand has been assassinated.

6 November
Medical inspection today, I expect to be discharged on Monday as I feel alright and I'm getting fed up. Went on the detail and received letters from home and John, Magnus [his younger brother serving in the Argyll and Sutherland Highlanders] has gone to France.

The weather conditions in the area began to change and it got much colder, especially at night. Angus's fellow soldiers still on the Gallipoli Peninsula suffered more, as they were still dressed in tropical kit that did little to keep out the cold and damp of the Mediterranean winter.

8 November
Very cold just like Scotland in January, my blood feels a bit thin after the Turkish summer season. Had a medical inspection and wrote home.

Mail call was keenly awaited by all the men, eager to see if the post NCO had letters or parcels for them.

9 November
Still in convalescence camp, this is my 30th day away from the battalion. Received a parcel containing two shirts, handkerchiefs and socks also a letter from John. Sent him a post card.

The routine in the camp went on as Angus awaited his discharge and return to his unit.

10 November
Usual routine. Cookhouse fatigues at 11am, we had rain during the night but the day was fairly warm.

11 November
Reported sick. Got medicine and duty. Fatigues at 2.00pm shifting refuse barrels weighting about 3cwt. I couldn't do it so I reported to the Corporal and then cleared out. I saw Lord Kitchener passing through our camp on his way to inspect the New Zealander and Australian camps.

Lord Kitchener, the British Secretary of State for War, had arrived on Lemnos Island to inspect the worsening state of the Gallipoli Campaign for himself. The British situation in the Dardanelles was deemed to be hopeless and decisions had to be made by the High Command as to what the next move should be. The British commander on Gallipoli, Sir Ian Hamilton, had been called back to London on 16 August 1915 and replaced by General Sir Charles Monro. Munro had now to decide what to do next: he could hold the small gains taken with such heavy losses carry out a total withdrawal. In a military dispatch sent after the campaign in the Dardanelles was over, General Monro wrote,

> The position occupied by our troops presented a military situation unique in history. The mere fringe of the coastline was secure; the beaches and piers upon which they depended on for all requirements of personnel and materials was exposed to enemy artillery fire. Our trenches were dominated almost through-out by the Turks; our artillery positions were insufficient and defective.
>
> The positions held were without depth, communications were insecure and no means existed for the concealment of fresh troops in a offensive. The Turks were in full observation of the battlefield, with abundant artillery positions and natural defences at his disposal.

The General decided to evacuate the Peninsula because

(a) it was obvious the Turks could hold us with a small force of men and still fight in Mesopotamia and Egypt or both.

(b) Any further advance on the enemy positions; could no longer be regarded as a reasonable military objective.

(c) Even if we had made any advance on the Peninsula, the positions we occu-pied could not be improved to any degree and an advance on Constantinople was out of the question.

(d) There was no purpose in remaining on the Peninsula, the appalling cost to the nation in embarking on an overseas expedition with no forward bases available for stores and equipment made it urgent we should divert the troops, locked up on the Gallipoli Peninsula to a more useful theatre of operations.

General Munro made his recommendations to the War Office for a total with-drawal from the Dardanelles and the abandonment of the plan to knock Turkey out off the war. When he visited Gallipoli Kitchener fully agreed with General Monro's assessment of the military situation and plans were quickly drawn up for the evacuation of all Allied troops.

As the plans for the evacuation were made, Private Angus Mackay was stuck in his convalescence camp, waiting for his medical board and a return to the battalion. However, he managed to find himself a job and a way to break the monotonous routine.

12 November
*Usual fatigue dodging before breakfast. The Adjutant wanted some officer's servants so
I volunteered, I start tomorrow. Rehearsal today, starting at dinnertime. Find I have to
look after the parson [battalion chaplain] he himself!*

Officers were entitled to employ a private soldier as a batman; the soldier's duties
included the maintenance of the officer's uniforms, boot cleaning, serving food in
the mess and other small tasks. The job meant extra pay and better conditions, as
well as better rations as officers' mess food was of a higher quality than that available to the lower ranks.

13 November
*First day as an officer's lot in the mess. Waiters like it alright as the grub is decent but
you're kept pretty busy.*

14 November
*Rose at 6.00am polished the parson's boots then woke him at 7.00am, brought him
shaving water. I then attended sick parade and tried to get out of my new job, I'm afraid
it's not for me. No good and I'm sent back to officers mess at 8.00am until 9.30am
when we breakfast on the remains. I was then told to clean out the parson's tent, and
then help at 12.00pm with lunch. Got generally cursed about my sarcastic sobs until
we finished at 2.00pm. Dinner at 4.00pm finished at 5.30pm, then supper at 9.00pm.
When the hell is a man to get better in this damned camp?*

Angus had clearly made a mistake in volunteering for his new job but it was only
to be for a few days. On 16 November 1915 he was finally declared fit.

16 November
*Declared fit and proceeded to detail camp. We are sleeping 12 men to a tent, rations
not bad. Received letters from John [his brother in Edinburgh], home and one from
Mr Stevenson dated 22 October. I also got a parcel containing a knitted jacket, socks
and underwear.*

17 November
*Attended medical officer's parade at 6.15am but was told to parade on Monday.
Declared A class [the highest class of military fitness] and received new equipment and
a rifle. Wrote home and to John.*

He rejoined the remainder of his battalion and training went on as the officers
tried to keep their soldiers fit, ready for the day they would rejoin the fighting.

18 November
Paraded for physical drill at 6.50am, then breakfast at 8.00am. Paraded for a route march at 9.30am. Dinner at 12.30pm then drill for one hour in the afternoon to finish the day at 4.30pm, served stew at 6.00pm.

Soldiers wrote poems and songs about their exploits in battle, some of which Angus recorded in his diary. The following was sung to the tune of 'My Little Home in the West'.

Landing of the 29th Division on the Gallipoli Peninsula. 25 April 1915

It was on the 25 April
That this gallant Brigade forced their way
With shots right and left,
As we climbed up the cliff, on that eventful day.
The General he gave us our chance
And we made such a glorious advance
The General was pleased when the Turks we chased
In their snug little homes in the trench.

The training went on day after day.

19 November
Skirmishing in the forenoon then kit inspection in afternoon. Weather getting very cold, reminds me of a winter's night in Leith docks.

20 November
Saturday morning fatigues for three hours, then wrote home.

The weather had begun to deteriorate and the troops suffered. On 21 November a terrific storm burst over the Gallipoli Peninsula, followed by a hard frost and a blizzard. The trenches in the Suvla area filled with four feet of water and many men were drowned; others froze to death as temperatures fell. Over 200 men died from exposure, with 10,000 men reporting sick suffering from frostbite and jaundice.

Conditions on Lemnos were not as severe as those suffered by the troops in the front line trenches, nearly twelve miles away. On the day of the storm Angus wrote,

21 November
Vicious sand storms. Paraded at 8.30am in the driving wind.

22 November
Fatigues all forenoon. Very cold, sandstorms etc.

The routine of military life went on with training carried out daily, even in the poor weather conditions.

23 November
Physical drill at 6.30am, then paraded at 9.30am for battalion drill. We were all then dismissed, for the purposes of reforming our unit. After tea sixteen of us slept in one tent, rum was issued to beat the damn cold.

Over the next few days the diary entries are all much the same as he writes about his daily routine of drill and physical training. Conditions were harsh and many men fell ill and had to report sick suffering from severe colds and influenza.

27 November
Reported sick with a cough, damn this cold weather. Received a MD [Medicine and Discharge]. We then received instruction on the machine guns. We are sleeping 10 men to a tent so things are quite easy. Good grub, I hope this lot can continue for the duration. Received a fag issue, five packets of Woodbines. Wrote letters and sent postcards.

The cold weather continued and Angus and his fellows on Lemnos got a taste of what the soldiers on Gallipoli were suffering.

28 November
Sunday morning and I'm duty orderly for the day. So cold we lay in bed all day except for meals.

29 November
No exercise today owing to the cold. Violent storms nearly blow our tent down and it's snowing here for the first time.

30 November
Usual parades. Water frozen it is very cold. Football match in the afternoon.

December 1915 began on a more positive note with football matches arranged between the various units in an attempt to keep up morale.

1 December
There is a football match between the garrison and our battalion in the afternoon. Result Garrison 2, the Battalion 1.

The next few days were busy for the battalion with the usual parades and drills, and the machine-gun section had a parade for a kit inspection. On 3 December 1915, things began to stir.

3 December
Usual parades. Rumours are going around that our battalion is going to return to Suvla Bay. I got paid in the afternoon, ten shillings.

Those rumours were partly correct; the 88th Brigade of the 29th Division was going back into the front lines at Suvla to help with the evacuation. They were to take over 3000 yards of the front and hold it until the evacuation was complete, then evacuate from the beaches at the rear. The 5th Royal Scots were not to be involved in the action due to the heavy losses they had suffered and were to be left behind on Lemnos Island.

4 December
Usual parades. Football match between the Dugouts and the battalion in the afternoon. Result Dugouts 0 the Battalion 0. Wrote home later and also to Robbie. Received a parcel containing writing paper, socks and 50 cigarettes.

5 December
Sunday. Wrote to G. Tweedie [Steads Place, Leith Walk, Edinburgh]. It has been a quiet day. Divine Service outside camp in the forenoon, then had a walk through the Greek villages in the afternoon.

6 December
Usual parades, mounting gun etc. I've received a letter from Donald dated 28 November, he's fighting on Bauchop's Ridge [on Gallipoli]. Wrote to Donald and then John, I've enclosed Donald's letter so that John can read it. Also sent a Christmas card drawn by Don Moodie from the machine-gun section. I came across George Mackay, 7th Royal Scots, today he is in the convalescence camp near us. He is now a full blown Corporal!

The letter from Angus's brother Donald, serving with 'C' Company, 9 Squadron of the Wellington Mounted Rifles New Zealand Expeditionary Force, had arrived from Anzac Cove on the Gallipoli front. The Wellington Mounted Rifles were fighting high up in the hills and nullahs above the landing beaches; the battalion had successfully captured Turkish outposts in an area of the front called Destroyer Hill and the Table-Top.

Fighting on Bauchop's Ridge was severe as the Turkish troops launched heavy frontal attacks, trying to push the Anzac troopers from their trenches. Casualties were heavy on both sides as the two armies fought for control of the area.

7 December 1915
Usual parades. Otherwise nothing doing, weather very warm and close.

8 December

Received letter from John, home and Robbie dated 18 November, the 16th and 13th of November. Hugh [brother serving in the Army Service Corps] has gone to Serbia and George [brother serving in the Royal Garrison Artillery] is expected home on furlough.

9 December

Went on sick parade then had a machine-gun drill in the afternoon. Received a parcel containing biscuits, cheese, sweets and Vaseline from home. I then met a Corporal of the Royal Engineers who was formerly a teacher at Leith Academy, he stays in Restalrig Road.

The routine for the following days was much the same, early morning parades followed by machine-gun drill and kit inspections. Angus continued to receive food parcels and mail from his parents at home in Scullomie.

12 December

We had a Divine service today then off duty. We are still at Mudros East. Expect we will have more machine-gun practice this week.

13 December

Still off duty, showers off rain during the morning. Football match in the afternoon, the battalion beats the A.S.C. [Army Service Corps] by 3 to 1. I wrote to John after receiving letter from him dated 26th November. In it, he says George has arrived in Scullomie on his 14 days furlough. Received parcel from M Sinclair containing fags and some socks.

14 December

Had our breakfast at 7.00am and paraded at 7.45am, to proceed to Mudros Island West for machine gun firing. The fog is so thick that we are delayed at the ferry for two hours. However, we got across eventually and marched 4 miles to the ranges, they are near the village of Conila. We fired 100 rounds, had some stew and returned to camp at 5.30pm.

Rumours about the evacuation from Gallipoli continue to sweep the British camps on Mudros Island.

15 December

No morning parade due to heavy rain last night. Heard rumours that Australians, New Zealanders and British are evacuating Anzac Cove. I hope I might run into Don if it's true. Wrote to Robbie then orderly for the day.

The evacuation of Anzac Cove and Suvla Bay was all set to take place over the nights of 18 and 19 December. The garrisons in the Anzac Cove and Suvla area were down to 20,000 men and so 10,000 men were evacuated each night by the Royal Navy. The arrangements made for the withdrawal went perfectly; the good weather helped alongside little Turkish military activity. There were no casualties and all Allied equipment left on the beaches was destroyed; even the sandbags in the trenches were slit open with bayonets. Rifles were left with water cans dripping into another can beneath, this can then pulled the trigger of a rifle maintaining the impression of trenches manned by snipers. A mine was fired on the New Zealanders' positions near Russell's Top at 3.30am; the whole Anzac area was empty of Allied soldiers by 4.00am.

Angus was unaware of events taking place twelve miles away.

16 December

An easy day. Parade in forenoon then played bridge etc. Bridge and whist is our only way to kill time. Rum is given out every night, enough to send a man spinning. Early frost.

17 December

Usual parades. There are still rumours of the battalion going to Suvla Bay to cover the retreat with our machine guns, probably firing off boats. This is pay day so I drew £2 and went for a walk to Greek village, bought a purse marked Athens.

18 December

Usual parades then a football match between the machine-gun section and the medical section, score 2 – 0. Bought a pocket book in the village for 2/6p and saw G. Mackenzie, he says he expects to return to the peninsula shortly.

19 December

Divine service at 10.30am. I then received a letter from Robbie dated 29 November. I took a walk up to the New Zealanders camp and came across one of Don's mates. He told me Donald was in the harbour and was expected to land during the afternoon. I hope I can see him tomorrow. When I got back to camp I wrote to Robbie and told him about my trip to the New Zealanders' camp.

Angus finally met his brother Donald at 2.00pm on 21 December.

21 December

Early morning parade as usual. I heard the Wellington Mounted Rifles were coming to a camp near here so I visited the New Zealand Highlanders camp. Met a chap who had been with Donald since he enlisted, he told me Don was with the last lot to leave Anzac. However, after dinner I was agreeably surprised to see a New Zealander, who looked like old Sandy hunting through the camp for me. It was Don and I was delighted to meet him, I had almost given up hope of finding him in the wilds.

We then visited the Greek village together and had spuds and fish together washed down with coffee, we then walked back to the New Zealanders' camp. Spent the rest of the afternoon together.

22 December

Got off duty for the day. I saw Donald again and he told me his battalion is leaving for Egypt tomorrow. He is busy on fatigues at the Egyptian pier and has no tucker [food], so I went and had a hunt for tinned stuff in the village. Saw Don again in the afternoon but when I went to New Zealand camp for tea; I was told he had been sent on board transport at short notice.

Angus was never to see his brother again; Donald's unit moved to Egypt the following morning where it joined the Egyptian Expeditionary Force, preparing to attack Turkish forces occupying Palestine. The Wellington Mounted Rifles served in the Desert Mounted Force in the Sinai Desert as mounted infantry. Donald Mackay had already served with distinction on Gallipoli in the thick of the fighting; his battalion was almost destroyed at one point as they held the Turks on Walkers Ridge and at Quinn's Post.

Angus prepared to spend his first Christmas away from his family.

24 December 1915

It is very wet and cold. Wrote to John otherwise a quiet day. Still in our rest camp and I expect we will spend Christmas and New Year here. We are saving up our rum issue for New Year. Had a few intermittent songs in our tent until 12.30am.

25 December

It is Christmas Day and no parades. Porridge, tea, bread and jam for breakfast. Dinner was turkey and roast followed by tea and plum duff. We then had tea and cake at 5.30pm. We all then paraded and proceeded to the local village. I was on picket duty at night.

26 December

Returned to camp and got between the blankets until dinner time then wrote home.

27 December

Came off picket duty at 7.30am and returned to camp to find our stores tent had blown down during the night. I was back on picket duty at 7.30pm.

28 December

Came off picket duty at 7.00am and then slept all day. Nothing doing.

29 December

Paraded for picket duty on Greek village at 7.30am came off at 5.30pm. Received a parcel containing cigarettes, chocolate and toffees. We were paraded in the afternoon to clean the gun tripods.

On New Year's Eve the soldiers make arrangements for a party.

31 December

Thick mist in the afternoon. I drew 10 shillings pay. Machine gun parade as usual, then arranged a feed to bring in New Year with style. Tea at 8.30pm with food Turkish Delight, cigars, tobacco etc.

4

Egypt

The New Year of 1916 began as the old one had ended; there was stalemate in France, the attacks at Aubers Ridge, Festubert and Loos in 1915 had been a costly failure. Industrialised killing with poison gas, machine guns and artillery fire had decimated the ranks of the British Expeditionary Force on the Western Front.

On the Gallipoli Peninsula, a small force of men from the 52nd (Lowland) Division occupied the forward trenches on the Helles front. Orders to evacuate the troops were issued by the High Command on 28 December; all preparations were to be made for a complete and orderly withdrawal. The withdrawal began on 1 January 1916 when the French Navy, in spite of the bad weather, took French infantry off the beaches.

None of those problems worried Angus Mackay.

1 January
Had a proper day off after our exertions of the previous night. Had our breakfast, dinner and tea in bed and then played bridge.

2 January
No church parade spent the day sleeping, playing cards and sleeping.

The break for the New Year was soon over and military training began again.

3 January
Spent forenoon filling cartridge belts. I've heard a rumour we are proceeding to Egypt to guard the Suez Canal. Played bridge in the afternoon.

4 January
Drill on the machine-gun mechanism in forenoon. Had a short route march in the

afternoon with Piper Peden playing all the time. Cards and football killed the rest of the time.

5 January
The usual parade. More rumours that we are proceeding to Alexandria.

The rumours were true; with the evacuation of the Dardanelles almost complete, the British High Command began to move all the troops from Imbros and Lemnos islands back to Egypt. The Allies now feared that Turkey would attack Egypt through the Sinai Desert and seize the Suez Canal. German agents in the area had been trying to stir up a holy war in the region, hoping to cause an uprising amongst the tribes forcing the British to withdraw from Egypt.

As the 5th Royal Scots packed up on Imbros ready to leave, Private Angus Mackay wrote in his diary,

6 January
Received letters from John and home dated 8 and 11 November. We are busy packing up. Received official confirmation of the rumours, we leave at 2.00pm tomorrow for Egypt.

The 5th battalion left their camp at 1.30pm the following day and marched to the Egyptian pier, headed by the garrison regimental pipe band. The Royal Scots then embarked on board the SS *Varsova* which moved out from the pier and anchored in Mudros bay for the night. On 8 January 1916, the SS *Varsova* set sail for Egypt; the Dardanelles campaign was over. The Royal Scots were placed on guard duty aboard ship.

8 January
As we set sail at 8.00am we mounted our guns on the upper deck. We are to remain on guard duty until we reach our destination. Escorted by two small destroyers.

As the SS *Varsova* sailed towards Egypt, the final evacuation of troops from Gallipoli was taking place twelve miles away. The troop evacuation went without a hitch and with no loss of life; over ten tons of explosives and huge piles of shells and small arms ammunition were blown as the last man left the beaches. The withdrawal from the Dardanelles was the only successful part of the campaign; the plan to knock Turkey out of the war had failed. The losses had been heavy: 5,241 officers and 112,308 other ranks were killed, wounded or missing in action. Turkey was still able to fight on in Palestine, Egypt and Mesopotamia; never again would Britain and her allies threaten the Turkish homeland.

Troops on the *Varsova* had no idea about the evacuation taking place on the Peninsula as they enjoyed their cruise to Egypt.

9 January

Still proceeding on our journey without any important incident. Saw some dolphins playing around the bow off the ship while I was on guard. Our transport ship has a small pom-pom [anti aircraft gun] on the stern; they had practice in the afternoon. We are sailing a zig zag course to avoid torpedoes.

Parody of 'Roamin in the Gloamin'

Roamin in the Gloamin,
On the banks of the Dardanelles,
Waiting for the Robin
To come down and drop her shells,
She came down the Shanak
But she damn soon went back
For the Lizzie she was
Roamin in the Gloamin.

As the SS *Varsova* arrived at Quay 45 in Alexandria, Egypt on 10 January 1916 Angus wrote

10 January

Arrived in Alexandria harbour at 8.00am. We are to go ashore about 6.00pm and proceed by train to Port Suez. Feeling the weather pretty warm. Went on board train at 7.00pm and proceeded to Port Suez, via Cairo. I enjoyed the run, as it was a fine starry night. We arrived in Port Suez [at the southern end of the Suez Canal] on 11 January.

As soon as we arrived in camp we erected our tent and settled down. We are sleeping eight men in each tent. We visited the town at 5.00pm. It was like civilisation again. Quite a lively little town of a mixed population. We can hear artillery fire in the distance all day; expect the Turks are attacking the Suez Canal.

In January 1915, about 20,000 Turkish troops under command of the German Colonel Baron Friedrich Kress Von Kressenstien had attacked the Suez Canal from the Sinai Desert. The Turks crossed the desert with all their artillery pieces and pontoon bridges in an attempt to launch a surprise attack across the canal. British Royal Flying Corps patrol planes attacked the Turks as they approached through the desert and foiled this surprise Turkish assault.

There had been no other threat made against the canal from Turkish forces since that time. In August 1915, Egypt was under threat from a rising by Senussi tribesmen, stirred up by German agents trying to start a holy war. The Senussi were defeated by a strong British force formed in November 1915. The Senussi tribes were finally defeated by May 1916 after heavy fighting throughout the region, mainly in the desert west of Alexandria, near Cyrenaica (now in Libya). The defeat of the Senussi ended with the rescue of the crews of HMS *Tara* and

HMS *Moorina*, by an armoured car squadron led by the Duke of Westminster. A German submarine had torpedoed both ships in November 1915 and the 91 crewmen had been captured by the Senussi. They were taken to the Wells of the White Doctor at Bir Hakim, about 75 miles to the west of Sollum and held there in terrible conditions by their captors. The armoured car squadron rescued them on St Patrick's Day (17 March 1916) and returned to Allied lines.

The artillery fire heard by Angus and his comrades as they arrived in Alexandria in January 1916 must have come from artillery ranges near Port Suez; there was no fighting going on in the region at the time.

12 January

Parade at 9.30am for gun mount drill. It's pretty cold at night; we only have one blanket each. Rations poor, living on biscuits and bully [beef]. Our battalion had a football match against the Gurkha troops; score Gurkha's 3 the Royal Scots 2. Had a walk through Suez on the pass.

13 January

Had usual parade, physical drill and machine gun parade during the forenoon. Received letters from John, home, Robbie and D McLeod dated 18, 20 and 27 December 1915. Also a Peoples Journal dated December 20, wrote to John.

14 January

Reveille at 5.30am. No early morning parade for a change. Machine-gun instruction etc in the forenoon. Had a stroll through Suez at night and visited the Bull Ring.

On 15 January, the 7th Royal Scots rejoined the 88th Brigade, 29th Division, having been absent since 17 October 1915.

15 January

We have moved camp again, only a short distance. Played cards in the afternoon.

16 January

Church parade in the K.O.S.B. [King's Own Scottish Borders] camp at 10.30am. It was very cold last night. Received two parcels containing 200 fags, 1 pair of socks, 25 Gold Flake [cigarettes], 2 handkerchiefs and a tin of shortbread from John. Splendid! It is winter weather and bitterly cold at night. We only have one blanket and a greatcoat.

17 January

Monday, inspected by the General outside Suez then returned to camp. Exercise in the forenoon and machine-gun parade in afternoon. Sent postcard to John and one to home. No pay, the whole tent is stony broke but plenty of fags etc owing to parcels and mail. Wrote home and sent letter to Donald telling him we are at Suez, sent postcard to Magnus.

18 January

Spent forenoon getting guns ready for firing range in afternoon as the reserve team are firing on a course. Heard a rumour that the 29th Division is to go to France in March. There is nothing for us here. However, I hope the Turks will give us a chance to get our own back before we leave. Wrote to Robbie. Put in some firing on the range in the afternoon. It was fine fun getting into action in the desert, true instance of the burning plains of Egypt.

The rumours of a move to France in March were true; the 29th Division's commanding General had received orders to prepare for a move to the Western Front. The 29th Division was to prepare to take part in a large attack and hopefully a breakthrough planed against the German lines, astride the river Somme in France.

19 January

Machine-gun parade in the forenoon. No bread and no biscuits. We did stoppage drills on the gun in the afternoon.'

20 January

Orderly for the day. Short rations again so I drew 20 shillings pay but could not get to town as the battalion is on Brigade duty. We have had a draft from Mustapha of about 30 men, which included Corporal Radcliffe and Sergeant Major Dunbar.

21 January

Exercise at 7.30am. We are still on short rations. Machine-gun parade in the afternoon.

22 January

Parade at 10.30am with an inspection by the Commanding Officer. Had a walk through Suez in the afternoon.

On 23 January, the Royal Scots moved camp again as the 29th Division made ready for its move to France. The soldiers were still on short rations and living in bell tents housing up to twelve men. The conditions were very cramped and there was only the routine of garrison duties to break up the day.

24 January

We are paraded with our company. Then had exercise before breakfast. In the afternoon, we built a defensive mud wall around our camp. Essex Regiment played the Manchester's in the last match at Brigade. The result was a 2-2 draw.

The daily routine went on for the soldiers in the Royal Scots Machine Gun Company; the diary mentions how the battalion attended the firing range for 'musketry' training and carried out fatigues. There was also a football match between the Royal Scots and the Royal Army Medical Corps, the Royal Scots winning three goals to one.

On 27 January 1916 Angus found himself in trouble for a serious breach of military law.

27 January

Exercise before breakfast. Three hours of circuit drill in the afternoon. I was collared for being deficient in my iron rations, expect I will appear in the orderly room tomorrow. The Worcesters played the Newfoundlanders at football in the afternoon, the result was Worcesters 1 the Newfoundlanders 0. We are having occasional showers of rain.

Iron rations were issued to every British soldier during the First World War for use in an emergency. They consisted of bully beef, cheese and hard tack biscuits, and only an officer could give the order for them to be eaten. To break into them at any other time was a serious breach of discipline. However, there is no further mention of this misdemeanour in the diary so presumably Angus's superior officers forgot about it, or the crime was overlooked in the preparations for the brigade inspection next day.

At 9.30am on Friday 28 January 1916 the 88th Brigade of the 29th Infantry Division formed up in the desert and marched past their Brigade Commander, Brigadier General Cayley. The march past was carried out in heavy rain, which persisted all day. In the afternoon there was another football match between two Brigade units, result Essex Regiment 4, Hampshire Regiment 1.

The monotony of routine in camp began to have a detrimental effect on the troops and they itched for some action.

29 January

Exercise as usual before breakfast. Commanding Officer inspection and then we had fatigues in the afternoon. I did my monthly wash after dinner. It was a splendid day. Worcesters and R.A.M.C. had a match in the afternoon, result 3-1. I received a gift containing shortbread, a pipe pouch and writing pad. This camp is getting very monotonous; wish we could have some excitement with J Turk again.

31 January

Usual parades. The battalion had a league match with the Newfoundlanders in the afternoon. Result Royal Scots 2, Newfoundlander's 0. It reminded me of a match at Tynecastle [Hearts of Midlothian Football ground in Edinburgh]. Great excitement.

1 February

The battalion sent eighty men on fatigue duties to Port Said, the rest of the battalion were put to work in a provision depot, Essex and Royal Army Medical Corps played football in the afternoon. Result Essex 4 and R.A.M.C. 1.

The football matches took on an important role in the daily lives of the soldiers in Egypt. It was a way to pass the time and inter unit rivalry was fierce.

2 February
Usual parades and drill forenoon and afternoon. Hampshire's and Worcester have had a match at 3.30pm. Result 3-0. It was a splendid day, very warm.

3 February
Usual parade. Football match between our battalion and the Essex during the afternoon, result 3-0. Another fine day, our battalion is now top of league.

It was not all boredom and football for the soldiers.

4 February
No parade. Battalion sent on fatigue party in forenoon unloading trucks. We were worked like dock gangs. We cleaned the spare parts for the gun in the afternoon. Hampshire's and R.A.M.C had another match, result Hants 6 and R.A.M.C 1. Wrote home at night.

5 February
Kit inspection in forenoon. I drew 12 shillings pay. Essex and R.A.M.C. had a match in afternoon, result Essex 2 the R.A.M.C. 1. We sent a hat around our gun team and purchased a football for 75pis [Piastres]. I also bought a belt for 20pis in Suez.

7 February
Usual parades. Royal Scots played football against Worcester's at 3.30pm. Result Royal Scots 0 the Worcesters 1. Our gun team was kicking a ball around during parade time. There are also boxing competitions going on all over the place.

On 8 February 1916 the commander of the 29th Division left his men in Egypt and headed off to France to prepare for his new sector of command.

8 February
We are paraded beside the railway at 7.00am to see the General off. Damn him for leaving so early. Battalion then put on fatigues. It's a warm day I am on picket duty around the canteen. We had a decent feed at 9.30pm.

9 February
We are on guard at H.Q. Football match between Royal Scots and the Hants, result Royal Scots 1 the Hants 1.

10 February
Relieved off guard at 9.00am. No parades for us at all today. We played football in the afternoon.

Divisional training began to get tough as the soldiers prepared for their move to the Western Front. The 29th Division was battle hardened; they had been bloodied by their spell in Gallipoli but were not ready for the conditions of trench life in France. Continental fighting was more ferocious than anything they had ever seen.

11 February
Breakfast at 7.00am. We then had a route march of 18 miles across the desert with no water bottles.

12 February
Exercise at 7.00am. Kit inspection at 9.30am. Football match between Royal Scots and the crew of HMS Glory. Result HMS Glory 3 the Royal Scots 2. The naval boys were splendid players and deserved to win.

13 February
Divine service passed rest of day playing football etc.

14 February
I am the orderly for the day. Parade at 9.30am in F.M.O. [Field Marching Order] for drill. It's a very warm day.

15 February
Parade at 7.30am. Had a march in F.M.O. for about six miles, across the desert to the Suez Canal. We were pretty done in by the time we got back.

16 February
Usual drills in the forenoon. It is very warm but weather prevailing.

17 February
Parade at 7.30am in full marching order for Brigade route march. We had a four-mile tramp through the desert. Saw several aeroplanes flying around. Football match in the afternoon between the Royal Scots and the Royal Field Artillery. Result Royal Scots 4 the Artillery 3.

The men from the machine-gun sections must have found the route marches very difficult, as they carried their heavy Vickers machine guns and all the ancillary equipment through the desert; the tripod for the gun weighed in at 50lbs alone. The gun with all its ammunition, water coolers and spare parts was equally shared out amongst the men, who also had to carry their personal equipment as well as rifles, webbing gear and .455 inch Webley pistols.

Their equipment consisted of the 1908 pattern webbing which was made up from a three-inch-wide belt and two two-inch shoulder braces, worn vertically in the front and crossed over the back like an ordinary pair of men's braces. Both belt and braces were fitted with various buckles and end-tags so that they could be fitted together in several different ways. The webbing was treated to be waterproof and was made up from the following items.

(i)   A pair of ammunition pouches, each of which carried 75 rounds of ammunition.
(ii) A haversack worn on the left hip.
(iii) A bayonet holder worn on the left side of the belt.
(iv) A water bottle worn in a sling on the right hip.
(v)   An entrenching tool, which combined a pick with a shovel.
(vi) A back pack containing a greatcoat, mess tin, washing kit, some spare clothes and a groundsheet.

The total weight of this kit was 60lbs; if the pack was discarded an extra 100 rounds of ammunition could be carried and the kit then weighed 55lbs. Add to this the Short Magazine Lee Enfield rifle weighing in at 8lbs 10oz or 9lbs 11oz with its bayonet fitted, although the section commanders and gunners carried the Webley revolvers weighing almost 3lbs.

The British High Command issued orders that machine guns were better suited to working together in attacks, able to pour down heavy fire on enemy lines, destroying counter-attacks before they could be organised. The battalion machine-gun companies would form together as Brigade machine-gun battalions and fight as independent units away from their original units. Men detailed to be the new battalion machine gunners were to be issued with the new lightweight Lewis machine gun, better suited to the rigours of life in the trenches on the Western Front.

The rumours of the formation of the Brigade machine-gun battalions began to filter down to the men in the battalions.

18 February

Parades in forenoon. We built a new cookhouse during the afternoon. We also heard our section is going to be attached to the Brigade Machine Gun Company. I drew 12 shillings pay.

19 February

Exercise before breakfast. We proceeded to some baths in Suez at 9.00am. Had a splendid wash in hot and cold showers. We got our clothes out of a fumigator they were actually steaming. Had our photo taken in Suez and then buggered about until 7.00pm.

The following day the 1st/5th Royal Scots machine gunners packed up their camp and left the battalion lines to join the 88th Brigade Machine Gun Company of the Machine Gun Corps. Second Lieutenant Baxendine led the men to their new unit, but he returned to the Royal Scots on 28 February and Lieutenant Chalmers replaced him.

20 February
Divine service at 9.30am. We packed up at 2.00pm and joined the Brigade Machine Gun Company at the adjoining camp.

The following are the men who transferred to the 88th Brigade Machine Gun Company of the Machine Gun Corps from the 5th Battalion Royal Scots, alongside Angus Mackay (Royal Scots 2428) Machine Gun Corps 20682, in February 1916.

20671 Sergeant A. Acquroff
Royal Scot 1316. Died of wounds 22 March 1918

20674 Private Erskine
Wounded in action 9 July 1917

20675 Lance Corporal Fairburn
Wounded in action 10 July 1917

20680 Private J. Jackson
Royal Scot 2882. Died of wounds 26 May 1917

20681 Private Tighe
Eenlisted 26 May 1915. Discharged 13 July 1916

20683 Private W.T. Muir
Royal Scot 2366. Died of wounds 13 October 1916

20685 Private G. Oliver

Private A.B. Scott
Royal Scot 2136. Killed in action 20 November 1916

Sergeant Veich G DCM MM

Private W.S. White
Royal Scot 2523. Killed in action 23 April 1917

The Machine Gun Corps was initially formed with 4000 officers and 80,000 men, formed up into companies and battalion-sized units. Each division would have three machine-gun companies, armed with 16 Vickers heavy machine guns, each gun manned by a crew of six men led by a corporal or sergeant.

21 February

This is our second day with the Machine Gun Company. Exercise at 6.40am machine gun drill in the afternoon, we then cleaned the guns.

The part time Territorial soldiers from the 5th Royal Scots machine gun section were now asked to sign up as regular soldiers for the duration of the war, in the newly formed Machine Gun Corps. This was an unusual step; most Territorial soldiers who fought in the First World War remained part of the Territorial Force.

22 February

Parades as usual. Did some washing in the afternoon. One of our officers wanted us to sign up as regulars in the Machine Gun Corps; he said we would get extra pay. I am not anxious to sign any more papers until we get more information. There are still rumours that we are off to France as a machine-gun battalion. Wrote to Robbie and Hugh.

23 February

Started on a route march at 8.00am, marched to the Suez Canal. Returned across the desert, we covered about ten miles in total. The dust and heat made it very heavy going. Received letters from home dated 5 February. Football match between Worcesters and R.H.A. [Royal Horse Artillery] result a 2-2 draw.

24 February

Exercise before breakfast. Machine-gun drills in the forenoon then drill and forming fours in the afternoon. The battalion and the Lancashire Fusiliers played a football match, result Royal Scots 0 the Fusiliers 1. It is a very warm day.

25 February

I am the tent orderly for the day. Usual exercise before breakfast, the section was then on fatigue duties. I received letters from John and Robbie which contained photos of George and Magnus also a Press and Journal and a Peoples Friend.

The inter unit rivalry continued in the newly formed Brigade Machine Gun Company.

26 February
Kit inspection in the forenoon. There was a machine gun competition in the afternoon at 4.30pm between the Worcester's, Essex, Hampshire, Newfoundlander and the Royal Scot gun teams. Result Worcester's 1st prize, we were second. We had a fag and baccy issue at night.

Rumours of the move to France persisted.

27 February
Church parade in the Royal Scots lines at 9.30am, we then spent the rest of the day in their camp. Rumour we are off to France in 10 days. We got our photos, but they are not up to much.

28 February
I am the orderly for the day. Lieutenant Chalmers has rejoined us from Port Said. Usual parades then we had the afternoon off. Football matches etc going as usual.

29 February
Usual parades and machine gun drill. We then had infantry drill, nothing much else doing.

1 March
Exercise before breakfast then had an easy day. We had fatigues and drew rations. More rumours of a move to France or England. The climate here is getting much warmer so I will not be sorry if we do shift. Wrote home and to Robbie.

Soldiers of the machine-gun companies were now allocated to individual gun teams and given an area of responsibility within their new sections. Angus found himself responsible for the ammunition.

2 March
Usual morning parades. I have been appointed as the number 2 [ammunition loader] on the number 2 gun. There was a bad sandstorm in the afternoon.

Angus and his fellow soldiers even had time to enjoy themselves.

3 March
Usual parade. I drew £1 pay and took a walk to Suez. We hired two donkeys and then raced back to camp, great fun. K.O.S.B [King's Own Scottish Borderers] and Lancashire Fusiliers played the final of the Division cup, result K.O.S.B 2, the Fusiliers 0.

The routine of garrison life went on as the soldiers began to prepare for the move to France.

4 March
Cleaning our guns in the morning. Spent the night in Port Suez.

5 March
Church parade at 9.30am in the Royal Scots lines. Spent rest of the day on fatigues, nothing else doing.

6 March
Usual parades. Received letters from John, also a Peoples Journal.

7 March
Just the usual parades. I am the orderly for the day. Nothing doing.

The ongoing preparations for the move from Egypt to France were almost complete.

8 March
We paraded at 8.00am and marched past the General in command of our Division. Nothing to do in the afternoon.

9 March
I am on guard for 24hrs. The rest of my section is away on a Brigade route march.

10 March
We were relieved of camp guard at 9.00am. Had a short parade in the afternoon. Nothing unusual.

11 March
Paraded at 7.00am for divisional manoeuvres. It was damn hot tramping through the desert carrying the machine gun.

Tension mounted in anticipation at the forthcoming move to France and began to affect all ranks in the 29th Division.

12 March
Church parade at 9.30am. The parson got ratty and stopped in the middle of his discourse; he said the men were not giving him enough attention. Sermon finished!

The Division's move to France finally began on 14 March 1916, with the transfer from the tented camp just outside Port Suez to Alexandria docks. The 29th made its move by troop train, finally ready for it's embarkation onto ships bound for France.

As a private soldier, Angus Mackay would have had little knowledge of the larger details of the Division's move; his diary concentrates on his own small part in it.

14 March

Usual parades before breakfast. Made our final preparations for departure. We had a test with a new gun tripod at the range, fired about 100 rounds with pretty good results. Struck our tents after dinner and drew 10shillings pay. Left Suez at 9.00pm and arrived at Alexandria docks at 9.00am.

15 March

We embark on the SS Transylvania and leave docks at 7.00pm. All the lights on board ship are out.

16 March

Going ahead on a north-north-west course. Nothing in sight except our escort.

There was a constant threat to shipping from submarines; troopships were prime targets for prowling U-boats of the German Imperial Navy. Infantry battalions were often tasked with guarding their own transports.

17 March

I am on submarine guard all day with our machine gun. Nothing in sight except our escort, we have sighted several ships travelling east. We have begun to steer a zig zag course.

18 March

We sighted Malta at 6.00am but have passed on without a call. Our escort ship has left us and headed off towards Valetta. We also passed an island called Sardinia about 4.00pm; I believe it is used as a convict settlement. Very calm sea.

19 March

We are passing islands and can see land; I think it is the Italian coast. We have no escort ships; I was on guard at 5.00pm.

The 88th Brigade machine gunners arrived in France the next day.

20 March

We have arrived at Marseilles harbour at 8.00am. Beautiful entrance, which seems to be well fortified, we can see German prisoners busy all over the place. When we leave the ship, we are marched to a station near the docks and boarded cattle trucks with 35 men in each; we are really roughing it. We could hardly stand up and as for lying down well no chance!

The machine-gun battalion arrived on the Western Front and headed for the front line trenches in northern France. The infantry battalions of the 29th Division travelled to the front with their support units of artillery, with medical units beside them.

The 1st/5th Royal Scots arrived in Marseilles on 22 March 1916; the battalion then left the command of the 29th Division. They were moved up to the village of Argueves, where they amalgamated with the 6th Battalion to form the 5th/6th Battalion Royal Scots. This new battalion, under the command of Lieutenant-Colonel Wilson, then joined the 14th Brigade of the 32nd Division to serve in France. Private Angus Mackay and his new unit, the 88th Brigade Machine Corps, formed from the machine-gun sections from the 4th Worcestershire Regiment, 2nd Hampshire Regiment, 1st Essex Regiment and the 1st/5th Royal Scots was ready to do battle.

5

The Western Front

When the 29th Division reached the Western Front in early 1916, the Allies were bogged down in the stalemate of trench warfare, fighting a strong German Army in a continuous trench line stretching over 300 miles from the Belgian coast to Switzerland. British and French mass attacks in 1915 had failed to break the enemy; disastrous offensives along the lines had destroyed the best of the British and French armies and reinforcements were desperately needed.

On 21 February 1916, the German attacked the French city of Verdun in an effort to break through and capture Paris. The defenders of the forts at Douamont and Vaux, just outside the city, fought valiantly to hold up the enemy attacks, but Fort Douamont fell into German hands on 25 February. French generals then poured reinforcements into Verdun and the slaughter began; the French Army lost 377,000 men.

The French Army were holding the front lines at Verdun at all costs as the 29th Division arrived in France in early March 1916, trying to stem the German advance on Verdun. Fighting around the low hill at Le Mort Homme (The Dead Man) was extremely fierce. Meanwhile the machine gunners from the 29th Division left Marseilles by train bound for northern France. The journey to the front was not a comfortable one; the men were jammed in cattle trucks like animals bound for market.

21 March
Proceeding on our journey. There are 45 men in each truck it is impossible to sleep, standing room only. This is a damn fine reception after nine months of fighting, beautiful scenery but food is awful, just bully [beef)]and die-hard biscuits. We passed Lyon about 6.00pm.

The journey took the men through the heart of France; the regions they passed through were untouched by war.

22 March

Travelling through the Rhone Valley, it is splendid scenery. The trees are so green and are a sight for sore eyes after Gallipoli and Suez. We have seen fair faces for the first time; they are a real treat after seeing nothing but Turks, gypsies and Greeks for a year. The carriage is so uncomfortable some of us climb up on top and hang on for five hours, pretty risky but at least there was plenty of fresh air.

The train journey ended the next day when the train arrived in the British rear close to Amiens.

23 March

We are disappointed that we did not pass through Paris, but we had a good view of the Seine. When we awoke at 4.00am, it was pretty cold and found we had arrived in a town called Abbeville. We unloaded our chattels and then marched to a village called Bellancourt, arriving there at 6.00pm; we are now billeted in an old house. Cleaned up our new billets and got a fire going. This is more home like and we soon had it looking like a palace after three days in those cattle trucks, there are rumours of leave. Received a parcel from home containing socks, some chocolate and a pencil.

The town of Abbeville was one of the main supply areas for the British front lines, in an area of France sat astride the river Somme. All British troops moving into the Somme area by train from the south, or from channel ports at Boulogne and Dieppe, moved through the railhead in Abbeville and on into the trenches. Villages in the countryside around the town became their camping and training area. The soldiers arriving by train and ship did not know it but they were heading for the Somme, a name that would become part of the British cultural identity just as much as Verdun would be for the French.

The newly arrived machine-gun battalions had now to acclimatise to the change in the weather, after the warmth of the desert sun. Angus Mackay felt the shock of the French spring climate.

24 March

It was a damn cold night as our fire died away and a snow storm hit the billet. We paraded in the morning for a route march; it is still snowing and very cold. We are not enjoying this much. Received parcel from home containing socks etc, I wrote to John.

25 March

We have shifted our billet to a nearby cellar. All our section is together and we have found plenty of straw to keep us warm. It is a much warmer day and the snow is disappearing. I received a Press and Journal from John.

The 88th Brigade of the 29th Division then began to gather in the Abbeville area, preparing its men for action in the line.

27 March
We are still in Bellancourt, France. I have received mail from John and Robbie also this diary, note from Sandy enclosed.

28 March
It is a wet and miserable day. We are sleeping in a cellar with 24 men in it; everywhere you go there is mud up to your knees. Section is on a route march in this wet and miserable weather. Wrote to William.

29 March
Better day today. There is a rumour we are moving tomorrow, I am the orderly for the day. Drew ten francs pay and received mail.

The rumours of a move were true; the 29th Division was to move closer to the front and prepare to enter the trenches for its first taste of action against the Germans. The Division was part of the build up of troops moving into the area for the summer push on the enemy lines; the British plan was to attack the Germans along the Somme river.

The attack on the German lines was initially to take place with the support of French units in the south; the Allies would break through the enemy lines and into the German rear areas. The Somme region was chosen as the axis of the attack not only because it was the junction of the French and British lines, but also because it encompassed strategic objectives. If the German Army pulled back on the Somme, the whole enemy line on the Western Front could crumble and cause a general retreat.

At the end of March 1916 the 29th Division began to make its way towards the front lines.

31 March
We packed up and got on a train at 11.30am, dress F.M.O. We have moved to a village called Gorenflos, it's about eight miles from Bellancourt. We arrived in Gorenflos at 2.00pm then billeted for the night.

1 April
Today we have marched eighteen miles to a village called Bonneville. My section is billeted in a stable; this is a decent size place with the whole 88th Brigade billeted within it. My feet are damn sore with blisters all over, very warm day. Leave is starting soon.

Behind the lines on the Somme new battalions of soldiers, brigade support units and divisional headquarters were moving forward to take part in the big push. It was one of the largest logistical movements of men and arms ever carried out.

The 88th Brigade remained in the village of Bonneville and rested on Sunday 2 April. As the Brigade prepared to move the next morning, Angus received some devastating news.

3 April

I have received a letter from John, my brother Magnus has been reported killed on the 19 March. We left our billets at 9.30am and marched seven miles to Beauquesne, where we are billeted for the night.

Memo – Magnus has been reported killed whilst guarding a bomb store, I hope it's not true. I'm afraid it is only too true.

Angus's younger brother Magnus had been killed in action early that month, whilst serving with the 11th Battalion Argyll and Sutherland Highlanders. He had joined up at the age of sixteen, having lied about his age to join the ranks of Kitchener's New Army, formed at the outbreak of war.

In early 1916, the 11th Argyll's were in reserve trenches, near the village of Loos on routine trench holding duties. The battalion men were busy improving their trenches and laying floorboards in good weather, in what was considered an extremely quiet sector of the line. They were readying themselves to enter the front lines and relieve the 7th Inniskilling Fusiliers, and as the preparations were being made for the move, enemy shell fire fell on the Argyll's positions and killed a number of men. During the attack a bomb store was hit and five sentries were killed outright; one man was wounded but he died later.

Private Magnus Mackay was one of the sentries killed that day; he was eighteen. His comrades buried his body in Loos village. His grave is now located in Loos British Cemetery France, Plot IX, Row G, Grave 20.

Angus had little time to grieve for his brother as he moved forward with his unit towards the front line trenches.

4 April

Today we marched 14 miles from Beauquesne to Colincamps. We are billeted in a cellar about 20 minutes walk from the front. Our village is a prime target for the German gunners.

The village of Colincamps was one of the main villages behind the battlefront, in an area the French civilians called the Zone of Occupation. Local civilians remained in their homes but the area was under military control; Colincamps was the final village for troops entering the trenches at Serre and in front of Beaumont-Hamel. It was only a short distance from there to the trenches; battalions heading for the front moved from the village up Euston Road and on past the *Sucrerie* (sugar beet factory) into the third line trenches.

The front was relatively quiet when the 29th Division arrived in the villages behind the lines on the Somme; the build up for the forthcoming attack was beginning slowly. They joined men from Canada, Australia, India, New Zealand and South Africa. The British Army had 58 divisions in the field, in four Army groups with a huge logistic tail dragging behind it. Many of the infantry battalions on the Somme were volunteer 'pals' battalions, groups of men who had worked together as civilians, joined up together and would, in many cases, die together. They were keen to get into action, but were totally unprepared for the slaughter that was to come.

Although the British sector of the Western Front in early 1916 was relatively quiet, all along the line soldiers were busy repairing and maintaining the trench defences. It was heavy work mainly carried out at night, shoring up shell damaged trenches, digging dugout shelters and opening up communication trenches between the third and first lines. In bad weather the trenches flooded, and pioneer battalions were kept busy. Heavily armed patrols moved out into no man's land at last light, searching for weak spots in the enemy line and taking prisoners. The latter gave the British intelligence officers indications of the types of German units they faced and the quality of their men. There were also proactive attempts to confuse the enemy. On one occasion near Arras, the 51st (Highland) Division carried out manoeuvres dressed in English divisional uniform to give the Germans a false impression of British troop movements. Overhead Allied and German observation planes photographed the lines and observation balloons were used by artillery spotters to observe the fall of their fire.

Both sides carried out extensive underground mining operations, using coal miners to dig long tunnels under the enemy trenches and packing them with explosives, the troops in the trenches above lived with the constant threat from a sudden underground explosion. The British miners were forced to live, work and fight underground, illuminated only by artificial light, digging quietly to avoid detection.

Life in the front line was both boring and terrifying; sleep or talk could be instantly interrupted by a sudden bombardment. At night there was the tiresome yet vital guard to be kept, keeping look out for enemy patrols probing into the Allied positions. If the enemy did get into the trench then there was the prospect of hand-to-hand fighting. This was usually done with the rifle and bayonet or hand grenade, but many soldiers preferred to fight with homemade trench knives, a metal cosh, a sharpened spade or an entrenching tool. Snipers and artillery spotters also moved out into no man's land at night, laying up in hiding all day to watch the enemy trenches. Soldiers on both sides lived in constant fear of the sudden bullet. Their rations did little to cheer them, being brought up by carrying parties at last light in large metal dixies. It was usually cold by the time it arrived.

The 88th Machine Gun Company were still in Colincamps, waiting for the order to enter the front line.

5 April
We had a parade and cleaned the guns. There are bags of shells flying around, but our billet is safe so far. Number 1 and Number 2 sections are going into the line.

6 April
We cleaned our guns in the forenoon, I received mail from Robbie and John dated 1st and 2nd of April. There was a terrific bombardment about 9.00pm and we were told to stand ready with our guns, but were not needed. The bombardment lasted about one hour.

It was at this time that the machine gunners got their first taste of the industrial warfare of the Western Front.

7 April
I am orderly for the day, cleaning guns etc as usual. Wrote to John and Robbie, then sent postcard to Sandy and Mother. Enemy bombarded us with gas last night, four men were wounded.

The German Army had first used poison gas in April 1915 at the Second Battle of Ypres; it had proved to be very effective and was soon used extensively by both sides. Many different types of gas were used but there were three main types: chlorine and phosgene attacked the lungs filling them with liquid, suffocating and then drowning the victim, and mustard gas caused severe blister burns to the body and blindness.

In the early days the poison gas was released from cylinders, but by early 1916, both sides were firing gas-filled ammunition from their artillery. Gas attacks did not cause heavy casualties, only 9 per cent of all wounded men treated by medical units from 1915 to 1918 were treated for gas injuries, and of them only 3 per cent died. However, it was highly effective at spreading chaos, especially in rear areas, disrupting logistics. Soldiers who came under a gas attack had to don gas masks and protective clothing, slowing their effectiveness when deployed as working parties. A man dressed in a gas mask could only work for a certain period before he had to rest, and all ammunition and supplies had to be decontaminated before use.

In early 1916 British troops had been issued with the 'PH' helmet gas mask; the mask dipped in a solution of sodium phenate and hexamine gave good protection from gas poisoning. The troops also received g training in anti-gas drills, which helped keep down the casualties from this terrible new weapon of war.

The troops in the rear areas also saw another new weapon of war in use for the first time.

8 April
Had gun drills during the forenoon. Later we watched four of our aeroplanes pass over our heads and saw them get a lively time of it, when about sixty shells were fired at them. We go into the trenches tomorrow. Wrote home and to P Burr.

The newly formed Royal Flying Corps was busy flying reconnaissance missions over the enemy trenches, in preparation for the forthcoming offensive. The aeroplane was an important new weapon of war, able to range far and wide over the battlefield, observing and photographing the enemy trench lines and gun positions. Machine gunners and artillerymen on both sides of the line tried desperately to shoot down the opposition's observation planes before they could return home with the photographs and intelligence gathered.

On Sunday 9 April 1916 the machine gunners from the 29th Division entered the trenches on the Western Front for the first time.

9 April
We are paraded at 9.30am and proceed to the 2nd line trench. We relieved the Essex gunners in a good position, several air torpedoes have landed near us but no casualties.

The soldiers entering the trenches went through a number of drills when they first arrived in their new positions. The men were usually allocated a dugout or shelf space where they could store their personal kit and greatcoat; they then loaded their personal weapons and if they had a rifle, its bayonet was fixed. Machine gunners set up their Vickers guns on top of the trench behind sand bags and loaded their ammunition belts onto the feed trays, ready for action.

Trench routine was then divided up amongst the sections but usually consisted of one hour on sentry duty, one hour on work party and one hour of sleep. At night men were sent out to repair barbed wire in no man's land, a 'stand to' (a general state of readiness against attack) was carried out at first light and last light, and the men could then try to catch up on sleep during the day.

The 29th Division had taken over trenches north-west of the village of Beaumont-Hamel in the northern sector of the Somme front. Regular army troops from the 4th Infantry Division were to the north and the 36th (Ulster) Division was to the south; this sector was considered to be quiet. The German defensive line around Beaumont-Hamel was well constructed and the German soldiers – who hailed from Württemberg – were able to sit deep underground, safe from British shelling. German trenches were more strongly built than those of the Allies, and more luxurious, often lined with wood and stocked with furniture looted from French houses. The deep underground bunkers built in and around Y Ravine near the village of Beaumont-Hamel were used as artillery shelters, and had running water and electricity.

Enemy bombardment of the British front lines continued as the build up for the attack went on.

10 April

This is our second day in the trenches. Rats as big as household cats come out in swarms after dark. There is a heavy bombardment going on our left flank but nothing doing around our position.

The rats were a common problem on the Western Front and moved in large swarms, feeding on the rubbish left by the troops, or on the dead littering no man's land. Hygiene was a major difficulty for the troops, as there was only a little water available for drinking, and none for washing or cleaning. As a result, body lice were a common problem.

11 April

Our third day in the trenches. We are still being shelled; no one has been hit yet. Received a parcel from home containing cake and a Press and Journal from John, it is heartily welcomed.

12 April

Laid down fire on enemy lines last night, and had a bit of a strafe. Heavy rain for the last 12hrs, the trenches are in a hell of a state. I received 200 Gold Flake and a letter from Jock, got a Press and Journal from Donald.

Offensive action and aggressive patrolling on the enemy lines continued, as the British High Command continued probing the enemy defences searching for week spots. Deep underground ex-coal miners serving in the Royal Engineers tunnelled under the German trenches and laid explosives. German miners and engineering units counter mined the British lines. On 13 April 1916, Angus Mackay and his comrades witnessed the blowing up of a German sap or observation trench in no man's land.

13 April

We exploded a mine under a German sap about 500 yards in front of our gun positions. There was a terrific roar and the ground shook for about a mile. We received some sniper fire and were relieved at 10.00am, then proceeded to Colincamps. Drew 10 francs pay, its very wet and cold weather.

Both sides dug observation trenches or 'saps' out into no man's land, to try to see what the other side was doing. The trench was usually dug out to a shell hole and a race often occurred between both sides to try to get there first. The saps were sometimes only yards from the enemy trench.

After a spell of four days in the front line trenches, the same time was then spent in rest camps just behind the lines. The period behind the lines resting was usually spent on fatigues or working parties.

14 April

We have settled down back in our cellar in Colincamps. We spent the whole of today carting manure from our billets, call this rest? There has been no more rain and the ground is a picture of mud and slush. We had a rifle inspection at 3.00pm.

The territorial soldiers of the 88th Brigade were once again asked to sign on as regular soldiers.

15 April

We have had showers of rain and some snow, gun drill in the afternoon. It is very cold. I wrote home and to John, sent postcard to Robbie. Germans have fired a strafe on us during the night. We have again been asked to sign on as regulars for the duration of the war in the Machine Gun Corps.

As a Territorial volunteer Angus was concerned about signing on as a regular Army soldier.

16 April

Had a parade at 9.00am. We were again asked to sign on in Machine Gun Corps for the duration, I'm afraid I want some particulars first. It is a splendid day. German aeroplane came over and dropped some bombs on us, no casualties.

The spell in reserve trenches was soon over and the battalions rotated back into the trenches for their spell of duty.

17 April

Went back into trenches at 9.00am. It is a rotten day, mud up to our knees. We have a good position and a dugout, about 1750 yards range from the enemy lines. Received 200 Gold Flake, a writing pad and letter from John dated 14 April. The shrapnel is really going some.

Shelling and counter shelling was going on all along the line; shrapnel shells were fused to explode above the trenches showering the infantry below with hot shards of metal. The many injuries put a severe strain on the stretched medical services. When there was heavy rain, wounded men often drowned as they lay waiting for stretcher bearers to take them back to the regimental aid posts, then on back to the casualty clearing stations behind the lines.

18 April

The weather is terrible, mud and rain in the trenches takes you to your knees all around. Shrapnel exploding beside our gun position has wounded two men. Wrote to John and George.

19 April
It's still raining the trenches are awful. It is simply a swimming matter on our 3rd day in the line. Things have gone very quiet and our artillery seems to have the upper hand. Received mail from George.

To the north of the Somme battlefield heavy fighting was going on around the Belgian city of Ypres; German attacks along the Ypres to Langemark road were repulsed between 19 April and 21 April 1916. The whole area was flooded in the torrential rain and it took one unit of the King's Shropshire Light Infantry several hours to cover 200 yards during the counter-attacks. The weather was then so bad that no wounded men were recovered until the 25th.

On the Somme the weather remained atrocious:

20 April
This is our fourth day in the trenches but there is sign of an improvement. Wrote letters at night. I was nearly potted by a Hun when I was on guard.

21 April
Fifth day in the trenches. We were relieved at 10am by the Worcesters' gun team and had a two-mile tramp, through mud and slush back to Colincamps. We are now back in our cellar and it is pouring rain, there are bags of shells coming over. Drew boots.

Units stationed in the front collected their rations from Army Service Corps supply depots, just behind the lines. The fighting battalions sent back their supply wagons with a small working party under the command of a junior NCO, to collect the rations and bring them up for issue. Angus was sent on such a ration run on 22 April.

22 April
I am orderly for the day. Better weather, we spent the day cleaning guns etc. I had a trip on the Transport Wagon to the village of Bus [Bus-les-Artois], about eight miles away for rations. We had a rotten time of it, raining all the way. Rations of Beef, cigarettes and matches are lying in about six inches of mud.

Mobile bath units were also set up behind the lines and rows of filthy, mud caked soldiers could be seen queuing up outside them, eager to bathe and get into new issue clothes.

23 April
It's a splendid day. We were paraded at 10.00am to have a hot bath for the first time since Egypt. I received a shift of clothing and I feel clean for the first time for ages. Sent postcard home and received an Ensign [local Highland newspaper].

The weather on the Somme battlefield gradually began to improve and so did the living conditions.

24 April
Another splendid day, very dry and warm. Parade for gun drill at 9.30am and watched aeroplanes busy over our heads. The Huns fired about 200 shells at once, in about ten minutes with out results. Wrote home.

25 April
Very sunny day it's like summer now, this is the anniversary of the Gallipoli landings. We are paraded at 9.00am and then head for the trenches to relieve the Worcesters. We are in a rotten position very open to sniping and machine-gun fire. I have decided to sign up for the duration in the Machine Gun Corps.

Artillery bombardments were a continual hazard. The Germans usually shelled one end of a trench and then worked along it a few yards at a time. The British soldiers would watch the shells fall and as the fire moved along the trench, they ran to the part which had already been shelled.

26 April
This is our second day in the trenches. We watched as one of our aeroplanes was shot down by shellfire inside the German's lines. The artillery is very busy but British guns seem to have the upper hand. We had some sniping and game shooting during the morning and at 1.30pm we came under heavy shelling, I had a very narrow escape. Received letter from Peter Burr.

Regular mail from home still arrived for the men in the front lines and the few minutes taken to read a letter or scan the pages from local newspapers, were a welcome break.

27 March
Received Press and Journal and Dispatch, from John. Today is our third day in trenches and it's much quieter, we have had only a few bombs and shrapnel thrown at us. Given a rum issue, splendid day. Spotted a German observation balloon, it looks pretty basic. We are going to do some strafing tonight. I spoke too soon the Huns strafed us at about 4.00pm with 9.2 inch high explosive, they were landing all around us in our gun position and dug out. They make holes six feet deep, no casualties.

The machine gunners soon make their first kill, when they retaliated against the heavy artillery fire landing on their positions.

28 April

Fourth day in trenches. The artillery is very lively, about 500 high explosives shells, shrapnel shells and air torpedoes have fallen all around us during the day, otherwise it was quiet. Had a pot shot at 7.50pm and killed a Hun. We have a splendid sniping post to keep the Bosches on the move. Splendid day, very warm and dry.

After five days under heavy artillery bombardment, Angus Mackay's section was relieved and moved back behind the lines. The soldiers soon realised that British Army discipline and bull was alive and kicking on the Western Front.

29 April

Fifth day in trenches. We packed up our chattels when the 192 section relieved us at 10 am and we moved back to our cellar in Colincamps. Received mail from John, Sandy and Robert then drew 10 francs pay. We have been put on guard from 5.00pm until 9.00am tomorrow, damn our luck as I expected a sleep tonight. Army red tape never dies out even on active service.

Guard duty behind the lines was necessary to guard against a surprise attack, saboteurs or gas bombardment. Soldiers on guard were usually under the command of a corporal, and patrolled the area so their fellows could sleep in relative safety.

30 April

Splendid day. Wrote to Robbie and Peter Burr. Came off guard at 9.00am and had a rest. We got very little sleep last night as our heavy guns were on the go all night. It was a fine firework display. I have just heard the gun that relieved us last night was knocked out.

Preparations for the Battle of the Somme were well underway by the end of April 1916 and artillery batteries were busy firing barrages on the enemy lines. Men and materials were pouring into the region ready to attack and relieve the pressure on the French around Verdun. The French situation was dire; thousands of their best troops were dying in the maelstrom of fighting around the city they vowed would never fall, while German divisional commanders were pouring troops into the attack as they tried to carry the line.

6

Close Shaves
in the Trenches

The German High Command was fully aware that the British were preparing for a large attack over the undulating wooded countryside around the river Somme. They could not fail to notice the build up of supplies and men gathering behind the British lines; the only thing the Germans did not know was the actual date of the attack. The British soldiers also knew the 'Big Push' was imminent, but knew no details beyond what they could see happening in their immediate sector. Only the Allied generals in the rear had a clear view of the battle plan.

1 May
We had a parade at 8.30am for physical exercise. Wrote letters home, to John and Sandy. Sent my Royal Scot cap badge to John in a registered envelope. The artillery is still very active.

The weather along the Somme had become very mixed as the 88th Brigade prepared to re-enter the front lines, near Beaumont-Hamel.

2 May
We had a parade at 9.30am for gun drill, and then wrote to Hugh. It started to rain again at 11.00am; there is a rumour we are getting leave on Sunday. Received mail from home and Peoples Journal I then wrote to George. We go back into the trenches tomorrow.

The following the day the machine gunners trudged their way back along Euston Road, entering the trenches close to the village of Auchonvillers (known as Ocean Villas by the troops).

3 May
We are paraded at 9.00am then proceeded to trenches, enemy about 600 yards range from our mounted gun. We have relieved the Worcesters in slippery muddy trenches, but it is a good position. We caught some of the Hun napping during the morning.

Danger in the front lines came from all sides and the threat of death was a constant companion.

4 May
2nd day in trenches. We had some shooting at us from a Boche aeroplane and then we were shelled. It was a pretty near shave at 600 yards, there is a heavy bombardment going on our right flank. The 29th Division is scrapping again.

The fighting was almost constant as each side harried the other, trying to cause casualties and disrupting work going on around the trench lines.

5 May
3rd day in trenches. Received letters from Donald Munro, William Mackay and a parcel from home containing socks. At midday, I was sent on a tramp for rations hard lines. We were busy in the afternoon observing machine-gun fire.

Harassing machine-gun fire or strafing went on daily along the front line and was carried out by both sides; the machine guns were laid on fixed firing lines and thousands of rounds of ammunition were fed through them. This constant stream of fire disrupted daily life in the line and made movement very difficult; sentries were unable to peer over the edge of the trench to see what the enemy was up to. Working parties mending barbed wire or repairing trenches were constantly seeking cover from the fire and the soldiers resting in the line were unable to sleep. The machine gunners, however, seemed to be enjoying their war:

6 May
Fourth day in the trenches. We are having some splendid sport clearing the Germans out of forward artillery observation posts and harassing working parties. We scored three bulls eyes. Received mail from Robbie and a letter from my old chum Andrew, who is Hawick, he seems to be enjoying himself. It has been a very quiet night, hardly a shot was fired.

This busy period in the trenches was soon over and the machine gunners marched their weary way back to Colincamps.

7 May
We were relieved about 11am and proceeded back to Colincamps. We did not manage to get our cellar this time but got a rather draughty resting place instead.

8 May

In Colincamps billets, and its damn cold. An ideal spot for draughts. Nine men have gone on furlough; expect I will get mine by the end of the month. Parade at 9.30am for gun cleaning and physical jerks. Wrote to Robbie, received letter from George.

9 May

Very cold and wet. Had a parade at 9.00am for baths, had a wash in some tubs, and received a clean shirt. It requires a strong imagination to call this a wash. Received mail from M.S. and then went on guard duty.

The soldiers did not get any time off after guard duty and had to report as normal the following day.

10 May

Came off guard at 6.00am, it is a splendid day. Cleaned guns etc during the forenoon then drew 10 francs pay and bought cigs in Bellancourt. The artillery is very quiet today. Wrote to M Sutherland.

The former Royal Scot machine-gun section soon returned to the front line trench.

11 May

Another splendid day. We paraded at 9.00am and proceeded to the trenches, where we arrived without incident. We have relieved the Hants in a splendid position with a good dugout; we are to stay here for eight days. Furlough is looking promising, received letters from home and John.

With some imagination the soldiers were able to make the trenches more homely.

12 May

Second day in trenches. I have rigged myself up a bed from netting and ammunition cases. We spend 2hrs on guard and then 8hrs off; there is a ration fatigue every second day. Received letters from John, it is very quiet all around.

The view from the machine-gun position out over no man's land must have been bleak: shell holes and barbed wire littered the 300-yard gap between the opposing armies. Corpses in various stages of decomposition littered the ground, and wooden grave markers showed the last resting places of those who their comrades had managed to bury. At night star shells and flares lit up the countryside turning it into a ghostly twilight world where men worked, lived and died.

Mail still arrived from home in a steady flow and helped to raise the morale of the men.

13 May
Third day in trenches. Very wet and cold, this trench is very muddy. I have received Press and Journal from John, sent a reply. Received parcel from home containing a towel, soap and pancakes, it is very welcome.

The build up for the attack went on all along the front, with Royal Flying Corps units still flying reconnaissance flights.

14 May
Fourth day in trench and a day of rest. We had some excitement during the forenoon as a British aeroplane did an exhibition above the gun teams. Received letter from home and Rob.

This spell in the trenches was over a little sooner than the men expected.

15 May
Fifth day in trenches. Another Royal Scots gun team has relieved us at 11am; we then proceeded to Colincamps and got our old cellar back. Wrote home and to George, received letter from John.

The men on the Somme now had a routine and soon settled in to their new way of life.

16 May
Had a parade at 9.30am and cleaned the gun. Very quiet day, warm and dry. I am really enjoying this spell out of the line, everything looks so fresh after the rain.

17 May
We have had a bathing parade at 10.00am, not bad. I received a couple of newspapers from John.

Battalion rations were collected from behind the lines every second day.

18 May
Went to Bus [the village of Bus-les-Artois, about 2 miles from Colincamps] on ration fatigue it was damn warm and a pretty long walk. Some of the chaps have returned from furlough, seemed to have enjoyed themselves.

19 May
Parade at 9.30am and had exercise then spent rest of day sleeping. It is splendid weather and the orchards are in full bloom. Trenches again tomorrow.

20 May

Parade at 9.00am and proceeded to the trenches to relieve the Hants. These are good trenches about 1,000-yard range; this M.G. [machine gun] position is called 'Trossachs'. We had some sport shooting at rats, swarms of them. Splendid weather again. Received Press and Journal from John, it is very quiet.

New units were arriving from England nearly every day, civilian volunteers who had completed their training and were eager to get into battle. These were not the professional soldiers who had fought in 1914; they were green and many would not see home again.

21 May

Second day in trenches. We have heard a new Company has arrived from Grantham to relieve us, expect we will rejoin the Brigade. Had some sport smashing up the Huns, perfect.

The weather on the Somme was improving daily.

22 May

Third day in trenches, splendid day a proper summer at last. Received letters from John. Single shot stunts, and then I went on ration parade. The new M.G. Company relieved us at 5.00pm. We got three more Huns just as we left.

The machine gunners returned to their cellar in Colincamps. On the following day a new commanding officer arrived to take over the unit.

23 May

We parade at 7.30am for exercise and meet our new Commanding Officer. Expect to move this afternoon. We marched to Englebelmer in the afternoon, about six miles away and billeted for the night, this is a very decent village two miles from the trenches.

The 88th Brigade had now moved into the small village of Englebelmer, about two miles west of the German-held town of Beaumont-Hamel. Englebelmer was and still is a typical rural French village, nestling alongside the river Ancre about five miles north of Albert. In 1916 the village was home to many soldiers billeted in the shell marked ruins. The 88th Brigade's ammunition and ration supplies were hidden and camouflaged amongst the houses.

With the 88th Brigade now fully up to strength and consisting of the 4th Worcester Regiment, 1st Essex Regiment, 2nd Hampshire Regiment and the Royal Newfoundland Regiment from Canada, the village must have been fairly busy. Brigade support troops such as Army Service Corps units, Royal Engineers, pioneer battalions and Royal Artillery gunners must have added to the pressure of finding billets.

The area around the town of Albert.

Within 24 hours of arriving at their new home the 88th Brigade were rotated into the trenches to relieve the 87th Brigade, a fellow unit from the 29th Division.

24 May
Parade at 10.00am and proceeded to the trenches where we relieved the Inniskilling's. This is a rotten position about 500 yards from the enemy. Received mail from Andrew.

The Brigade was now in position opposite the German lines around Beaumont-Hamel; the enemy line was strong and well constructed, especially in and around Y Ravine. The two front lines were approximately 500 yards apart, over flat shell marked muddy ground. The village of Beaumont-Hamel was out of sight of the British lines in a hollow behind the ravine.

Soldiers entering the front line came up into the badly damaged village of Auchonvillers and then moved along St Johns Road communication trench. As they approached the front line the soldiers would pass through the unit they were relieving, collecting valuable information on the enemy positions opposite. Once in the first trench the relief would take place very quickly and in total silence so as not to warn the enemy of what was going on, as units changing over positions were extremely vulnerable to a surprise enemy attack.

25 May
Second day in the trenches. We have been shelled and had bags of bombs chucked at us in the forenoon. Trenches are in a rotten state, the Newfoundlanders are holding the line behind us.

British front line positions were laid in three lines of defence with the front line trench closest to the enemy; the trench was dug in a zigzag line to protect from flanking fire and grenade and infantry attacks. Troops fought in the front line from fire bays and lived in dug-outs or 'funk holes' dug in the side of the trench. The trench was about six feet wide and seven feet deep with a fire step for men to stand on and fire on the enemy line; they were built up with sandbags giving added protection from shellfire. Behind the front line was the support trench, a trench very similar to the front line one and constructed along the same lines, connected to the first trench by communication trenches. Regimental first aid posts, small arms ammunition, grenade dumps, battalion headquarters and latrines were also to be found in the communication trenches. The reserve trench housed the reserve troops, ready to rush forward in the event of an attack.

Life in the front line trench was hectic and an attack could come at any moment:

26 May
Mine exploded in the morning and then a bombing raid went in after it. Rotten weather, it has been raining all night. Received letter from William dated 20th May, wrote him a reply. I was sent on a tramp for the rations but I got lost.

Getting lost in the trenches was a very easy thing to do, especially in the dark. Private soldiers were not given maps and the men were forced to find their way by trial and error. Soldiers named their trenches and one could tell which units had been housed where; Scottish names likes 'Princess Street', 'George Square' and 'Sauchiehall Street' appeared alongside 'Trafalgar Square', 'Euston Road' and 'Waterloo Bridge'.

27 May

Fourth day in the trenches. The weather is splendid but I expect we will shift tomorrow. I will not be sorry as this position is not much good, a case of hanging on by your eyebrows. I had a sleep of nine hours during the day, not bad! Very quiet night, the Newfoundlanders have been out in front cutting the wire, no casualties.

Both sides carried out wire cutting at night, as they tried to find a path through the belts of barbed wire in no man's land and into each other's trenches. Paths cut in the wire were usually marked with tape and a machine gun trained on them to prevent surprise enemy attack.

The trench relief went on in the front lines:

28 May 1916

Fifth day in the trenches. The weather is splendid with hardly a shot being fired; there are a few of our aeroplanes up above. Received letter from home containing a ten shillings postal order heard that my brother Hugh [serving in the Army Service Corps] is off to India. We were relieved by the 82nd Brigade's Machine Gun Company and proceed to the village of Mailly Maillet at 4.30pm, where we settle in for the night. We have a decent dugout about two miles from the trenches, received letters from Alan and John.

Mailly Maillet was another small village just behind the front lines; the 88th Brigade's machine gunners were probably sent there to occupy their relief's vacant billet. Mailly Maillet was one of the main build up points for troops attacking Beaumont-Hamel and the villages of Serre and Gommecourt.

Time out of the trench line was spent on the usual military routine of garrison duties.

29 May

I am the orderly for the day. Number 23 section has gone back into the line; we are getting a few days rest in Mailly. It is a splendid warm day and I am on guard at 7.00pm. Wrote letters home and to Buchanan.

Although the mail and treats from home were welcome by the soldiers at the front they did not always arrive in perfect condition:

30 May
Wrote to Andrew and Robbie. Came off guard at 6.00am and then had a parade at 9.00am for rifle inspection. Received a parcel from home containing cakes, but they had gone mouldy and were not much good.

31 May
Had a parade for saluting etc what damn rot. We had a rifle inspection after. It is very quiet around here and our billets are lucky regards shells, splendid weather.

The quiet would soon be shattered; behind the lines thousands of artillery pieces from the Royal Field and Royal Garrison Artillery were being moved onto the Somme. Over 1,500 guns of every calibre were being prepared to fire the largest and longest artillery bombardment ever fired by the British Army, intent on destroying the enemy wire and sweeping aside the German lines. The great British and French offensive was now only weeks away.

The Germans knew the attack was coming; on 2 June near Ypres, heavy enemy attacks failed to draw troops away from the Somme, much to the frustration of the German High Command. Heavy fighting along the Menin Road east of Ypres, on the Ypres Comines Canal to the south of Hooge and around Hill 60 took place as German infantry tried to smash their way through Canadian held lines. Battalions of brave Canadians stubbornly held the line and refused to pull back from the annihilated front line trenches; many units were completely cut off yet fought to the last man and bullet.

The lines east of Ypres were reoccupied after repeated counter-attacks pushed the Germans back; the enemy assault was unsuccessful as they failed to consolidate their gains. Heavy British artillery batteries fired over open sights to destroy the German attackers before they could continue and overwhelm the Allied lines.

In Mailly Maillet on the Somme, Angus Mackay and his comrades were unaware of these attacks, taking place 80 miles to the north.

1 June
It is a splendid day. We had a parade at 7.15am. I then wrote to John and received a Press and Journal and postcard from M Sutherland. We went into the trenches on fatigue duty at 8.00am and spent most of the day carting bricks. Several more men have gone on furlough.

Trench maintenance on the front line trenches was a continuous job, as units tried to improve their living conditions and repair shell damage. Bricks – often from demolished houses just behind the lines – were used to build makeshift roads or improvised bunkers. As the Canadians were fighting desperately around Ypres, nothing much happened on the Somme front.

2 June
Parade for exercise at 7.10am Received mail from John, sent reply. We then got our guns ready for the trenches and spent the rest of the day buggering about.

The 88th Brigade machine gunners were soon on the move back into the front lines.

3 June
Parade at 7.00am. We proceeded into the trenches at 9.00am and relieved the 4th Division in another prominent position, where we are very likely to get aerial torpedoes when the Hun bombards us. We have a new sergeant with twenty years service and a head as thick as a house! The range is 650 yards and we foresee us carrying out a strafe tonight, I expect we will get a hot time of it.

A British artillery barrage often attracted a German counter barrage, and it was the 'poor bloody infantry' in the front line who usually suffered under this bombardment.

4 June
Our guns are firing a terrific bombardment. It was a grand sight but soon got so hot we had to dismount our guns and take cover. Our trench has been knocked about a lot and I think we were lucky to escape, about thirty men have been killed and twenty wounded around our place. Our bombers have also raided their trenches.

Artillery fire was the biggest killer of soldiers during the First World War; shells and trench mortars caused over 58 per cent of the total casualties. Many men who were close to exploding shells suffered from 'shell shock', becoming nervous and incoherent. The condition was often debilitating in the long term, as depicted in novels such as *Regeneration*.

The situation on the battlefield was beginning to heat up:

5 June
A heavy bombardment on our right flank lasted for four hours. There are slight showers of rain falling. I expect the Hun will bombard us tonight, as it's the Kaisers birthday. We did some firing during the afternoon, banging our guns and knocking out fifty 'Boshes'.

6 June
A heavy bombardment started at 11.00pm. The night was dark and the flash of the guns is lighting up the countryside for miles around. We fired off 500 rounds, the show then stopped at 1am. We were lucky as usual; one of our shifts has gone on furlough.

Danger was a constant companion and death could strike the unwary soldier, at any time or in any place.

7 June
Had a very quiet night but I nearly got caught by a Hun machine gun when sticking up aiming marks. Received letter from John. Our relief has been postponed until tomorrow. This is our fifth day in the trenches and the weather is rather broken with rain.

The battalion and brigade supply dumps were just behind the lines, usually run by the quartermasters from the battalions; the 88th Brigade's stores were in Auchonvillers.

8 June
Had a tramp to the village a mile away for ammunition. The trenches are very muddy and it is still raining but at least it is quiet. The 86th Company have relieved us, I had a narrow shave just before 4.00pm when a shell blew the gun while I was sitting there.

We have now marched to Louvencourt, about seven miles behind the lines and settled into decent billets at about 7.00pm. Received an Ensign [local Highland newspaper] from John.

The periods of rest behind the lines were not always popular:

9 June
Had a parade at 7.15am. Exercise and rifle drill etc in the forenoon. I drew 10 francs pay at 3.00pm. If this is what you call rest I would sooner risk the trenches.

Training for the forthcoming attack began in earnest; the infantry battalions were informed that he attack would be easy, heavy artillery would destroy the German trenches. The assault was then to be made slowly; the attacking infantry were trained to move across no man's land in successive waves, carrying all their personal equipment and trench stores. Each soldier would be heavily weighed down with his webbing gear, a rifle, his ammunition, a spade or pick, sandbags, food and water. The weight of this equipment meant that they did not have to be trained to move slowly. The volunteers of 1916 obeyed their superior officers, believing them when they were told the attack into the destroyed German lines would be a 'walk over'.

Experienced front line soldiers like Angus Mackay knew what to expect and did not think it would be so simple.

10 June
I am the orderly for the day it's a damn rotten job. It is raining pretty heavily so all parades are off so far due to the weather. I have heard that we are to start training for the advance. I don't expect it will be a picnic but we will shift them all right. Received letters from Donald, Moodie and Robbie, wrote them all a reply.

11 June

Rose at 8.00am. There is nothing doing so today is a day of rest, I don't think! Better weather and the sun is shining. Some of us had a little ramble through the countryside in this peaceful place.

The soldiers, used to the cramp of the trenches, began to train for the new type of warfare they would use when they broke through the enemy lines, out into the open countryside beyond.

12 June

Parade at 9.00am with 88th Brigade and began to practise advancing over open ground. This will be for the big advance. Wrote letters home and to John.

The soldiers were not enthusiastic about the weight of equipment they would have to carry into battle.

13 June

Had a parade as usual. Brigade training carrying 1,000 rounds for the machine gun, I'll not be happy carrying that lot when the scrap comes off, a rifle and bayonet would do me. We had a decent concert in the CA [Church Army] hut last night.

Theatre companies regularly entertained the troops, taking their minds off life in the front line, singing songs such as 'Tipperary' and 'Pack Up Your Troubles in Your Old Kitbag'.

The training period was soon over and the units were told to prepare for the front lines.

14 June

Wrote to John and home we then had bags of parades. Brigade training during forenoon, there are rumours we move forward tomorrow. Things are getting very busy, move soon, I hope we are successful.

15 June

I got no sleep last night until 2.00am, as rats were running across my face. Reveille was at 4.00am; we paraded at 4.45am for Brigade Training and had six hours of tramping through cornfields etc in F.M.O. [Field Marching Order]. Dinner was at 11.30am, after that we packed up and marched seven miles to Englebelmer where we had tea. We then got our goods together and tramped into the trenches to relieve the 87th Brigade. This is a decent position but we are all dead beat, red tape again.

The 88th Brigade's machine gunners had now returned to their positions west of Beaumont-Hamel, near the village of Auchonvillers. The company held a number of fortified positions just behind the British lines called Fort Anley, Fort Moulin and Fort Prowse. Ammunition dumps, containing millions of rounds of rifle and machine-gun ammunition were set up just behind the forts, ready to feed the troops in the front lines when the attack began.

Trench routines went on as usual for the soldiers holding the line.

16 June

Stand to at 3.00am. It has been a very quiet day. Received 2 Press and Journals and an evening newspaper from Jock. I am afraid this peace is only a lull in the storm. We are all pretty well off here. We saw H.E. [high explosive artillery shells] kicking up a terrible row 500 yards away at 9.30pm.

17 June

Third day in the trenches. We are having a splendid rest of it, I am writing this on top of our gun pit, some war this. We have spent the forenoon cleaning ammunition, drawing range cards and reading, this beats our billets to sticks and only too good to last. Splendid weather, very warm and dry, we are in a position called Fort Anley.

The fighting was not confined to the front line trenches; the troops had a grandstand view of the battle in the skies above their heads.

18 June

Usual routines going on, received an Ensign from Jock. The airmen are very active today and we saw several fights overhead. I saw two German planes come down behind their lines. We are to get 10,000 rounds so I guess the show starts in the next 24hrs. We are going to be among the first guns to advance, I expect we will get it pretty hot and heavy.

The great advance was still twelve days away but the soldiers in the field were unaware of this as they were not told of the actual date in case they were taken prisoner. Rumours and counter-rumours spread along the lines as men tried to guess what the battle plan was. They were eager to meet the enemy and speed up the end of the war so they could go home.

19 June

Received mail from home, this is our fifth day in the trench. Things have gone very quiet and there is no firing. I have heard the advance is postponed for a day or two. I really think we are up against it this time.

20 June

It's another quiet day, sent postcard to John, George and home. I am really enjoying this spell in the line; this is the best rest we've had since coming to France.

21 June
Seventh day in the trenches, I had to tramp for rations at 5.00am. We have been told the scrap starts soon so if we stay here we will really see something. I hope this is really the beginning of the end.

The period of quiet was soon shattered as the British artillery began its heavy bombardment of the enemy lines once more.

22 June
Eighth day in the line. Received mail from George and Robbie. Our artillery is starting to get busy once again. One of our machines [aircraft] has crashed a short distance away.

After an extended period in the front the 88th Brigade Machine Gun Corps returned to the villages behind the lines.

23 June
This is our ninth day in and it is very wet. We were relieved at 7.00pm by number three section; we then marched to Englebelmer for tea and started for Louvencourt at midnight. We had an eight mile tramp through the pouring rain and it was damn rotten.

The machine gunners now joined the 1st Battalion of the Essex Regiment who they were to support when the attack was launched. As the men were busy settling into their new billets, all along the lines the Royal Artillery were loading shells into the breeches of their guns and preparing to fire the largest artillery barrage ever seen in history.

24 June
We have joined the Essex Battalion and have settled down in billets. It is not too bad but a bath and a change would be welcome. Went to an open-air concert and it was splendid, I believe the company came from England. We can hear the guns from here; the flashes are lighting up the sky. I expect the artillery is beginning to clear the way. I hope this will finish it as we are all fed up, some hopes I don't think.

The artillery barrage would last around the clock for the next six days, in an attempt to pulverise the German line and allow the British Army to pass over with the minimum of casualties. High explosive and shrapnel shells rained down onto the German trenches in an effort to inflict the maximum number of casualties and the greatest amount of damage. The British soldiers in the villages behind the lines could hear the bombardment going on.

25 June
We had an inspection of our equipment etc during the day. Heard our guns going at it all day, so I expect that the big push has begun. I have received a parcel containing cakes from M Sutherland.

Troops from the 29th Division received a visit and a briefing from their commanding general:

26 June
We have been inspected by General H de B Lisle and he said the attack was coming off this week. If his estimates of the German forces are correct we will win hands down. Received Scotsman *from Robbie.*

The final preparations for the attack were almost complete.

27 June
I have wrote home to mother and to Bob. We have had a Brigade parade in the forenoon; it's the final one. Next time we move it will be towards the German lines and I think we will have our work cut out.

As the soldiers prepared for the forthcoming attack, Angus Mackay and his comrades knew they might not survive and accepted the fact in the hope that a victory would be achieved.

28 June
We are supposed to be having a day of rest. We have a shot of finishing the war tomorrow morning that may be a success. If I go under it will be in a good cause, so roll on the adventure. I have just heard that the attack goes in on Saturday.

All along the front lines from the Somme to Ypres over 70 trench raids were launched to try and unsteady the German troops. Gas attacks also took place in approximately 40 other positions. The attacking formations behind the Somme front lines made their final preparations and rested the men, ready for the move forward.

29 June
We are still at Louvencourt trenches, I have received letters from home and from John with a photo. There is nothing much doing today expect we are getting a rest before the stunt wheels off We have heard that raiding parties are going in at night.

The soldiers were nervous as they waited to go forwards and it was a tense time for them all.

30 June

Another quiet day of it, we move up to the trenches tonight and I expect we will be well into it in a few hours. The guns are booming all the time and it is better weather.

That night after dark, the 29th Division moved forward through the dark lanes of the French countryside and into the front line trenches. As they moved forward through the villages of Colincamps and Mailly Mallet, the sky would have been lit by the flashes of artillery guns, raining their shower of steel on the enemy lines.

As they marched silently into the line they would have passed the field ambulance units waiting to receive the wounded; they would also have seen the grave registration units digging graves for those who would not survive. By midnight, thousands of British soldiers were in the front line ready to move across and capture the German line, among them the men of the 'pals' battalions who were about to do battle for the first time.

On the other side of the line the German defenders sheltered deep inside their dugouts and waited for the British artillery to lift their heavy fire. The Germans knew that when the artillery stopped the British infantry would climb out of their trenches and advance, The German soldiers knew they had to stop them.

7

The Battle of the Somme

Saturday 1 July 1916 was a warm sunny summer's day. The British hoped that this push would bring an end to the war. It was not to be. At 7.20am, ten minutes before zero hour, the British artillery lifted their fire on the German second and third lines and a huge mine, containing 40,000lbs (over 18 tons) of explosives was exploded under Hawthorn Ridge Redoubt west of Beaumont-Hamel. These explosives not only obliterated the German defenders in the redoubt, but also acted as a warning of the forthcoming attack allowing the Germans time to man what remained of their trenches.

Three larger mines and seven smaller ones were then blown at 7.28am; the biggest two were either side of the road at the village of La Boiselle. One of them, which contained 24 tons of explosives, formed the biggest crater to be found on the Western Front, at Lochnagar.

The larks were singing at zero hour (7.30am), when the British climbed out of their trenches and lined up ready to move forward in a large set piece trench assault. The men moved off shoulder to shoulder, in a straight line 100 yards apart, eight waves of men straight towards the enemy wire.

In the German trenches the infantry were struggling out of their bunkers and deep dugouts, ready to set up their machine guns to repel the British assault. As they came above ground they found the British artillery had destroyed most of their trenches, but they managed to set up defensive positions and when they looked over the parapet they could not believe what they saw. The British Army was marching slowly towards them with their rifles at the port; they presented the finest target the German machine gunners could ever have hoped for.

The British soldiers had only gone a few yards from their trenches before the killing began, the German machine gunners cutting them down like ripe corn in the summer harvest. Men fell dead and wounded in long lines, those coming on behind walking over their bodies. German soldiers poured fire into the British ranks; some of the enemy soldiers were even seen to climb out of their trenches so that they could fire their rifles more accurately at the targets lined up below them.

At Beaumont-Hamel the 2nd Royal Fusiliers, 86th Brigade of the 29th Division, stormed across no man's land and tried to occupy the steaming crater on Hawthorn Ridge. They failed to take the eastern edge when German machine gunners and riflemen beat them to the objective and held up the attack. The Royal Fusiliers lost 561 men that day.

South of Y Ravine the 1st Battalion Inniskilling Fusiliers from the 87th Brigade attacked the enemy and were held up by uncut wire, taking heavy casualties of 549 men, as they bunched up and tried to break through. The 2nd South Wales Borderers, 87th Brigade, sent some men to the left of Y Ravine but they were forced back 100 yards by fire from three German machine guns. The 1st King's Own Scottish Borderers and 1st Border Regiment both from the 87th Brigade, attacked in support of their sister battalions at 8.05am but were also forced back, suffering grievous losses as they did so.

The attack was not going well; the 29th Division's commander was forced to use his Brigade Reserve in the attack, and it was now that the 88th Brigade moved forward to try and maintain momentum and take the enemy line. Both units took 552 and 619 casualties respectfully.

Private Angus Mackay and his comrades seem to be totally unaware of the carnage going on to his front. As he sat waiting in the trench for his turn to go 'over the top,' he wrote in his diary.

1 July

It is 7.30am and we are in the trenches having a smoke before we go, terrific bombardment going on. Our artillery is really going at it and making plenty of noise, I think old Fritzy is having a hard time. We have been told the 86th and 87th Brigades have failed to take the enemy lines, 50 per cent of them have been washed out. We are next. 10.00am – we have had to retire under a hail of fire. Our team has been lucky so far only one man wounded. If I am still living expect to be through the German lines, Non Comprey!

The 88th Brigade had moved forward to attack at 8.45am, with the 1st Battalion Essex Regiment on their right flank and the Newfoundlanders on their left. It was decided that the Brigade would advance without any artillery barrage; however 22 men from the 88th Brigade Machine Gun Corps (Angus Mackay's unit) would lay a strafe of fire to give support.

As the Brigade moved forward into the front line trench the Essex men were delayed as they were forced moved through the dead and wounded coming in from the first attack. Bodies were piled high in the communication trenches making movement forward difficult.

At 9.05am, the Newfoundlanders moved out of the communication trench and into the open, arriving in the front line slightly ahead of the rest of the Brigade. As they moved over the open ground they began to sustain heavy casualties, losing 710 men to the accurate machine-gun fire pouring into their ranks from Y Ravine. The majority of the Newfoundland Regiment fell dead or wounded in the gaps in the British barbed wire, their bodies piled on top of each other. The battalion was totally destroyed, the worst loss suffered by any army unit during the First World War. Today a memorial stands in Newfoundland Memorial Park at Beaumont-Hamel to commemorate those who fell.

The 1st Essex attacked on the Newfoundlanders' right a little later; they also suffered heavy losses, losing 200 men to enemy artillery and machine-gun fire as they left the front lines. By noon, parties of soldiers isolated on the edge of the crater at Hawthorn Ridge were driven back; an attempt to reinforce them with the 1st Lancashire Fusiliers who had sustained casualties of 486 killed and wounded, totally failed. The 29th Division's attack had been a failure, and the survivors struggled back to their original front line trench. Over 5000 of its finest officers and men lay dead and dying in no man's land.

Over the whole attack front of 15 miles the offensive did not go well; only in the south was some success achieved and then only with French Army support. Objectives at Montauban were taken with little loss of life, however along the remainder of the assault front the attack was generally unsuccessful. At the village of Thiepval, the 36th (Ulster) Division took the heavily defended Schwaben Redoubt with serious losses; ten battalions of Irishmen attacked that day, winning four Victoria Crosses in the process, but over 5,000 of them fell dead and wounded. They were forced to withdraw at nightfall, and no reinforcements could reach them when the attacks on the flanks were not maintained.

North of the slaughter at Beaumont-Hamel, the 4th Infantry Division took grievous losses as they attacked a German defensive position called the 'Quadrilateral', British units including the 2nd Seaforth Highlanders and the 2nd Lancashire Fusiliers gaining a foothold in the enemy line. The 2nd Essex and the 1st King's Own managed to penetrate into the German lines as far as Munich Trench, about 1000 yards, but they were forced back by German hand grenade attacks. Those positions were held until 11.30am the following day, then the few survivors fell back to the original British lines taking their wounded and as much equipment as they could carry.

By nightfall on 1 July 1916, the British Army had suffered its greatest defeat in a war, a total of 57,470 officers and men had been lost, 19,240 were dead and 35,493 were wounded. The survivors lay in the front line trenches listening to the screams and cries of their injured comrades lying in no man's land. Many brave stretcher-bearers risked their lives working through the night to bring in the men. Medical units were completely swamped as they tried to deal with the flow of wounded being brought in, and many of the uninjured soldiers left holding the line were deeply traumatised by what they had seen.

The volunteers of Kitchener's New Army were destroyed on the first day of the Battle of the Somme. The battlefield today is covered with war cemeteries. The attacks went on as British Generals tried to exploit their small gains, (just over three miles). Further attacks on Beaumont-Hamel were cancelled and the 29th Division was told to hold the line. Soldiers like Angus Mackay were now aware of the slaughter that had taken place in their sector of the front, but still did not know what was going on elsewhere.

The following is an extract from the 88th Machine Gun Company's war diary for 1–2 July 1916.

7.30 a.m. Headquarters left Englebelmer and proceeded to concentration point in our front trench at Q.17.b.70.30. The 'UP' trench (Withington Avenue) was clear and had not been damaged by bombardment but its parapets were being subjected to continuous MG fire. From Knightsbridge forward progress was interrupted by wounded and in a few places trenches were damaged by shell fire.

8.20 a.m. Concentration point was reached at 8.20 a.m.

8.30 a.m. The concentration of the eight reserve guns was completed at 8.30 a.m. Officers in charge of sections at once reconnoitred our front trench with a view to finding suitable points at which their teams could leave the trench and pass through our own wire. During the reconnaissance they found that enemy MGs and snipers had all the lanes in our wire covered.

The Brigade attacked at 8.50 a.m. but was held up by MG fire. The company was ordered to remain where it was till further orders. The nearest available dugouts were used for cover for men and guns, the enemy shelling being very heavy on the front line. Orders to move were issued at 2.30 p.m. when the reserve half company was ordered to take up gun positions in the front system with a view to defence, an hour later the guns from the units were ordered to rejoin the company at Hyde Park Corner. As they assembled they were detailed to occupy positions for defensive purposes. When all were in position the company had six guns in the redoubt line and ten in the front line.

Casualties: during the day we lost two NCOs of the company and two ammunition carriers.

Company HQ were fixed at Knightsbridge and telephone communication was established with the redoubt line. Everything was prepared with a view to a probable counter attack that night. Each gun was supplied with 6500 SAA rounds and a tin of reserve water while spare numbers were accommodated in deep dugouts while all precautions were taken against gas.

2nd July

The night of the 1st/2nd passed without other incident than the heavy shelling of our lines both by high explosive and heavy shrapnel. Our guns had orders to prevent the enemy from repairing his wire. Fire was limited by the fact that we had many wounded in no man's land, many of them near the enemy wire and by the work of our stretcher bearers and rescue parties.

The 88th Brigade's Machine Gun Corps sat in the front line trench and listened to the fighting going on to either side of them.

2 July

We tramped about all night looking for a decent gun position. We are still stranded somewhere in France. I have heard our Brigade casualties are 1,400 men, so I consider my self damn lucky to be alive. We have spent most of today in a dugout on the firing line; the divisions on our left and right have advanced, so I expect we will have another shot at it. Better luck next time? We have now moved to a new gun position behind the second line, overhead fire during a bombardment.

No advance had been made on the right at all; the small gains made by the 4th Infantry Division were given up later that morning. To the 4th Division's north, the 31st Division had attacked the village of Serre on 1 July; this attack also failed when the Division's Yorkshire 'pals' battalions were mown down in no man's land.

In the south, the Germans counter-attacked at Bernafay Wood twice, once at 3.00am and then at 4.00am. These attacks were repulsed by shrapnel fire, an the wood finally caught fire when it was shelled with Thermite (flammable) shells. A successful attack was made on the village of Fricourt by the 17th Division, who captured 100 prisoners; the Division then managed to push on as far as some clear ground in front of Mametz and dug in.

Soldiers in the trenches at Beaumont-Hamel could clearly hear the attacks and counter-attacks going in on the right flank.

3 July

We can hear a terrific fight on the right. Fritzy is busy counterattacking. We have seen some of our airmen being brought down, three machines this morning. Our right and left flanks have advanced several miles but are getting their work cut out to hold on. Received a letter from John dated 27 June. An attack is expected so we are moving up to the front line.

The men in the front line had little knowledge of the overall military situation, as we can see from Angus's diary; he was completely unaware of the disaster that had befallen the attack.

A German counter-attack was now expected at Beaumont-Hamel, and the severely weakened 29th Division stood to and prepared to repel the German advance. As they did so it began to rain.

4 July
Still have our gun mounted in the firing line, this is a pretty hot quarter. Fritzy has not attacked yet, received mail from Hugh dated 28-3-16, [Hugh his brother, was serving with the Army Service Corps in India] and a parcel from home containing socks and cakes, a real Godsend. The trenches are in an awful state; mud and water up to our knees.

Even in the midst of this appalling war there was a flicker of humanity left in some of the combatants, who were otherwise so desperate to kill one another.

5 July
Still in same place, feeling wet and needing a good sleep. Corporal Stevens was killed on rations last night. Our gun position is getting shells galore chucked at it. The ammunition carriers have rejoined their battalions so I expect that means we do not attack again for some time. The Germans carried our wounded to our trenches last night, good for them.

Thousands of badly wounded men lay out in no man's land, and many of them bled to death before help could reach them. Corpses often lay for months, hanging over the barbed wire defences they had tried and failed to breach.

The battle to the south of Beaumont-Hamel still raged on; attacks by the 7th and 17th Divisions on Mametz Wood failed in the face of heavy machine-gun fire. Attacks by the 23rd and 19th Divisions around the east side of the village of La Boisselle met with little success, however the 25th Division did obtain a foothold in Hindenburg Trench and Leipzig Salient.

Enemy artillery batteries were now busy firing on the British lines, in an attempt to disrupt any build up of British forces and a further attack on the German line. Soldiers in the front line had a miserable time under the enemy fire:

6 July
Sixth day in trenches and still in the same positions. Sent 7 postcards to home and John. Wet and miserable weather. We worked on our gun position until 12.00pm.

In order to help the attacks and small gains being made in the south, the 29th Division was ordered to feign an attack on the line at Beaumont-Hamel. The Division was really in no fit state to attack but the enemy was not to know this; the Germans had to be prevented from reinforcing the southern end of the attack front.

7 July

Troops are attacking on our right so we are to bluff the Huns here with smoke bombs etc. We had to dismount our gun at 8.00am this morning owing to the heavy bombardment. Received a Press and Journal, an Ensign and a Scotsman. It is still raining. The official report says that 15,000 prisoners and 97 machine guns have been captured from the enemy.

Angus Mackay seems to be quoting these figures from newspapers in this diary entry; the papers were told that a great advance was being made and a victory over the 'cowardly Hun' was being achieved. It wasn't until the telegrams began to arrive in households all over Britain that the true loss of life on the Somme became known. Reports of the war in the media were sanitised and its horrors watered down.

Rain was now falling steadily on the battlefield and it turned into a quagmire. Constant shelling of the line was churning up the ground making living conditions almost unbearable. In the line at Beaumont-Hamel, the soldiers just existed in the trench line and tried to stay alive.

8 July

This is our 8th day in the trenches. It is raining steadily and the trenches are in an awful state, almost levelled by shellfire with mud up to the waist. I had a two-mile tramp through them in the afternoon. We are still in the same gun position and getting shells galore.

Most of our gun team is going around barefoot; it seems to be warmer that way. Our artillery fire is very busy, we saw an enemy aeroplane being brought down in the afternoon, and it had British colours displayed on it [possibly a British aeroplane incorrectly identified as German].

All along the line the attacks on the German lines continued; to the south assaults on the line at Trones Wood and Berfnay Wood were launched by the 30th Division. The 9th (Scottish) Division attacked Trones Wood at 8.00am on 8 July, but assault failed when it was broken up by fire from enemy field guns. At Mametz Wood the 38th (Welsh) Division attacked under cover of darkness but were stopped by heavy mud and barbed wire, other assaults by the 17th, 23rd and 19th Divisions made little headway in the face of relentless enemy opposition.

At 3.00am on Sunday 9 July 1916, the 30th Division renewed its attack on Trones Wood, south of Longueval. Immediately following the 40-minute bombardment, the 2nd Royal Scots Fusiliers successfully reached the German-held Maltz Horn Trench and the sunken road at La Briqueterie.

The battalion then bombed its way north along Maltz Horn Trench and took 109 prisoners; the fighting continued until 7.00am when the entire trench line up to a track leading to Guillemont was in British hands. The 17th Manchester Regiment on the eastern edge of Trones Wood then joined the Scots Fusiliers, but a heavy bombardment forced the Manchesters to withdraw to Bernafay Wood at 3.00pm.

Counter-attacks by the enemy on this sector of line were beaten back by the Scots Fusiliers and one company from the 18th Manchesters. The 3rd Division relieved the 18th Division on Montauban Ridge, whilst in other sectors of the lines the 17th, 23rd and 32nd Division launched attacks.

There was little improvement in conditions in the front lines at Beaumont-Hamel, where Private Angus Mackay and his comrades were still living in shelled trenches.

9 July

This is our 9th day in Slush Lane. I started my trench duty at 4.00am and it's feeling damn cold, some Black and White [whisky] would go down well. The trenches are pretty rotten. We have been heavily shelled all day and our team has been lucky so far but we have hit a hot corner.

The weather on the Somme began to improve; Monday 10 July was hot at 80 degrees Fahrenheit, and there was heavy cloud cover with no wind. On the 30th Division's front the 4th South African Regiment from the 9th Scottish Division moved through Trones Wood. To the west, bombing parties occupied some of Longueval Alley. There was also some fighting in Central Trench, which ran through the centre of the wood.

At 4.15am, Mametz Wood was attacked by the 38th (Welsh) Division, moving behind a 45-minute bombardment which devastated the German lines. The 13th and 14th Welsh Regiments, followed by the 10th and 15th Welsh, carried the right flank of the attack. On the left flank the 14th and 16th Royal Welsh Fusiliers from the 113th Brigade remained in support, as the right flank of the attack pushed on into the wood and dug in.

The 17th Division launched other attacks in the afternoon around the village of Contalmaison, where stubborn hand-to-hand fighting took place clearing the enemy-held Quadrangle Support Trench, a trench line connecting Contalmaison and Mametz Wood. The 23rd Division's 69th Brigade launched attacks on Bailiff Wood with the 8th and 9th Green Howards who attacked a trench line 2000 yards west of Contalmaison.

At Beaumont-Hamel the shelling of the British lines went on, the troops trying to hold their nerve.

10 July

It is a splendid day. Trenches have begun to dry up a bit. We had a bit of mud larking in the afternoon. The shelling has become more frequent and some of us have had miraculous escapes, I just hope our luck holds.

A Royal Scots gun crew, 1914.

Standing: Gunner W. Hughes; Private Wilson (East Lancashire Regiment); Private Gartredge (Royal Marines). Seated: Private Angus Mackay (Royal Scots); Private Nugent (Inniskillen Fusiliers); Private Allan Fraser (Royal Scots). Seated on the ground: Private Lawson (1st Royal Inniskillen Fusiliers). This photograph was taken on Lemnos Island, 1915.

Men of the 11th Battalion Argyll and Sutherland Highlands. Left to right: two unknown men, Private William Mackay, Private Peter Burr and Private Magnus Mackay.

The remains of the bunker at Eskmouth in Muselburgh, where Angus Mackay spent the winter of 1914.

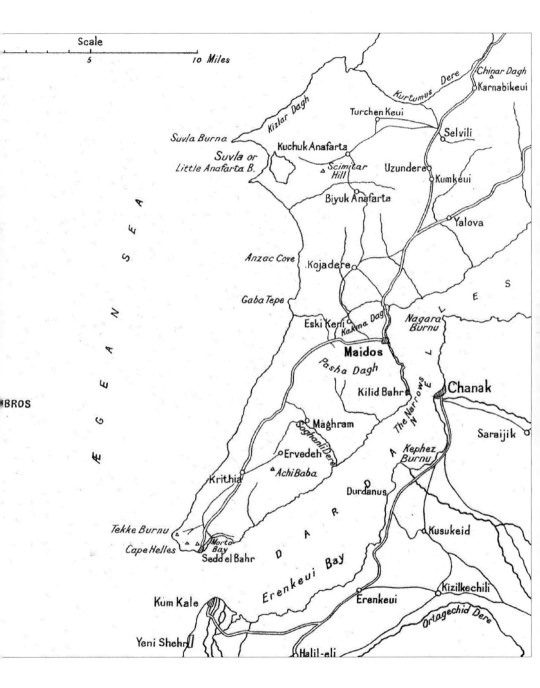

The Gallipoli Peninsula. (The Seaforth Highlanders War Diary)

Anzac Cove, Gallipoli, 1915. It was always under the Turkish guns at Gaba Tepe to the south.

An Australian trench at
Gallipoli, 1915.

The capture of Gird Trench at Gueudecourt, 26 September 1916.

The potential of the tank was realised during the Somme campaign, as barbed wire and machine guns proved no match for it.

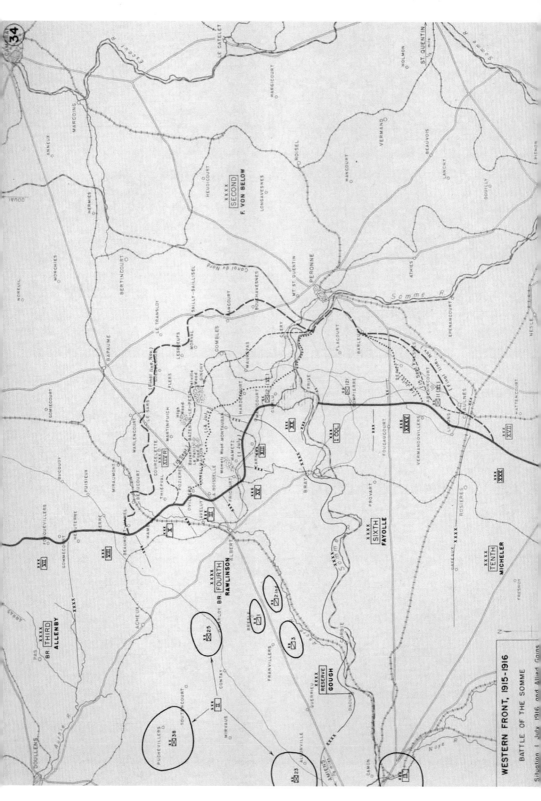

The Battle of the Somme.

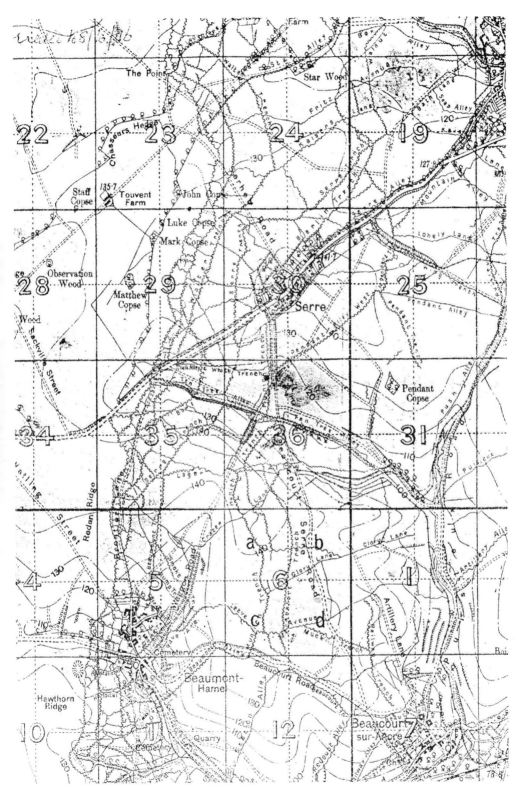

Trench lines north of Beaumont Hamel, 1916.

19 Sunday—2nd in Lent. *Afraid it is only too true, I only ask to do the same aus.*

Mg.—Gen. xxvii. 1-41. Mark xiv. 27-53.
Evg.—Gen. xxviii. or Gen. xxxii.
1 Cor. xi. 2-17.

○ 5h 27m After.—

* *Magnus reported killed while guarding a Bomb Store. Hope it is not true.*

20 Monday. Sun rises 6.5, sets 6.11
Steamed into Marseilles Harbour. Beautiful entrance seems to be well guarded. Numerous German prisoners working in the Docks. Marched to Station about 10PM and got stowed away in Cattle Trucks.

21 Tuesday. Sun rises 6.2, sets 6.12
Proceeding on our journey 35 men in each Truck. Impossible to sleep. Standing Room only. Damn fine reception after nine months fighting. Beautiful Scenery. But feeding awful Bully and die hard Biscuits.

22 Wednesday. Sun rises 6.0, sets 6.14
Travelling through Rhone Valley. Splendid scenery. Trees quite green a sight for sore eyes after Gallipoli and Suez. Carriage so uncomfortable that some of us climbed up on top and stuck on for a few hours. Pretty kisky but plenty fresh air & scenery.

23 Thursday. Sun rises 5.58, sets 6.16
Wakened up at 4am feeling pretty cold and found that we had arrived at Abbeville. We unloaded our chattels and marched to Bellancourt a few miles away and got billeted in old houses. Got a fire going.

24 Friday. Sun rises 5.55, sets 6.17
Had a damn cold night got as our fire died out and a snow storm on. The Billets seem to be a collection of army parades for a Route March still snowing. Very Cold. Received a pc from Home sent Sockets WROTE JOHN.

25 Saturday. Sun rises 5.53, sets 6.19

Annunciation. Lady Day.

Shifted Billets to a cellar nearly. plenty straw to lie on. Warm all our section together. Received a PC dated 11th March from John.

Week-end . . . .

The 19 March 1916 diary entry where Angus recorded his brother Magnus' death.

The grave of Private Magnus Mackay, 11th Argyll and Sutherland Highlanders. Loos British Cemetery, France. Plot IX, Row G, Grave 20.

Vickers Gun.

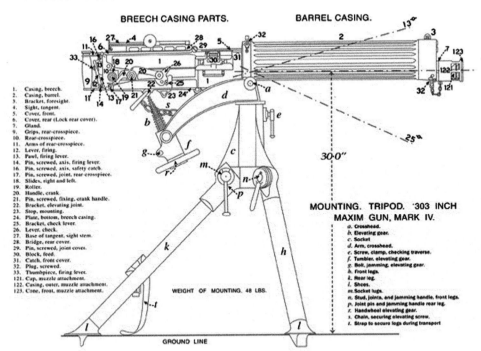

The stalwart Vickers machine gun, as used by Angus Mackay.

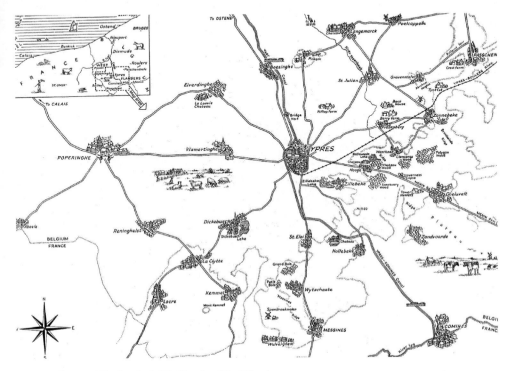

Ypres, Belgium. (The Seaforth Highlanders War Diary)

Remains of Fort Prowse, Beaumont Hamel, France.

The remains of Fort Anley, Beaumount Hamel, France.

The 29th Division (Machine Gun Corps) Memorial at Beaumont Hamel, France.

The Caribou Memorial at Guedecourt, France, where Angus Mackay fought beside the Newfoundland Regiment on 12 October 1916.

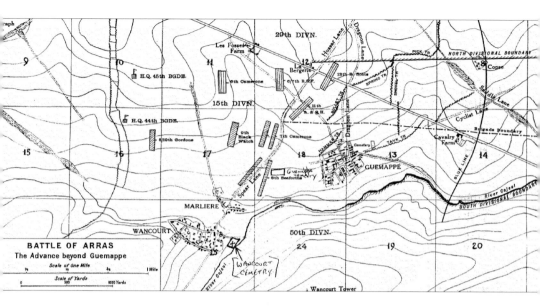

Trench lines south of the 29th Division, Arras, April 1917. (The Seaforth Highlanders War Diary)

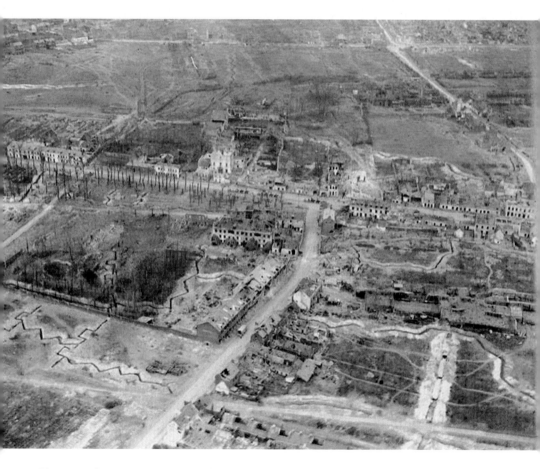

The ruins of Arras in 1917. (The Seaforth Highlanders War Diary)

146

The death card of Private
John George Mackay,
who lived in the village of
Skerray, near Angus's family
home in Scullomie.

In Loving Memory
OF
Pte. John George Mackay
(SEAFORTH HIGHLANDERS),
Beloved Husband of Jessie Mackay,
CLASHNASTRUAG, SKERRAY,
Who was killed in France,
On 9th April, 1917,
AGED 33 YEARS.

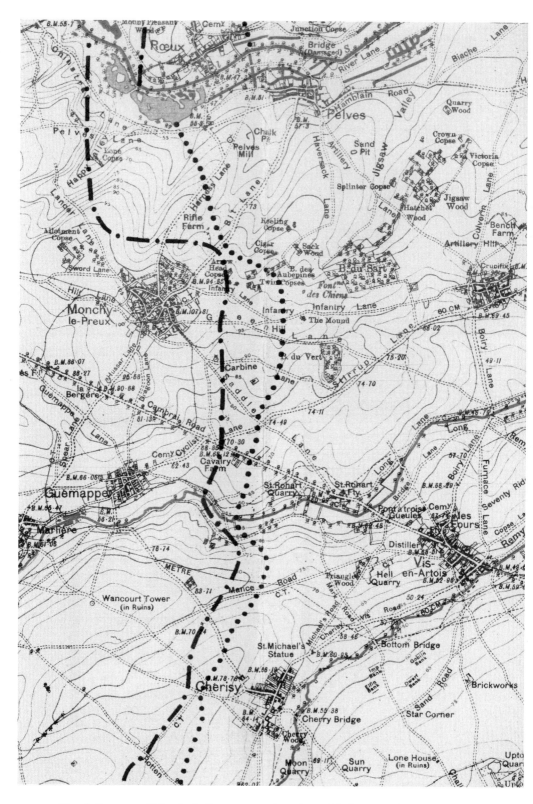

Trench lines east of Monchy le Preux, 1917, where Angus Mackay was taken prisoner.

The ruins of the Mackay family home at Scullomie, Tongue.

5 **Sunday** [217—148]
   9th after Trinity.

9 THURSDAY [221—144]
   ☾ *Last Quarter, 7.56 p.m.*

6 MONDAY [218—147]
   Bank Holiday.

IO FRIDAY [222—143]

22ⁿᵈ YEAR. DONT. EXPECT. TO. SEE. IT. ANYHOW
I WILL. BE. DAMN LUCKY. IF I. DO.

7 TUESDAY [219—146]

II SATURDAY [223—142]
   Half Quarter Day.

8 WEDNESDAY [220—145]

Angus' final diary entry.

The Tongue war memorial.

All along the front the British tried to push on and take ground. At 1.00am on 11 July the 30th Division's 90th Brigade relived the 89th Brigade to the east of Montauban. A British artillery barrage was then laid on Trones Wood at 2.40am, which was followed by a night infantry attack in which the 20th King's Regiment initially bombed their way along Malz Horn Trench. The 2nd Bedfords then advanced northeast into the wood where they were forced to swerve right as they came under heavy machine-gun fire; the battalion then occupied the south-eastern edge of the wood. Two companies also entered Trones Wood between Trones Alley Trench and the light railway.

The fighting in and around Trones Wood was very confused and fluid at this time and the front line became very disorderly, with no one really knowing where it was. When the 17th King's entered the wood at 10.30pm, from the sunken road near the village of La Briqueterie, they met no enemy opposition and dug in.

In Mametz Wood the 38th (Welsh) Division's 115th Brigade began to clear it of Germans at 3.30pm and met little opposition. Only on the left flank did the 16th Welsh fall back slightly as they came under fire from machine guns and flamethrowers. In Angus Mackay's position at Beaumont-Hamel things were improving as the weather dried up the trenches.

11 July

This is our 11th day in the trenches. I have received mail from home dated 6th; they have evidently heard there is a war on! Expect we will get a relief soon. Sent postcards home and to John. The weather is getting better, our trenches are almost dry.

On 12 July the Germans launched the first of a number of counter-attacks on 30th Division positions in Malz Horn Trench and Trones Wood. The 62nd Brigade relieved the 38th Division at dawn and throughout the morning the 10th Green Howards cleared their way through Mametz Wood, alongside the 12th and 13th Northumberland Fusiliers. These three battalions eventually managed to link up with the 7th Division on their right and the 1st Division on their left. The 62nd Brigade held this section of line until relieved on 16 July, having lost 950 officers and men. Night attacks on the village of Ovillers by the 16th Cheshires' 7th Brigade battalions, the 8th Border Regiment and 2/5th Lancashires achieved considerable success, pushing their opponents out of their trenches and allowing the British a foothold in the enemy line.

At Beaumont-Hamel the 29th Division were finally relieved from the front line trenches.

12 July

Our 12th day in the trenches. I had a tramp for rations the shellfire has quietened down a bit. We have been relieved at 10.00am and have returned to Englebelmer.

I wrote to John, home and sent postcards to Robbie and William. I then drew 15 francs pay.

As the 88th Brigade machine gunners cleaned their equipment in the village of Englebelmer, the fighting went on in the front line. At 7.00pm on 13 July the fighting in Malz Horn Trench continued, as the 7th Buffs failed to take enemy strongpoints after several attempts.

An assault by the 7th West Kents on Trones Wood lost direction and came under heavy fire from Central Trench; however 150 men did manage to reach the edge of the wood south of Guillemont track and dig in. An attack by the 7th Queens across open ground from Longueval Alley did not get within 100 yards of Longueval Wood and was forced to retire in darkness at 8.45pm.

13 July
Wrote to Hugh and George. We had cleaning parades in the afternoon and a rifle inspection etc. It is a very quiet day, no rain and our heavy artillery is very quiet. I have heard our troops are doing well on both flanks.

Angus's information was wrong; only to the south of him was the attack being pushed on but at a terrible cost. The attacks to the north, on the 29th Division's left flank, had come to a halt with many casualties taken at Serre and Gommecourt. Heavy losses at Gommecourt had occurred amongst the 56th London Division and the regular army 4th Division at Serre. This had led to the assault being postponed in that sector of the front.

The early morning of 14 July also saw the real resumption of the Battle of the Somme, with the first organised attacks taking place with a dawn attack on the Bazentin Ridge. An assault by the 9th (Scottish) Division's 26th Brigade was launched on Delville Wood at 3.25am who arrived in the German trenches before a shot was fired. After some delay south of Longueval village, the Scots Division captured all its objectives, including the edge of the wood. However when they failed to take Waterlot Farm (a sugar refinery), and Divisional headquarters was forced to send parties of Seaforths and Cameron Highlanders to occupy Longueval Alley Trench.

The attack on Trones Wood was resumed at 4.30am, when the 18th Division launched an assault into the south-western edge of the wood. An enemy redoubt in Central Trench was taken at 6.00am; the advance then continued on but lost direction when the eastern side of the wood was mistaken for the northern end. The wood was finally cleared of German troops by 9.30am and the position was consolidated.

An attack by the 3rd Division then captured the village of Bazentin-le-Grand, while troops from the 7th Division attacked over 1200 yards of no man's land in front of Caterpillar Wood. Both these attacks were successful, taking valuable territory as the British assaulting battalions pushed forward into German lines.

British cavalry (consisting of the 7th Dragoon Guards and the Indian Army's 20th Deccan Horse) were then moved into high ground between Delville Wood and High Wood, but were spotted by enemy artillery spotters and came under shellfire. The Dragoons charged the enemy line at 9.30pm, taking up cover for the horses behind a high bank, beyond a rough road.

The news of these successful attacks began to filter its way back to the troops resting behind the lines.

14 July

Usual parades. Our artillery has been going at it all night. I have heard we have captured several villages on the flanks. One of our guns has been knocked out. The weather is splendid.

At daybreak on 15 July 1916, one company from the 5th Cameron Highlanders – later supported by two companies of South Africans – tried to take Waterlot Farm, west of Longueval. The attack eventually succeeded but was so heavily shelled by an enemy counter barrage it was not consolidated until early on the morning of the 17 July.

At 6.15am on the 15th the South African Brigade, consisting of 121 officers and 3,032 men, began its assault on Delville Wood. The Brigade attacked behind an artillery bombardment and cleared the southern half of the wood in just less than two hours. A further advance then secured the remainder of the wood, except the northwest portion, which the enemy held in strength.

Attempts to secure the area were made under heavy machine-gun fire, as the Germans tried to counter-attack from three sides and push the South African troops back. The enemy mounted a spirited defence of the wood as the South Africans dug in amongst the trees and tried to lay barbed wire defences. German machine gunners got to within 75 yards of the Afrikaners and took a terrible toll, picking the men off as they worked.

The 1st South African Regiment then reinforced Delville Wood and the 9th Seaforth Highlanders – the 9th Division's pioneer battalion – sent a company to lay wire towards the north-eastern edge of the wood. An enemy counter-attack was spotted massing in their section of the wood but was stopped before it really began. Intense shellfire rained down on the South Africans as they worked on the wire, causing heavy casualties.

On other parts of the front, the 12th Royal Scots attacked Longueval village at 8.00am, bombing their way along North Street Trench. Further attempts to attack through the orchards on the west side of the village made little progress. All gains made were later retaken by enemy counter-attacks.

The 7th Division was launching frontal attacks on High Wood, west of Longueval. These attacks came under heavy machine-gun fire from enemy trenches – called The Switch Line – and the attack failed. At 11.45pm a general withdrawal was ordered and the wood was heavily shelled by the 7th Division's artillery.

The 33rd Division, on the Switch Line west of High Wood, launched other attacks near the village of Bazentin le Petit. These went on well into the night but were abandoned between 4.00pm and 5.00pm, because of the heavy casualties being taken from machine-gun fire from High Wood.

Other attacks were made by the 1st Division and the 34th Division but in each case the story was much the same, one of heavy loss of life with little gain made. Any German counter-attacks made were beaten back, but slaughter occurred on both sides as the Germans attacked with bomb and flame-thrower, the British fought back with shell and bayonet.

It was quiet at Beaumont-Hamel; the troops there would have had little knowledge of the heavy fighting at Longueval, High Wood and Delville Wood. As the South Africans fought their dreadful battle in 'Devil Wood', Angus Mackay was in good mood.

15 July

I am orderly for the day. Received mail from John, wrote back to him. We are in splendid billets but were heavily shelled last night and have now moved into a cellar. The shelling set houses on fire, some shelling in the afternoon but our cellar is going strong yet. I have heard we are going for a long rest so roll on.

The fighting at Delville Wood took on a new intensity on 16 July, as the South Africans and the 11th Royal Scots tried to push on and take the area. Attacks along the woodland rides (alleyways between the trees) called Princess Street and North Street towards Longueval both failed under heavy machine-gun fire. The fighting in the area continued without gain by either side, the South Africans repelling a German counter-attack at 11.00pm.

The 7th Division pulled back behind the village of Bazentin le Grand, after falling back from High Wood with little difficulty. The 1st Division (III Corps) made further attacks on the Switch Line at 2.00am, bombing their way forward and building a defensive position in Black Watch Alley Trench, west of Bazentin le Petit. An attack by the 25th Division on Ovillers was successful and the 48th Division relieved them at nightfall. These positions were consolidated that night.

16 July

Wrote Allen, P Burr and D Munro. We proceeded to the trenches at 9.00am on fatigues, digging gun pits. Our cavalry has been in action on the flanks, Bengal Lancers. Received Press and Journal dated 8 from John.

At 2.00am on 17 July the 9th (Scottish) Division launched a fresh attack into Delville Wood, with the South Africans moving along the rides Princess Street and the Strand into the wood. The attack was again stopped by German machine gunners that the earlier bombardment had failed to destroy; losses on both sides were heavy. The Germans then bombarded Longueval and Delville Wood with high explosives and gas all night.

The 28th Division made a further assault on an enemy trench line south of the village of Pozieries, after a heavy bombardment. The attack, carried out by the 12th Durham Light Infantry, stalled early on under heavy machine-gun fire. At dawn the next day the 48th Midland Division's 144th Brigade, took 300 yards of enemy trench west of Ovillers.

At Englebelmer the machine gunners came under heavy shellfire, as the German artillery tried to stop any build up of British troops around Beaumont-Hamel.

18 July
We had a hot time of it last night. Bags of 5.9 shells dumped into our billets but our cellar is still surviving. The house beside ours was knocked down; we are busy making a dugout for transport during the afternoon.

There was a lull in the fighting on 19 July, although the 18th Division made a push onto Longueval and Delville Wood. The attack launched at 7.15am had little success; only a small portion of the wood fell into British hands.

19 July
On orderly room duties. I had a six-mile tramp for a bath during the afternoon. Received a pint of water for washing in and a clean shirt, the shelling goes on.

Thursday 20 July 1916 was a fine clear day on the Somme battlefield. The 3rd Division attacked High Wood at first light, using the 2nd Suffolk and 10th Royal Fusiliers from the 76th Brigade. When the Suffolks advanced from the west at 3.35am its lead companies were almost wiped out by heavy German fire; the Fusiliers' attack also went somewhat off course and they were shelled by a British barrage, losing most of their officers. The surviving Fusiliers then went on to launch a futile attack on the German line, losing many more men in the process. The 35th Division attacked High Wood at 5.00am after a 30-minute bombardment, with one company of Sherwood Foresters attacking just south of Arrow Head Copse. Another company attacked Maltz Horn Farm but suffered heavy losses from machine-gun fire and had to fall back; those parties of men who entered enemy-held trenches were quickly shelled out of them.

At Delville Wood, the 76th Brigade relieved the South African Brigade and the surviving 29 officers and 751 South Africans marched back down the road to Montauban. Their losses had been horrendous; over 2300 men from the South African Brigade were dead, seriously wounded or prisoners of war. Today there is a memorial to those men lost over four days in 1916, as well as a museum built by the South African government. The wood has re-grown and is now a beautiful place, but it still bears the scars of war. A bullet marked tree stands on the spot where the South African Brigade had its headquarters, and deep in the undergrowth the remains of the trenches can been seen. Most of the Brigade's dead were never found, blown to pieces by shells, so the wood is a living war grave, a cemetery for the brave men who died so far from home.

Angus Mackay and his comrades in Englebelmer would have had no idea of the losses suffered by their South African brothers at arms; they were too busy trying to survive themselves.

20 August
We were paraded at 9.00am and proceeded to the trenches where we had to dig gun pits, water and mud up to our knees, this is damn fine rest. Received letter from Robbie dated the 10. All is well; the shells are still coming down.

Friday 21 August 1916 was a quiet day on the Somme front; at High Wood the 51st (Highland) Division moved up into the front line and relieved the 33rd Division. South of the village of Pozieres the 1st Australian Division, veterans of the Gallipoli campaign, took over a trench called Black Watch Alley near 1st Division positions west of Bazentin-le-Petit.

Even at Englebelmer, Angus and his fellow machine gunners were having an easy day of it.

21 July
Usual parades, and inspections etc. Splendid day, I wrote to Robbie then had a walk to Mailly ([Mailly Mallet village is about 1km from Englebelmer] canteen. One of our billets was knocked down in the forenoon. Received Press and Journal in the post.

The canteen Angus talks about was one of many set up just behind the front lines during the war; they sold basic items such as soap and toothpaste, as well as food to supplement army rations.

The attack was again pushed forward on Saturday 22 July; little bites were being taken from the enemy lines all along the front, but at a heavy cost. Back home in Britain the first wave of telegrams were arriving, telling families of their sons lost on 1 July.

At Maltz Horn Farm, a battalion from the 35th Division unsuccessfully assaulted an enemy trench, near Arrow Head Copse. East of Delville Wood an advance by the 3rd Division, towards Guillemont railway station from Waterlot Farm, was forced back by heavy machine-gun fire.

The 88th Brigade machine gunners at Englebelmer were sent on fatigue duties back in the line.

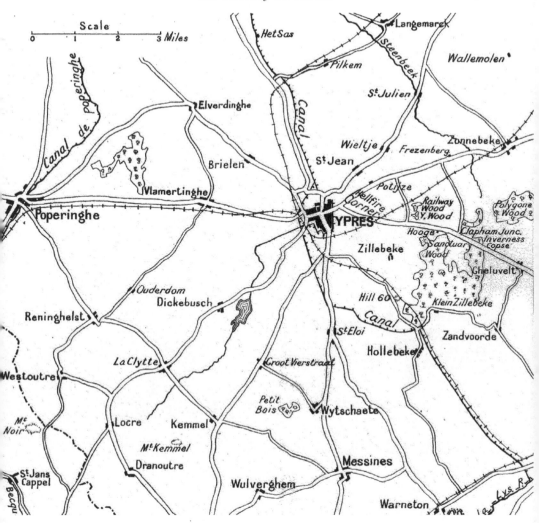

The Ypres Salient. (The Seaforth Highlanders War Diary)

22 July

Our section went back into the trenches digging gunpits. I was off that parade because we had been working until 1.00am carrying timber from the R.E. [Royal Engineers] dump. Weather is keeping splendid and the offensive is progressing well. I wrote to Andrew. I have heard we are moving to another part of the line tomorrow night, we might get a rest and furlough before we go into the trenches again. I would love to see the Rean [the burn which runs below the family croft in Scullomie] once again.

Rumours of the move were true; the 29th Division commander had been ordered to pull his division off the battlefield. The 29th were to move north to the infamous Ypres salient in Belgium to refit, and get a little rest.

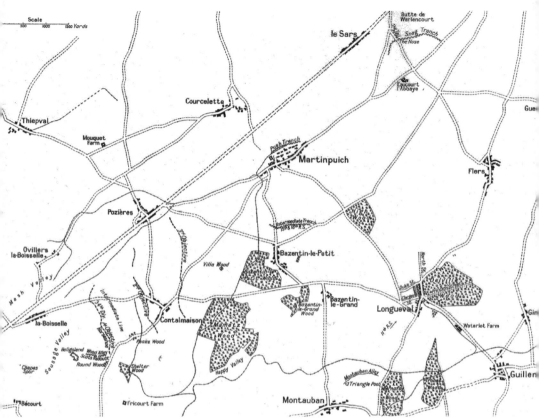

The Somme battlefield in the area of Martinpuich.

At 3.40am on Sunday 23 July the 30th Division attacked Guillemont, with the 21st Brigade in the lead. The 19th Manchesters assaulted the village from Trones Wood, with the 2nd Green Howards attacking from the north. When the Manchesters reached the enemy wire they found it uncut, however they managed to breach the wire and enter the village, the battalion managed to stay in Guillemont until 2.00pm when they were forced to withdraw.

To the north an attack by the 2nd Green Howards managed to get lost in a smoke screen and the poor light, scattering the men in different directions. One party did manage to take a trench near a railway line, but most of the men fell back to Waterlot Farm and Trones Wood, badly disrupting an advance being made by the 3rd Division.

The 3rd Division's attack was being made on Delville Wood, with supporting attacks being made on the orchards north of Longueval by the 5th Division. Assaults made by the 1st Northumberland Fusiliers at 3.40am were followed by those of the 13th King's and 12th West Yorkshires. Considerable progress was made at first, but heavy machine-gun fire from the front and the left flank forced all these advances back, first to Piccadilly Trench and then back to the attack start line in Pont Street Trench.

Attacks were now being made all along the front line; the 5th Division mounted an offensive on the Switch Line Trench to the east of High Wood and took Wood Lane Trench before 10.00pm. German flares later caught the Division crossing a ridge line and casualties were taken when the German machine gunners opened fire. Heavily defended enemy strongpoints defied the assaults being made on them, and fire from these and High Wood brought the British attacks to a standstill. Further attacks at 1.30am from the 2nd King's Own Scottish Borderers and the 15th Royal Warwick Regiment also failed, and they made their way back to the start line having lost over 1,000 men. The 51st (Highland) Division finally took High Wood and went on to over 600 yards of the enemy-held Switch Line. The Gordon Highlanders lost their way and came under heavy machine-gun fire, which caused many casualties. The 9th Royal Scots also suffered heavy losses when they were shelled as they advanced southwest of the wood.

South of Martinpuich as the 1st Division formed up outside the British wire and prepared to advance over no-mans-land, the 1st Cameron Highlanders and the 10th Gloucesters came under machine-gun fire from long grass to their front. This held up the attack and both these battalions failed to reach the enemy trenches on the Switch Line.

Two other battalions from the 1st Division – the 2nd King's Royal Rifles and 2nd Royal Sussex – attacked enemy trenches along the Switch Line Trench towards Munster Alley but failed to take their objectives. The 2nd Loyal North Lancashires attacked Munster Alley Trench at 2.30am with little success; other units tried to push into the German lines on their sector of front but failed.

On the 48th Division's front, the 1st/6th Gloucesters were mowed down by machine-gun fire as they attacked up Mash Valley into the Schwarzwald Graben Trench line, west of Pozieries. Only a few of the battalion's grenade bombers entered the German trenches near the railway line, supported by the 1st/4th Gloucesters on their left flank. The 1st/5th Gloucesters were decimated by enemy fire on the left flank as they attacked; however the 1st/4th Ox and Bucks Light Infantry and the 1st/4th Berkshires managed to take the enemy line to the south of the railway line.

A German counter-attack from the cemetery, launched by the 117th German (Burkhardt) Division, was pushed back at dawn; the 1st/1st Bucks then took the railway line and trenches to the east. Over on the right flank the enemy still held trenches running into the village of Pozieries. The village was later taken and held by the 1st Australian Division.

At Beaumont-Hamel the 29th Division was preparing to move out, away from the butchery on the Somme. As Angus Mackay and his colleagues packed up ready for the move he wrote in his diary,

23 July
Reveille at 5.00am as we are getting relieved by some company. We then lay about all day and cleared out of the village at 3.00pm as it was being heavily shelled, one man was wounded. We finally got on the move at 5.00pm and marched to Beauval twenty miles away wearing F.M.O. [Field Marching Order]. It was hellish and I was hardly able to walk by the time I got there.

The 29th was on the move north towards Ypres and the soldiers found they were once more behind the lines amongst the machinery of war which fed the front line trenches. The village of Beauval would have been a hive of activity when the 29th Division arrived, crowded with new units heading for the fighting, as well as British stockpiles of ammunition and food. Artillery shells moving up the road that day were heading for the ammunition dumps that fed the heavy fighting going on around Pozieries. Heavy artillery was busy firing on German units dug in around the OG lines, near Pozieries mill, and to counter the attacks being made by the 86th (Reserve) German Army on Munster Alley Trench east of the village. German artillery units counter barraged Australian units in Pozieries throughout the remainder of the day.

In Beauval the machine gunners had a lie in.

24 July
We rose at 10am feeling stiff and sore, no wonder! Beauval is a fine place with plenty of shops and canteens but we have no money. I have received letters from home and John, also a Scotsman *from Bob.*

Back at the front line on the Somme, the 3rd Division were relieved by the 2nd Division, south of Delville Wood. At Pozieres the 1st Australian Division attempted to bomb their way out of the village; by 2.00am the 5th Battalion had taken the enemy trench line called OG1. Following a barrage OG2 was entered by the 5th Battalion but enemy bombing on their flanks forced them back into OG1; the Germans kept possession of all trench lines up to and including the railway line.

Behind the lines the men were training.

25 July
Started of on a route march off 15 miles. I felt damn sore but stuck it all right. Got 10 francs pay and received a parcel containing two shirts, socks and hankies from John.

The battle for Pozieres raged on as Australians from the 1st ANZAC Division and British troops from the 48th (West Midland) Division linked up northwest of the village on 26 July. A further raid at 3.00am on the trench line OG1 was unsuccessful; in the afternoon bombers from the 17th and 18th Australian Infantry Force (AIF) attacked enemy positions in Munster Alley.

To the left of Pozieries two companies of Welsh troops, left behind when the 1st Division moved forward, attacked the Switch Line at 3.00pm but were driven back. A further attack made later alongside the Australians was somewhat more successful in pushing the line forward.

At Beauval the machine gunners began to hear rumours of where they were going this time:

26 July
Several small parades in the morning. I received a letter from John and home also an Ensign *and a* Scotsman. *The rumours say we are going to Ypres tomorrow.*

The Salient at Ypres was a battlefield feature that projected into German-held territory; the salient was surrounded by the enemy on three sides, making the troops occupying it very vulnerable to enemy fire. An enemy's line facing a salient is referred to as a re-entrant (an angle pointing inwards). A deep salient is vulnerable to being 'pinched out' across the base, forming a pocket, in which the defenders of the salient become isolated. The 29th Division was bound for Ypres to release other units from that area, so that they could join the fighting on the Somme. The 29th would also receive new replacements for those men lost on 1 July.

As the machine gunners prepared to move north, the slaughter of troops from both sides in and around Delville Wood continued, when the 2nd Division advanced behind a heavy barrage on 27 July. At 7.10am the 1st Battalion of the King's Rifles advanced to about 50 yards inside the wood, followed by the 23rd Royal Fusiliers. Consolidation of these positions then took place with the 1st Royal Berkshires clearing enemy positions towards the eastern edge of the wood as German artillery shelled British support positions in Princess Street Trench.

A further advance by the 5th Division was made behind the 2nd Division into the wood and against an enemy position in the northern end of Longueval village. The fighting was severe in this area and the orchards at the junction of Duke Street and Piccadilly trenches were left in enemy hands. A German counter-attack at 9.30am got in behind Princess Street Trench (in Delville Wood), forcing the British line back a little; the sniping and bombing continued for the rest of the day.

At Beauval the 88th Brigades machine gunners were on their way north.

27 July
We were paraded at 11.30am and marched to Candas 4 miles away. We then boarded cattle trucks and proceeded north to a town called Poperinghe in Belgium, where we arrived at 1.00am. It is a decent sized town only seven miles from Ypres. I have heard we go into the trenches in a couple of days.

8

Holding the Ypres Salient

The Ypres Salient had formed around the ancient cloth-weaving city of Ypres (known as 'Wipers' by the British soldiers) in Belgium, during the First Battle of Ypres in October 1914. The salient came about as the remnants of the BEF fought to stop the German Army reaching the channel ports in what became known as the 'race to the sea'. The stakes had been high: if the ports had fallen, the British supply lines would have been broken and Germany might have won the war.

At 1.00pm on 7 October 1914, the first German shells fell on the Grote Markt (Great Market). The German Army then occupied the city for the following three days before falling back to take positions up on Passchendaele Ridge to the east and the Messines Ridge to the south.

The truly savage fighting in Flanders began on 19 October 1914, continuing right up until the end of the war. Over 350,000 soldiers from each side had been killed or wounded in the slaughter of the Ypres salient by the summer of 1916.

During the Second Battle of Ypres (22 April to 25 May 1915) the German Army used poison gas for the first time, almost breaking through the Allied lines. French colonial troops, who took the brunt of the gas attack, broke and ran when the clouds enveloped them, and only a stout defence by British and Canadian troops stopped a German breakthrough to the channel ports.

The fighting in the salient in the summer of 1916 was one of constant trench and siege warfare; no large scale offensive action had taken place since the fighting in May 1915. Soldiers on both sides sat it out, shivering under frequent shelling and gas attacks, at the mercy of snipers and on the alert for the nightly trench raids carried out by both sides.

When the 29th Division's machine gunners arrived on their train at Poperinge (known as 'Pop' by the British soldiers) the area was already a huge military camp. All the supplies and men bound for Ypres came through the city en route to the front lines; the railhead fed the salient on a miniature railway system maintaining a constant supply of shells and bullets to the troops.

Poperinge was well within range of the German guns on the ridges overlooking Ypres and was already badly damaged by the summer of 1916, as the German artillery men tried to disrupt the British rear area. British soldiers had amenities laid on by the YMCA and the Church Army; there was even brothel controlled by the Military Police.

The soldiers found the normality of Poperinge strange when first they arrived, but soon adapted to their new surroundings. After walking around the city Angus wrote in his diary,

28 July
We had a splendid shower and a bath in the forenoon, then had a walk around. The town is a bit smashed up by 5.9s but is the best billet we have had so far.

Only 75 miles to the south of Ypres the fighting on the Somme went relentlessly on, as the 5th Division advanced towards the village of Longueval. An attack by the 12th Gloucesters and the 1st East Surreys was made at 3.30pm on Saturday 29 July, but achieved little.

The 51st Highland Regiment was also in action at High Wood, trying to secure an enemy bunker in the eastern corner of the wood. An attack by the 1st/4th Seaforth Highlanders (154th Brigade) at 9.20pm was brought to a standstill by enemy machine-gun fire.

Other attacks by the 23rd Division's 69th Brigade near Bazentin-le-Petit on Gloster Alley Trench were successful, and by 5.30pm they had entered the enemy Switch Line. Australian troops from the 2nd Australian Division overran the enemy line at OG1 Trench at 12.15am, but further attacks were stopped by heavy enemy barbed wire.

In Ypres Angus Mackay and his comrades were preparing for their first taste of trench life in the salient.

29 July
Parade at 9.00am to get our gun ready for the trenches. We are about to go into the trenches in the Ypres Salient. Received a parcel from Hugh and a Press and Journal from John. I sent a postcard home and to John. Entrained at 9.00pm and proceeded to Ypres where we arrived half an hour later. We have entered the trenches and relieved the 6th Division. It is much quieter here than it was on the Somme but very bad trenches all blown in.

The Ypres salient had seen almost two years of war and was in a very bad state of repair; the trenches were continually shelled and required daily restoration and refurbishment. Some of the trenches had had to be built above ground because of the lack of water drainage; any soldiers who had to dig trenches immediately found water just below the surface of the earth.

It was bleak and exposed in the front line and the soldiers felt very vulnerable. The view over the parapet in to the enemy lines was one of total destruction; no vegetation remained, the Belgian hamlets were ruins and forests were black and flattened. Scattered across no man's land was the detritus of war: abandoned wagons and artillery pieces lying between and in the shell holes. Out among the barbed wire defences dead soldiers from both sides laid scattered; the smell of decaying flesh hung over the salient mixed with the smell of cordite and high explosives.

On 30 August Private Angus Mackay was sent as his platoon runner back to the Brigade Machine Gun Company, near Ypres.

30 August

We are in the x2 trench, I was sent on a tramp to Ypres. No trenches available so I had to do a VC [Victoria Cross] act across the open ground. It is very quiet here but the German machine guns worry us a bit, I expect we will soon see them in open positions. We can see 1,100 yards into the salient, but we are fired on from three sides.

The German positions overlooked the British positions from the low ridges and the artillery spotters were able to direct accurate fire onto British saps and trenches below them. To the rear of the British lines lay the ruins of Ypres, a city the British High Command had pledged not to give up to their enemy.

There were few civilians left in Ypres by the summer of 1916; the city had been reduced to rubble and any troops stationed within the walls lived in cellars and underground bunkers. Troops on their way to the front moved through the city in the early evening or at night, through the Grote Markt past the ruins of the cloth hall, destroyed by fire in 1914, out through the Menin Gate and onto the Menin road. Ypres was quiet at this stage of the war, mainly because the fighting was concentrated along the Somme. The Allies were struggling to carry the fight beyond High Wood and Longueval; as the ANZACs fought along the Bapaume road towards Courcelette and Martinpuich, the 51st (Highland) Division tried to take High Wood.

31 July

Splendid day. I made some char at 4.30am, some change. It is very quiet so far, the famous Yp [Ypres] Salient is a rest camp compared to the Somme. Wrote home and a PC [postcard] to John. Went on a tramp for rations.

1 August

Still keeping quiet but the snipers are getting busy. Eight chaps got it during the night. Enemy machine guns also very active they worry us a lot on rations, as we have to go over the top and into the open. Received letter from William. Splendid weather but there is bags of mosquitoes around.

The many shell holes created swamps in no man's land, the perfect place for mosquitoes to breed.

2 August
4th day in the line, still very warm. Flies are now becoming very troublesome. Bags of HEs [high explosives] being chucked at us today, some chaps knocked out. We have started to build a dugout next to our gun position. We worked all night very quiet.

3 August
Splendid weather. Wrote to Hugh and George it is very quiet so far. We will continue to work on our dugout filling sandbags etc all night.

The soldiers in the front line positions spent most of the day asleep; when awake they did sentry duty on their trench fire step, went on ration parties or repaired shell damage. Most work was carried out at night, the better to elude the enemy snipers hiding in no man's land. The only illumination came from the flares fired by both sides. Other soldiers guarding the working parties had to keep their ears open for the sounds of enemy raiding units, or even worse the deadly smell of gas released from the enemy lines. If raiders were heard the soldiers manned their stand to positions ready to repel the attack, if gas was smelt they quickly donned their gas masks and capes, sheltering until the gas dissipated and they could return to their tasks.

4 August
We spent most of the day sleeping there is nothing doing. We are to get relieved on the 9th and go to Poperinge for a rest. It is proper summer weather now but damn the flies.

On the Ypres Salient observation and fighter aircraft were busy, and soldiers in the front line were treated to a daily air show as aircraft fought duels to the death in the skies above.

5 August
I have received a P.J. [Peoples Journal] and an Evening News from John. I was on ration fatigues at night, received mail from Scullomie. German aeroplanes are busy around here, our machines are not so good as on the Somme. The German Archies [heavy machine guns] also out class ours. This is our 7th day in and not a fag for love nor money. No sleep tonight I guess it is all in a days work.

Things were quiet all along the salient but the unknown to the British soldiers the Germans in the trenches opposite were preparing to attack in strength. Enemy artillery constantly shelled the British line before the assault, forcing the sentries to hide in dugouts and preventing observation of the built up in the enemy trench line.

As the Germans prepared their attack Angus Mackay wrote in his diary,

6 August

Very quiet day. Weather is splendid but it is getting colder. We have been putting the finishing touches tom our dugout. There are more shells coming over so the old Div is getting lively again.

At the rear of his diary he wrote a breakdown of the previous few days and the move to Ypres from the Somme.

We moved from Englebulmer on the Somme to Beauval and on from there to a place with an unhealthy reputation, commonly known as Wipers. We had heard all kinds of tales about this quarter and it was with rather mixed feelings we moved to into our sector. However after doing a few days in the trenches I must say it is much the safest we have struck yet. Very little shellfire and only an ordinary amount of M.G. fire and sniping and one can generally dodge that lot. Our rest billets are also a welcome change. A decent sized town called Poperinghe or Pop as it is generally known, with its picture houses pubs and shops is the nearest approach to civilisation we have struck yet. It does get dumped on sometimes but that only adds to the joy of living when it is all over. But all said and done in all my wanderings I have not seen a spot yet I would exchange the Rean for. The old home is ever in a Highland mans mind.

As Private Mackay wrote those words, the Germans were about to attack him and his comrades with one of the most deadly weapons of the First World War.

As the fighting continued in Delville Wood on the Somme front, Private Angus Mackay and his fellow machine gunners were told they were on a bonus payment scheme at Ypres.

7 August

Received letter from George and slept most of the day. We have been put on anti-aircraft duty with our gun today, told we will get £5 for each we knock out, some hope! We are to be relieved tomorrow night, I have a night in tonight so much to the good.

Angus's 'night in' and his relief never materialised; it was spoilt by a surprise German trench raid, launched that night on the 29th Division's positions. The raid was intended to probe the British line looking for weak spots, taking prisoners for intelligence purposes and gathering up documents from dead British officers or company command posts. The intelligence would then be used in the planning of further attacks.

8 August

This is our 10th day in the trenches and the night was a farce. We were turned out at 1.00am to help number 3 gun to shift. Our relief for tonight has been cancelled, so I expect we will have another ten days in the line. I heard the gas alarm going as we tramped into our position.

In the early morning of the following day Angus wrote in his diary,

9 August

We got our gas masks on and in a few minutes we were in a cloud of gas. We spent a very rotten couple of hours under gas, all the time we were under heavy shellfire. Thanks to my Box Respirator I only received a couple of mouthfuls. Horrible stuff.

Phosgene gas was the new terror weapon of the First World War, and could inflict severe injuries on soldiers not wearing gas masks and protective gas capes. Soldiers had to sit out the attack until the wind dissipated the nauseating fumes.

Not far from Angus Mackay another young soldier of the 29th Division panicked when he heard the gas alarm and fled from his position. On his return to his battalion support lines after the attack, he found that seven of his comrades had been killed and 46 wounded in the gas attack. Private John Bennett was arrested and charged with misbehaviour before the enemy; his court martial heard that he had gone pieces under shellfire. Bennett, a veteran of the fighting, was shot at dawn alongside two other men who had been charged with desertion.

10 August

A number of men were gassed last night; I saw some of them our gunners. This is the most inhumane weapon used yet. It is my 21st birthday today, I wondered if I would live to see it at Colincamps on 7 March. It is a very quiet day, the battery are still carrying the dead and gassed out.

As he wrote this entry his comrades and the soldiers around him would have been cleaning up the carnage caused by the previous night's assault. Wounded men were taken back to the first aid posts in the support trenches. Those blinded by the gas were led to the rear, walking in lines, each man with his hand on the shoulder of the man in front.

The dead had their identity disks taken from around their necks to be logged in the unit's casualty state for return to Brigade HQ. They were then wrapped in groundsheets or gas capes and taken to the rear for burial by the graves registration units. They were interred just behind the trench line or in one of the large cemeteries that had been built in the rear areas. Many of the bodies buried near the trench line were never identified after the war – when bodies were dug up for transfer to the official war cemeteries – as shell fire destroyed many grave markers. Today many men lie unnamed under gravestones inscribed 'known only unto god,', or are listed as 'known to be buried in this cemetery.'

The soldiers seemed not to dwell on the death and the carnage that could descend on them at any moment; they just struggled on. On the day after the gas attack, life in the lines at Ypres seemed to return to normal.

11 August
Quiet day today. We have played cards and read all day as we are in the middle of a field and can only move about at night. Our fags are done, pretty rotten living here without a smoke. This is our 13th day in the trenches.

Front line soldiers were totally dependant on their nightly supply of rations brought up from the rear, and cigarettes – or 'gaspers' as they were usually known – were a very important part of their allotment. They also valued their daily rum issue, and the soldiers would crowd around to get their share when it was doled out.

12 July
Wrote George and Rob. Received mail from M.S. [Murdo Sutherland] and George respectfully. It has been very quiet all day so we have been killing time playing cards etc. There was a short bombardment at 8.00pm; I am on rations at 11.00pm. We keep awake all night then try to sleep during the day. Splendid weather all the time sometimes just a shade too much.

It is hard to imagine soldiers in the trenches around Ypres being bored and having the time to play cards, but they sat idle for a lot of the time, although always alert for the sounds of a raiding party. Some would pass the time by volunteering for extra duties, which could have their benefits; those on the ration carrying parties usually managed to scrounge a hot meal as they waited to carry food into the line.

Enemy artillery was a constant threat, although it wasn't always accurate. Sometimes the enemy fire landed all round a position, as the enemy spotters and range finders failed to direct the shells onto their target. On 13 August the machine gunners of the 88th Brigade became the target of one such inept spotter.

13 August
15th day in trenches. We have received a new O.C. today. The artillery is very busy today; the Huns are dropping them near our position. Received letter from Robert.

14 August
Things are quiet. Played bridge etc passed time all right. Wrote home and to George. On rations 10.00pm.

Down on the Somme the battle raged on, as British and Commonwealth troops pushed against the German lines trying in vain to break through. Around the village of Pozieries, Australian troops tried to carry the lines towards Courcellette, on the Hardecourt-Guillemont road. British troops from the 3rd Division failed to reach enemy strongpoints in Trones Wood.

In the trenches at Ypres the machine gunners in their dugout enjoyed a peaceful day in the line, even thought the stress of combat was beginning to show.

15 August
Our 17th day in. We are having a very quiet time of it. There is a rumour we will be relieved on 19 August. There has been slight rain and the mosquitoes have been damn bad. I'm getting tired.

Even in the line training went on as normal, as the men set up mini firing ranges to practise their marksmanship skills, though not everyone enjoyed firing the Webley .455-inch six shot revolver, longing for something more solid to use on the enemy.

16 August
We had some revolver shooting outside our dugout this morning; I still prefer my old rifle. We think the beggars [Germans] are saving up their shells, aeroplanes very busy but we have got better [anti-aircraft] guns now.

As the First World War went on, both sides dramatically improved their weapons range and killing power, countermanding the other side's improvements on the battlefield in a constant arms race. Anti-aircraft artillery improved as gunners tried to knock the opposition's spotter and fighter aircraft out of the skies. Proximity fuses set to explode near aircraft, and shrapnel shells rigged to go off at a set height, were both used in the daily war to deny the opposition free passage over the front line.

Even the variable weather in Flanders was a friend to the British 'Tommy', stopping surprise enemy gas attacks and turning the chemicals back onto the perpetrator. This is what happened the day German gas troops launched a surprise attack on the lines east of Ypres, on a night of heavy rain. Once the attack had passed Angus Mackay felt some pity for his enemies in the opposite trench.

17 August
Heavy rain in forenoon, I have received a Scotsman. *We heard the gas alarm at 3.00am. There was heavy shelling at the time but the wind changed and drove the gas back again. Hard lines on the Bosches otherwise quiet and peaceful.*

'Quiet and peaceful' is clearly relative; the stress of being under fire one minute, in total silence the next must have been unimaginably stressful.

The day after the attack the 88th Brigade Machine Gun Corps was relieved and headed for a rest in the line behind Ypres, after a long spell in the trenches.

18 August
Our 20th day in trenches. Received letter from John and Sandy. It is a very quiet day and we have been relieved by the 86th [Brigade Machine Gun Company] at 1.00am. We then marched to Brandhoek, where we arrived at 4.00am.

Brandhoek village is just west of Ypres on the road to Poperinge and was the location of one of the many rest camps built behind the line during the war years. The journey back from the front line that night would have taken place in total darkness and with little sound, less the enemy were alerted to the change of troops taking place. The march back into the shattered city of Ypres and through the Menin Gate was a journey made by thousands of Allied troops, and many died during attacks on the British rear, intended to destroy the roads and rail lines.

A permanent memorial to the missing thousands of Ypres now stands on the road leading into the salient along the Menin Road, built after the war to plans drawn up by Sir Reginald Bloomfield. The Menin Gate memorial lists the names of 58,896 men who died from the outbreak of hostilities to 15 August 1917. At 8.00pm each evening, local volunteer firemen play the Last Post in memory of those men killed in action defending the city so long ago, a simple yet very moving act of remembrance.

When Angus Mackay and his fellow machine gunners passed along the way laden down with their weapons no gate existed, just a gap in the ramparts around Ypres guarded by two stone lions on either side of the road. As they moved back that night their only thoughts would have been on sleep, a warm bed and a good hot meal.

Base camps behind the lines were built to try and improve the soldiers lot and give them some home comforts, away from the trenches Tented camps soon gave way to wooden billets with proper kitchens, dining rooms and bathing facilities. A simple hot breakfast was a godsend for a tired, wet and battle-weary soldier.

19 August
Had our breakfast at 9.00am then cleaned our guns in forenoon. We are billeted in huts with beds, a paradise after the trenches. I have drawn 20 francs pay but the buzz is not good. Heavy rain all day.

The heavy rain was turning the Ypres Salient into a quagmire of filth and mud, destroying the water table causing flooding in low lying British positions. Even behind the line the ground was ankle deep in mud, which clung to clothing, boots and equipment. Uniforms became covered with mildew and boots rotted. Even protecting one's living quarters from the elements was a daily battle.

20 August
Scrubbed out our hut during the morning then we had a clothing inspection. Splendid day having a decent time of it.

Time behind the line was mainly taken up with administration and training, the latter to keep the men fit and ready for battle. In their spare time the men read welcome mail from home and took the chance to clean up.

22 August
Morning parade forming fours etc then lectures. Received parcel from home containing 50 cigs, soap etc. got my photo, which had been taken, at Beauval. Bathing parade at 2.00pm.

Behind the lines daily guards were laid on to protect against surprise German attack or sabotage acts by enemy intelligence agents. Occasionally the best turned out soldier was excused guard duty for that evening and walked away; in the modern British Army the 'stickman' is the same as the 'walking man' of the First World War. On one occasion Private Mackay was awarded 'walking man' as best turned out soldier on his guard duty:

23 August
Wrote letter to M.S. enclosing a photo. On guard walking man, practised mounting gun for Brigade sports with gas masks on. No cop.

The Brigade sports were inter-unit competitions laid on to keep the soldiers occupied behind the line and to hone their fighting skills. Athletic events such as running, jumping and shot putt took place beside gun mounting drills, first aid tests and shooting skills. The sports day also gave an opportunity for some friendly inter unit rivalry as each team tried to out do the others.

The days leading up to the sports day were quiet even though the machine gunners' new billets were in range of the German artillery.

24 August
Wrote to John, home and George enclosing photo. Another quiet day, off all parades. Splendid weather. Received letter from home.

There were many range areas set up around Ypres, allowing the machine gunners time to practise their skills.

25 August
Did some target shooting at the range in the forenoon. We then cleaned our gun etc afterwards. Splendid weather.

Cleaning the Vickers gun after the range day would have been a job for the whole section, ensuring the gun was in tip top condition and ready for further use. If the gun was left dirty or any part was damaged, it would jam in action and leave the men open to attack while they tried to clear the stoppage.

Another job carried out by the machine-gun sections behind the line was the filling of ammunition belts for use in the line. The canvas belts held 250 rounds and were filled by hand from cardboard boxes each containing 100 rounds; however a mechanical loading device was sometimes available, helping speed up the process.

The Brigade sports day gets hardly a mention in Private Mackay's diary and seems to have been a bit of a non event.

26 August
Usual parades, got a Scotsman *from Leith. Very wet day, bags of mud. Brigade Sports day in the afternoon, it was not much good.*

Behind the line there were some recreational activities laid on for the troops where soldier could spend their pay and relax. Their money was mostly used to supplement the boring army rations, a plate of egg and chips, cigarettes and *vin rouge* (red wine) from a local *estiment* (café) run by enterprising civilians.

27 August
Church parade at 9.00am, what a change. I drew 15 francs pay then had a walk around during the afternoon.

All too quickly the machine gunners' time behind the lines was over and preparations were made for a return to the trenches; it was someone else's turn for a break.

28 August
Got our guns ready for the trenches. Parade was at 8.00pm then got a ride to Ypres in G.S. wagons [general service horse drawn carriage]. We have relieved the 86th Brigade at B2 position 550 yards range.

As rain fell around Ypres the machine gunners trudged back into the line with their equipment. The going would have been hard as they moved up the communication trenches through the third line, then second line trench and into the front line. The only consolation would have been that the rain was also falling on the enemy line and they were having as miserable a time as the British troops.

A constant battle was fought with the elements to stop the trenches flooding. Mud and water up to the knees was an uncomfortable way to spend a day. The continual immersion of soldiers' boots resulted in wet feet and socks, often leading to a painful condition called 'trench foot' which incapacitating many soldiers and further burdened the overstretched medical services. The symptoms of trench foot included burning and tingling of the feet and often a loss of sensation. The effected parts of the foot and toes could appear grey and blotchy, and if the feet were warmed after cold exposure then the burning sensation became severe. Lacerations and fissures of the skin were common, as were blisters, redness and peeling of the skin. Many soldiers lost their feet to trench foot, as gangrene set in when the body failed to re-circulate blood to the affected area.

In the trench line the 88th Brigade's machine gunners were kept busy in their flooded gun pit, bailing out water. The situation would become even worse by the time of the Third Battle of Ypres in the summer of 1917, as increased shelling further undermined the already delicate Flanders water table. Many wounded men would drown in flooded shell holes before help could reach them.

29 August
Rotten weather it has been raining all day. We have spent all day bailing out the gun pit as two of us sleep beside the old gun.

Even in the foul weather the shelling went on, but the use of poison gas was severely restricted. Ideal conditions for gas attack were a light wind that would carry the gas over the enemy lines, but it couldn't be too strong or it would travel too quickly and dissipate without doing much damage. Rain ruther curtailed the effectiveness of the gas, dampening the gas clouds and causing them to break up to quickly.

An attack on the German lines was planned. It was hoped that gas could be used to distract the defenders, which would be followed by a small attack force who would take prisoners and capture equipment, especially machine guns. The following day followed the familiar routine of trench life; only the talk of action seemed to warrant any comment in Angus's diary.

30 August
Today ditto. We are going to gas the Germans if the wind is favourable. I expect we are going to have a lively time of it.

Around 7,000 men a day were casualties during the quiet periods on the Western Front, lost to shelling and trench raids rather than frontal assaults. Angus's unit's planned trench raid was postponed due to bad weather.

31 August
Received a letter from John and 200 fags. There has been no attack tonight owing to the
rain.

As the fighting went on in the front lines the rear echelon supply troops fed the rations into the line, it was still the job of company runners to collect them from the third line trench and bring them forward. At the start of a new month Angus Mackay was sent to collect the rations.

1 September
Had a tramp for rations and received a letter from Bob, there was also a letter from
home and a Press and Journal from Jock. It has been very quiet all around we fired 750
rounds between 9 and 10.00pm.

The 88th Brigade moved into the first line trench to relieve another gun team. In the German lines the enemy were preparing gas cylinders for a surprise attack on the sector.

2 September
Relieved No.4 gun team in the front line, we are 30 yds from Fritzy in a pretty decent
gun position. We heard the gas alarm ring on our right at 10.00pm. However the wind
changed and sent it back over to the German lines again, we then had heavy artillery
fire for half an hour. I gave them 500 rounds to let them know I had survived.

The action in the line at Ypres intensified the following day.

3 September
I have received a Glasgow Herald from Jock and a letter from M.S. Fritzy has chucked
several grenades and a few trench mortars around our gun pit. During the morning we
gave them 250 rounds in return.

Sometimes soldiers were able to throw grenades back into German trenches, although that was a risky business. There were also cases of soldiers lying down on top of an grenade, absorbing the explosion and protecting their comrades, at a terrible cost to themselves.

The weather was getting worse and living conditions deteriorated. In their front line position Angus Mackay and his comrades did their bit for the Allied war effort.

4 September
Weather is getting very wet, spent some time smashing up some of Fritzy's sniping
posts with our gun during stand to. We got some bombs in reply. We are getting to know
each other quite well now only Fritzy gets angry sometimes.

With little shelter and the constant rain, life in the trenches around Ypres was not pleasant for the British Tommy. Khaki serge uniforms soon became sodden with water and added 20lbs to the weight of the equipment the soldiers already carried. Their boots were not made to withstand moisture and feet were permanently damp. The soldiers often lived knee deep in water, and many drowned when they fell off duckboards into shell holes. When the temperature dropped they suffered from frostbite; a total of over 74,000 British soldiers were treated for the condition. The trenches also swarmed with rats, with one pair of rats capable of producing 880 offspring in a year, and the rodents fed off dead bodies and even attacked the wounded and sleeping men.

In the line at Ypres, Private Mackay could hear the enemy mining below his feet.

5 September
Got letters from home and from John and Hugh. Rotten weather, bags of rain and mud. Bombs still coming over and the Huns are digging a mine below us. Hope they don't get nasty and blow us up. Received letter from George.

Both sides used miners to dig long tunnels under the opposition's trenches; explosives were then set off at the end of the tunnel in the hope that they would create a gap in the line. Those in the trenches could sometimes here the clank of spade and pick beneath their feet, but there was little they could do but listen and hope that their engineers could stop the enemy by countermining.

Angus didn't have to listen to the mining for long. The 88th Brigade machine gunners were to be rotated back into the ruins of Ypres for their break.

6 September
Wrote to Hugh and Sandy. Had a walk to Ypres to see our next position, an anti-aircraft trench that we take up tomorrow. The mortar duals are still going on and it's damn unpleasant.

The city of Ypres was held by British stubbornness born of pride and an unwillingness to give ground to the enemy even though straightening the line behind the Ypres salient would have saved many lives.

Many soldiers lived in the ruined city during their rest periods; the cellars gave some respite from the elements and the constant rain of German shells. The old city ramparts and medieval defences, built by the French occupation troops in 1678, provided valuable shelter to the British Tommy in a new type of siege warfare.

7 September
It was very quiet last night, but they have started to strafe with the Stokes gun [trench mortar] again. The Huns replied with rifle grenades and trench mortars, this is a very

*unpleasant place I don't think. We have been relieved by No4 section at 6.00pm and
proceeded to the ramparts in Ypres where we arrived at 8.00pm.*

The 3-inch Stokes Trench Mortar, developed in 1915, was a simple weapon but
devastatingly effective. It consisted of a steel tube like a drainpipe, down which
was dropped small explosive projectiles. When the projectile reached the base
of the pipe a percussion cap on the base hit a striker which propelled it back up
the barrel and out over no man's land into the enemy lines. This new method of
loading made rapid firing possible; a good mortar crew could fire 20–30 rounds
a minute, and could have several projectiles in the air at one time. The Germans
also had good heavy mortars – or '*Minenwerfer*' – and numerous smaller mine
throwers called '*Granatenwerfer*'. The German 25cm heavy mortar fired a projectile weighing 200lbs which created a room-sized crater.

Larger mortar shells could usually be seen as they flew over no man's land and
the soldiers became adept at guessing where the rounds would land. Soldiers
who spotted mines and hand grenades in flight, would yell a warning or blow
prearranged blasts on a whistle to warn their comrades of where the munitions
would fall.

On the ramparts surrounding Ypres the 88th Brigade machine gunners were a
few miles behind the lines and relatively safe from the shellfire and mortars.

8 September
*We got our gun cleaned and fixed up for aircraft. Very quiet day and a splendid billet
almost. Shell proof! Received letter from George, still very busy.*

Part of the ramparts at Ypres today is the site of the Commonwealth War Graves
Commission Cemetery known as 'Ramparts', containing the graves of 153
British, 11 Australian, 10 Canadian, 14 New Zealand and 5 unknown soldiers. The
cemetery lies in a quiet suburb of the city next to the remnants of the moat; close
by are the remnants of trenches and dugouts.

Apart from the odd artillery barrage on Ypres it was fairly quiet in the city in
the autumn of 1916; the civilian population had mostly fled to avoid the shelling.
Angus and his fellow machine gunners would have spent much of their time on
personal administration and guard duty manning their section gun. Occasionally
a German spotter plane flew over, shattering the silence and sending the gunners
sprinting for their weapon.

9 September
*Had a pot shot at a Fokker during the afternoon. Our four guns drove him off pretty
quick as he was flying low. Rumours say we are going back for six weeks rest. Then over
the top I suspect.*

The German Fokker aircraft was the main fighter and reconnaissance platform used by the German Air Force during the First World War. In previous wars cavalry units had been the eyes and ears of the generals but trench warfare had made the horse obsolete, at least in an offensive context (millions were used for haulage). In their place, aircraft flew over the lines photographing enemy positions. The reconnaissance planes over Ypres were searching for supply depots, artillery positions and formations of troops moving into the lines. Machine-gun units played a valuable role in deterring them; the Vickers machine gun with its high rate of fire could bring down a plane at the right range.

10 September
Bombardment of the Hun lines starts tonight. Raiding parties will be busy soon all along the line. Received parcel from M.S. containing socks and cake. We are digging an anti-aircraft gun pit on the ramparts of Ypres. It has been very quiet all day. We hear furlough starts soon. Roll on.

The raiding parties were sent over at night to try and take prisoners, gather intelligence, maps and documents. One of the most important things to be learnt from a raiding party were the names of the German units holding the line opposite, as when crack German troops appeared in the line this could warn of a forthcoming attack.

11 September
Still digging out gun pits and building dugouts. There are some H.E.s flying about but otherwise quiet. Splendid weather.

Improved dugouts brought unwelcome visitors in the form of rats scrounging for waste food or a warm place to build a nest. The soldiers made light of this unpleasant enemy and turned rat hunts into a macabre sport.

12 September
We have finished our gun pit and it is a quiet day. Spent the afternoon shooting rats etc at revolver practice all along the canal.

The canal was actually the old moat. Only the ramparts on the eastern and southern part of the city remain today, but one can still see the remains of the workshops, stores and garages built into the casements by the troops. The casement where the famous trench newspaper *Wipers Times* was printed is close to the Lille Gate in Aalmoezenierstraat.

After months of action in the lines, the machine gunners found being anti-aircraft gunners rather dull. Angus longed for an enemy aeroplane to come along so he could try out his marksmanship.

13 September
We are still on anti-aircraft duty. Having a decent time but wish a few Huns would come across and give us some sport. Only one gone across so far.

The work to improve conditions continued behind the lines as dugouts were constructed and enhanced, in the expectation of long term occupation.

14 September
Building a dugout for the O.C. It is raining and rather cold. Very quiet all around but we hear a bombing raid is coming off soon. Rumours of furlough [leave] when we get back.

Raids into the enemy trenches were regular nightly occurrences, a useful way to find weaknesses in the enemy lines. Artillery was used to soften the position before men armed with grenades attacked the stricken trench. Apart from grenades the attackers were armed with guns, bayonets, entrenching tools and clubs, sweeping across no man's land under the cover of darkness. The machine gunners' role was to lay down covering fire into the rear of the German lines and stop reinforcements rushing into the line to help repulse the attackers.

15 September
Received letter and P.J. from John. It has been a quiet day bombing raid goes in tonight. Artillery to open at 11.00pm. Lively scrapping all night, the Huns reply was very weak.

Private Mackay's diary gives no indication of how successful the trench raid was or of his units' involvement in it; however for the troops in the line the raid would have been judged by the intelligence information gathered. Many soldiers taking part in the nightly raids would have had no idea of what was going in the rest of the line but knew their sector well; if the intelligence gathered was valuable then perhaps the lives lost had not been lost in vain. Some soldiers positively relished raids; the war poet Siegfried Sassoon saw them as a break from the boredom of trench life and a chance to fight back, to be active rather than passively waiting for death via shell or sniper's bullet.

On the ramparts in Ypres, news filtered through to the machine gunners that the trench raids might have been successful.

16 September
Wrote George and John. Received letter from home. Splendid day. I expect we will be relieved tomorrow night. There are rumours Fritz is retiring to a shorter line. I hope so. I am on rations at 10.00pm, tramp to Headquarters.

All the food and supplies (including ammunition) for the British Army on the Western Front came to France from England through huge supply depots at

Boulogne, Calais, Dieppe, Le Havre and Rouen. The food was then distributed through warehouses, bakeries and cold storage facilities and then into the rear areas by light railway. The supplies were then sorted out into truckloads depending on a division's requirement.

The rations were then taken by truck, mule or horse drawn wagon to the rear of the communication trench, ready for carrying parties from the battalions to collect the supplies. The backbreaking carrying work was both arduous and dangerous, and the most difficult part of the entire supply chain; the Germans knew the British re-supplied their front line at night, and shelled the rear areas in order to disrupt the process.

On the ramparts the machine gunners were given bad news.

17 September
Quiet day our relief has been postponed until tomorrow. Heavy bombardment last night, the 29th had a raid and breached the 2nd line.

The fighting at Ypres in the autumn of 1916 was at a stalemate; hundreds of men were killed daily in a war of attrition, which was slowly wearing both sides down. The British knew they had to break the German lines to win the war, the Germans knew they had to hold their line to stop that breakthrough. Meanwhile on the Somme a new weapon of war was being introduced, a weapon the British hoped would sweep the Germans aside: the tank.

9

The Landships of Flers-Courcellette

The tank was born out of a project set up by the First Lord of the Admiralty Winston Churchill in February 1915, called the Landship Committee. It was charged with designing an armed and armoured 'landship' capable of breaking the deadlock in France. This committee consisted mainly of Admiralty personnel because of the Royal Navy's experience in the use of armoured cars in France; there was little interest from the Army.

In the summer of 1915 the first tank built at William Foster's of Lincoln's factory was under test by the experimental Armoured Car Squadron (Royal Navy), at Wormwood Scrubs. The first tank – a three-track tractor based on a combination of British and American designs – was found to be unsatisfactory and the company was instructed to build one with two parallel tracks.

The new tank unveiled in September 1915 was christened 'Little Willie', and went through obstacle tests near the Foster factory in Lincoln. These revealed some faults, mainly with the tracks, but this was soon overcome and by December 'Little Willie' was up to the tasks it had been designed to complete.

During the construction of 'Little Willie' a second tank design was devised for a battle tank, with construction completed in January 1916. The new design performed perfectly and dealt with a mock battlefield easily. The test was so successful that the British thought they had the weapon which would finally break the deadlock in France and ultimately end the war.

The new tank – the Mark 1, nicknamed 'Mother' – was constructed with an order of 100 tanks split between Fosters and the Metropolitan Carriage, Wagon and Finance Company of Wednesbury, near Birmingham. This order was increased to 150 with the first tanks delivered to the British Army in May 1916. The tanks would be manned by a new unit formed for the purpose called Heavy Section, Machine Gun Corps under the command of Colonel Swinton, an original exponent of 'landships'.

'Mother' was available in two types; the male tank (cannon armed) had two 6lb quick firing guns and four 8mm Hotchkiss machine guns. The female tank (machine-gun armed) had four .303 Vickers machine guns and one 8mm Hotchkiss machine gun. Both tanks required a crew of eight: three drivers, four gunners and an officer or sergeant commanding.

The Mark 1 was covered in armour ranging from 6mm to 12mm thick; it was 32 feet 6 inches long, 8 feet high and between 13 feet 9 inches and 14 feet 4 inches wide. It weighed around 30 tons and was powered by a Daimler 6-cylinder inline water cooled 105 horsepower petrol engine, giving a top speed of 3.7 miles per hour. It had range of 23.5 miles, could climb over a 4 feet 6-inch vertical objective, cross a 11 feet 3-inch wide trench and access a gradient of up to 24%. It could also cross ground successfully displacing a ground pressure of 26lbs to the square inch with a sinkage rate of 1 inch.

Forty-nine Mark 1 tanks arrived in France during the Battle of the Somme and were immediately prepared for action, to the dismay of those who had wanted a surprise attack by mass tanks over suitable ground. The tank crews who arrived on the Western Front were inexperienced and the ground to be attacked over was not good; however the attack on the Somme was not going well and it was hoped that the first use of the tank at Flers-Courcellette would be a success. This took place on 15 September 1916, part of the ongoing Somme campaign. In the event too few tanks arrived on the battle line to guarantee victory; the Mark 1 was prone to breakdowns and the crews were not able to reach their designated start positions.

XIV Corps attacked Flers at 6.20am from Leuze Wood, the 169th Brigade attacking with a tank in support. The first enemy trenches were quickly taken and the tank gave great assistance to the attacking units of the 1st/2nd London Regiment. This attack was stopped by machine-gun fire from Loop Trench in the morning; bombers then attacked Loop and Combles Trench in the afternoon. The Mark 1 was hit near Loop Trench and knocked out; however the machine gunners on board stayed at their guns and held the Germans at bay.

Two other tanks were due to help with the attacks in this area but one threw a track before the attack began; the other moved to Bouleaux Wood 20 minutes before the attack began. When the 167th Brigade attacked at 6.20am the 1st/1st London Fusiliers became bogged down in heavy barbed wire and fierce machine-gun fire; the unit eventually penetrated German lines as far as Middle Copse. The tank assigned to support the attack remained at Bouleaux Wood.

On the 6th Division's attack front three tanks were allocated to assist but only one reached the start line, near the crossroads at Guillemont. As it moved along the railway line towards the Quadrilateral (trench system) its machine gunners mistakenly opened fire on the 9th Norfolks. This fire was soon checked and the tank moved north towards Straight Trench.

Further attacks made on the Quadrilateral by the 16th Brigade were stopped by machine-gun fire, but attacks by the 1st Buffs on the Leuze Wood and the Ginchy road achieved some success. Other attacks in the area of the Quadrilateral met uncut wire and heavy machine-gun fire that forced the attackers to hide in shell holes.

The Guards Division had been given ten tanks to assist with their attack but only five made it to the start line; the rest either broke down, ditched, lost direction or ran out of petrol as they moved up. The Guards attacking from Ginchy into the enemy-held Serpentine Trench achieve some success, and reinforcements then moved up in the late afternoon to consolidate the gains made.

On the 14th Division front, three tanks were due to attack alongside two companies from the King's Own Yorkshire Light Infantry to the east of Delville Wood. By 5.15am only one of these tanks was still serviceable but it still attacked accompanied by the Yorkshire battalion's bombers from Pilsen Lane Trench. It was then immobilised by shellfire and the Yorkshires' attack came under fire from the rear of their right flank; however these enemy positions were soon overcome by bomb and bayonet attack. At 6.20am another three tanks made for Cocoa Lane Trench with only one tank reaching the objective on time; one of the others was late, the last one ditched in the morass of the Delville Wood.

The attack from Delville Wood towards Flers went well and the 14th Division's Light Infantry battalions were advancing behind the few tanks that had made it to the start line; 36 of the 49 tanks available had arrived, but of those 14 of them then ditched or broke down, 10 were damaged by shellfire and were of no further use and 7 were slightly damaged.

The 41st Division took Flers village behind a creeping barrage at 6.20am, with Tea Support Trench and the Switch Line Trench falling by 7.00am with little resistance from the enemy. By 7.50am the main trench line in Flers had fallen and was consolidated by the 10th Queens, the 21st Battalion King's Rifles and two companies of the 23rd Middlesex. Enemy trenches to the east of the village were then taken with Flers village coming under attack at 8.20am. Tank D16 entered the village with infantry from the 122nd Brigade following on behind. Three further tanks (D6, D9 and D17) then worked their way along the eastern flank of the village smashing houses and destroying machine-gun posts as they moved along.

By 10.00am the Bavarian defenders of Flers had fled back into the German lines towards Guedecourt, with some British units reaching the third objective line. There was then little action between 11.00am and 1.00pm as the British consolidated their gains and collected stragglers before moving on. The tank attack had been a limited success but at a heavy cost: only D16 tank returned from the action with D6 catching fire near Guedecourt. D9 tank was knocked out near Glebe Street Trench and D17 tank was abandoned after taking two shell hits near Flers.

An attack by British troops with the New Zealand Division to the west of High Wood went well at first, but suffered a limited set back when it came under a British barrage and machine-gun fire from High Wood. The New Zealanders of the 2nd New Zealand Brigade did manage to push on and capture the enemy held Switch Line and by 6.50am had dug in 60 yards beyond it, and took their second objective Flag Lane Trench at 7.20am.

A further attack was then pressed home at 8.20am by the 2nd and 3rd Regiments (New Zealand Rifles), taking enemy trenches in Flers Trench and Flers support lines before coming under heavy enemy fire near the Flers/Abbey Road. This area, a well-known and difficult area to attack, was a sunken lane 20 feet deep containing many German dugouts.

The 47th (London) Division's attack to the east of High Wood began at 6.20am, with an advance on the enemy-held Switch Line. As the Londoners linked up with the New Zealanders, four tanks advanced with only two reaching the southern edge of the wood; they then turned east onto open ground. Only one of these tanks made a real impression on the battle (the rest were all ditched in trenches or shell holes), when it crossed into the German lines and laid fire into the enemy support lines until it was put out of action by returning fire.

An infantry assault by the 47th Division into the wood was then stopped by heavy machine-gun fire, with a chaotic struggle taking place along the edge of the trees. A few men from the 1st/6th London Regiment managed to reach the Flers Trench line after attacking Cough Drop Trench, but failed to hold these positions. The positions taken in Cough Drop Trench did hold on and an attempt was made to dig eastwards, to link up with the New Zealanders. The 140th Trench Mortar Battery then shelled High Wood for fifteen minutes with 750 Stokes mortar rounds, forcing the wood's German defenders to start surrendering to the London Regiment bombing parties on the flanks of the attack. Several hundred German prisoners were taken were quickly moved back towards the old British lines, as the British consolidated their newly won positions. By 1.00pm the wood was in British hands and the survivors of the 141st Brigade 1st/17th London (Hackney & Stepney) Rifles, 1st/18th London Irish Rifles, 1st/19th London (St Pancras) Rifles and 1st/20th London (Blackheath & Woolwich) Rifles) 47th Division prepared to hold on until reinforced.

Reserve troops from the 47th Division's 142nd Brigade attacked the enemy-held strong points in the Starfish line at 3.00pm. This attack failed to consolidate the ground taken early on and as night fell the 47th Division units were badly fragmented and held no real dedicated front line positions. Only on the eastern edge of the Division's positions was a link up made with the New Zealanders at Cough Drop Trench; however German positions lay heavily defended all around this position.

Elsewhere on the line, in front of the village of Martinpuich, the 50th (Northumbrian) Division's 149th Brigade attacked Hook Trench at 6.20am, taking the line by 7.00am and joining up with their 150th Brigade by 7.00am. The 1st/6th and 1st/5th Northumberland Fusiliers were then sent to support bombing parties from the 1st/4th Northumberlands moving towards the 47th (London) Division in High Wood. Fighting then continued in a sunken road, named The Bow, as the Northumberland Division protected the flank of the

High Wood attack from enemy reinforcements. Elements of Starfish Trench were then taken later in the morning but at a heavy cost.

The 150th Brigade then sent two tanks forward in an attempt to support their infantry; one of these reached Hook Trench and fired its guns along its length. This enfilade fire continued until the tank was hit by two shells from a nearby artillery position and blew up. The second tank crossed over into the enemy lines and went on to knock out three German machine-gun nests in Martinpuich; it then returned to refuel and rearm.

British divisions were by this time on the edge of Martinpuich and poised to advance into the enemy positions around the southern edge of the village. One of these divisions was the 15th (Scottish) Division, which had already fought south of Martinpuich in August taking heavy casualties in an attack on the enemy held positions in Switch Line Trench.

The 15th (Scottish) Division spent the time before the attack on Martinpuich in the village of Lavieville behind the British lines, near Albert. The men had carried out training and the Division had received new drafts of men and reorganised its battalions into specialist bombing squads. The machine-gun teams also underwent important training, learning how to use the new Lewis guns delivered to the infantry after the reorganisation of the heavy Vickers machine guns into machine-gun battalions.

On 12 September the Division had moved into reserve positions and then on the morning of the 14th moved forward into their assault positions. Before they did so the soldiers handed in all their papers, letters and maps to their battalion quartermaster for safekeeping or to be forwarded on to their families if they did not return. They could not risk going into battle with valuable intelligence material on their person, a map showing gun positions or even a letter home that mentioned the location of a barracks.

The battalions moved forward at 8.00pm and entered the line in total darkness under a constant artillery barrage which kept the enemy under cover. Some men were killed as the British barrage fell short onto the British line, a rare occurrence by late 1916. In the early days this had happened all too often, but the British artillery men had learned their trade well for the most part.

By 1.00am the Division was in position and remained there until 6.20am when they heard the shrill of the whistles calling them to climb out of their protective trench and move forward into the attack. As the Scotsmen fell in, the British artillery fire quickened in a last attempt to assure the destruction of the German barbed wire and machine-gun posts.

The assault was planned to be made in four waves; the first wave would attack enemy trenches in Tangle Trench, Tangle North and South and then into the village its elf. Once the village was taken and secure, the attacking waves would consolidate on the railway line embankment north of the village, and reinforcements would then secure the line before the next move forward.

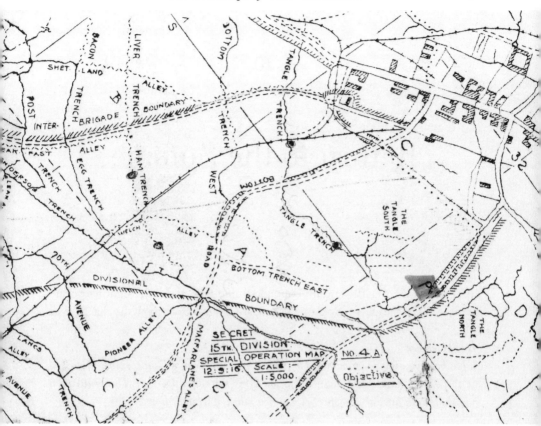

15th Scottish Division trench map, 12 September 1916.

The first wave met little opposition as it swept into Tangle Trench, with bombing platoons assaulting Tangle North and South. Heavy resistance did occur as the 15th Argylls assaulted a railway cutting, forcing the Highlanders to clear a number of deep dugouts with hand grenades and bayonets. One well directed hand grenade was thrown into a bomb store and killed all the occupants; the residents of the nearby dugouts quickly gave themselves up.

By 7.00am some of the 15th (Scottish) Division's battalions had passed through Martinpuich and reached the objective on the railway embankment and began to dig in; casualties had so far been reasonably light. In the village a tank helped the 6th Cameron Highlanders clear German troops from Bottom Trench (see map) with the Gordon Highlanders clearing the village of all enemy defenders by 2.00pm.

The attack had been a success with only a few enemy snipers causing problems for the rest of the day, along with some sporadic artillery fire. Martinpuich was secured ready to be used as a strong position or a base from which to push the attack forward.

10

Return to the Somme

In Ypres Private Mackay and his comrades cared little about the fighting on the Somme. When the relief arrived on the ramparts, Angus wrote about the change over.

18 September
It has been pouring down all day. The 86th Brigade [Machine Gun Company] arrived at 12.00pm. I have to stay with them for 24hrs to show targets etc. The Huns then bombarded our lines at 4.00pm. Several men killed, 9 wounded.

The outgoing unit had to leave a spotter behind to show the incoming unit the ranges to the enemy lines, fixed firing points for a strafe fire, range cards, fixed enemy positions and enemy observation points. A spotter could also be useful in noticing anything unusual in the enemy trench line which had not been there previously, such as a covered window in a building providing cover for an artillery observer or a camouflaged sniper position in no man's land.

Positions on the Ypres ramparts looked over the British salient into the German lines, giving a good view of the enemy trench system. The position was useful in laying strafing fire on fixed lines into the enemy line, the flatness of the ground giving the opportunity of the fire laid down by the Vickers to fall accurately on the target area.

19 September
I stopped all day with the 86th M.G. Company with no rations. At 10.00pm I marched to HQ then entrained on to Brandhoek rest camp where I arrived at 1.00am. It is raining all the time.

The journey from the ramparts in Ypres would have been made through the darkened rubble strewn streets of the town, in the unreal world of shellfire and the flashes of the artillery men's guns. Angus would have met the constantly patrolling military police who checked for spies and deserters behind the lines. He would have also passed by the long columns of reinforcements marching into the line, columns of Army Service Corps trucks and horse drawn wagons carrying the food, ammunition and the million other items required to supply an army at war.

Once behind Ypres, Private Mackay travelled on the light railway which fed the supplies into the Salient from the main railhead at Poperinge. As the carriages were emptied of their supplies, the foot weary soldiers returning to the rest camps in the rear could be carried back for a well-earned rest. In the rest area the soldiers found their units and were allocated a sleeping area in one of the large tent camps which sprang up beside the railway.

Alongside the camps were the field hospitals that patched up the wounded men not badly injured enough to merit transfer to the Channel ports and back to England. Around the field hospitals – their nicknames of 'Dozinghem', 'Mendinghem' and 'Bandaghem' reflecting the soldiers' humour – sprang up cemeteries full of the bodies of men who had been painstaking carried through the trenches by brave stretcher-bearers but had succumbed to their wounds.

Even behind the lines there was no rest from the threat of gas attack. Gas training went on in and out of the line as the British tried to keep casualties to a minimum. Protection drills were carried out to make sure soldiers wore their gas masks and gas capes correctly, keeping the gas away from the face and mouth. While these were necessary precautions, as Angus noted, they were not pleasant to wear.

20 September
We had a gas course in the forenoon, it was damn unpleasant. We went to Pop [Poperinge] at 2.00pm for a bath. I have received a parcel from home containing socks and biscuits and a Scotsman *from Jock.*

A break in Poperinge was welcome after the privations of the front line trench; it was a chance to clean uniforms and remove body lice, although this was done in the knowledge that they would return once back in the trenches. Uniforms were fumigated and occasionally new kit was issued, but this was rare, and usually soldiers were given back their old clothes.

A rest camp also meant an opportunity to tend to one's feet. In the line soldiers rubbed whale oil on their feet in an effort to waterproof their skin, as their boots and socks were rarely dry. Once in the rear they applied foot powder and were able to wear dry boots, but there was rarely time for their feet to heal from the ravages of trench foot and other maladies associated with standing up to one's knees in water for days.

Behind the lines training and parades continued, to the annoyance of the soldiers.

21 September
Exercise in mud at the farm. Regular mud bath. Petty parades all day until 4.00pm. Drew 20 francs. Received Press and Journal *from John.*

Mud was a constant companion. It made life difficult for every soldier, and also had a financial cost for the British Army in general in terms of damage to equipment, uniforms and men made ill by the damp conditions.

The daily routines and supply of fatigue parties continued behind the lines.

22 September
Exercise in the morning, splendid day but it is getting very cold. We were paraded at 7.00pm and proceeded to the Salient on digging fatigues.

Units out of the lines supplied men at night to carry out routine repairs to the front line, the darkness ensuring they could move around in relative safety. Whilst some of the fatigue parties carried out repairs to the shell smashed trenches, others dug new trenches, buried any dead they found or carried them back to the hundreds of makeshift cemeteries for a proper burial.

If the soldiers were not on digging fatigues they helped in the huge logistics lines feeding the front, hundreds of men sweating nightly as they moved supplies. Everything from sewing needles to the largest calibre of shell had to be moved into the lines by hand, a difficult business balancing on the duckboards that lined the trenches. The backbreaking work usually continued well into the early hours of the morning, but even a night on fatigues did not excuse a soldier from his other duties.

23 September
Returned from trenches about 2.00am. No parades in the forenoon so we cleaned our room. Several German planes over the camp. I am on camp guard at 6.00pm. Damn rot, Red Tape every time. It is a splendid day.

Guard duty was usually uneventful, a boring routine of checking passes, saluting officers as they passed by and guarding the perimeter of the camp. There were many German spies behind the Allied lines, trying to gather information on British plans. The guard also helped deter the theft of military equipment by civilians, deserters and black marketers looking for food, petrol and other items to sell on for a profit. The day following his stint on guard was a good one for Private Mackay.

24 September
Got off guard and had a day of rest. I have received letter from John with photos, also photo from W Mowat.

25 September
Paraded at 7.00am and then went to the range, for revolver range firing and Machine Gun tests. Wrote to Bob and sent postcard to John. There was a football match and a concert in the afternoon.

Time on the firing ranges was essential to ensure the smooth operation of the soldiers' weapons and their correct operation of the Vickers gun when they returned to the front. In the mild autumn weather the 29th Division's machine gunners trained and paraded behind the lines in Ypres.

26 September
Wrote to John and M.S. and home. Usual parades and a splendid day. There are rumours that we are going back to the Somme.

The rumours were true; the 29th Division was going back to the Somme to try and break the German lines in a new attack beyond Longueval and Deville Wood. The Allied generals knew that the Germans were badly beaten up and one last push might just break the enemy line. However, British losses had been severe and winter was near; they had one chance to use a rested division to break the line and roll up the enemy trenches.

At Ypres the mundane life of trench duties went on. As they waited to see if the rumours were true, the machine gunners went back into the line.

28 September
Cleaned our guns and got packed up for trenches during forenoon. We then proceeded to Ypres Salient and relieved 86th at 74 G.P.

Once the relief was complete the gunners found that they were in a quiet part of the line.

29 September
Good gun position with 800 yards range guarding marshes, there are no trenches in front of us. There have been showers of rain all day. Had a tramp for rations at 8.00pm. Fired 250 rounds.

The machine gunners were in the northern sector of the Salient where the Belgians had flooded the land in 1914; this flooding stopped the German advance on the Channel ports, as the water cut through the northern part of the line, alongside the Ypres canal towards Boezinge and Steenstraat, with the German lines on the high ground beyond. The daily strafe would have just let the Germans know that the line was defended and to keep their heads down, and the 250 rounds fired high in the enemy line probably caused few casualties and were likely no more than an inconvenience. However the machine-gun fire did receive a response from the Germans in the form of artillery.

30 September
Several shells flying around during the day. There was a strafe at 8.30pm. 9.2-inch trench mortars combined to make the Salient a hell where the 18 pounders give it a sort of finishing touch. Fritz must be getting it to as we are getting shelled up to 800 yards away. Received Press and Journal from John and fired 150 rounds.

These daily exchanges in the line around Ypres were nothing compared to the constant battles being fought along the Somme valley, but the attrition rate was still high as men were picked off in the daily low-key exchanges. However, the press ignored the many small battles, their memory kept alive today only by battalion war diaries.

By October 1916 the Battle of the Somme was not going the way the British had hoped; advances had been made but at a terrible cost. They had taken a large swathe of the battleground but whole battalions had disappeared daily as the fighting progressed. The new cemeteries appearing along the battle lines were testaments to the extent of the killing.

On 25 September the British had attacked the German held village of Combles, east of Deville Wood, during the Battle of Morval, forcing the enemy to withdraw. The 6th Division also captured part of the village of Lesbœufs, consolidating the line on the road to Morval; a link up was then made with 1st Guards Division before the remainder of the village was taken.

Combles was taken on 26 September by the 56th (London) Division, linking up with French units in the village, near a light railway. The 168th Brigade was then ordered to maintain contact with French units by attacking the German-held Mutton Trench. Little progress was made in this attack; two tanks sent to help push the line forward were ditched and the assault was called off.

The 21st Division – assisted by a tank – then attacked the hamlet of Gueudecourt; the tank then withdrew when it reached the southwest of the town. Infantry patrols then entered Gueudecourt accompanied by a squadron of cavalry from the Cavalry Corps, the South Irish Horse. The Irish Horse were then sent on to reconnoitre the high ground beyond, where they were to be joined at noon by the 19th Indian Lancers from Mametz. However they came under heavy fire at 2.15pm and had to dismount, entering Gueudecourt from the southwest.

In the meantime the 110th Brigade slowly began moving forward to dig in along the northern edge of the village, taking up the positions consolidated by the forward units. The final positions taken were just short of the Le Transloy road, on the junction with the Lesbœufs road; the 110th were in touch with the Guards and the 10th Green Howards. These were the positions that the men of the 29th Division were to take over in October when they moved down from Ypres.

Fighting was also going on in other areas of the Somme; Thiepval Ridge, an objective of the first day on the Somme, also fell on 26 September. Heavy and confused fighting took place on the ridge, especially around the ruins of Mouquet Farm, known as 'Mucky Farm' by the British soldiers.

In Ypres the 88th Brigade's machine gunners were unaware of the carnage awaiting them on the Somme.

1 October
We have fired 250 rounds. Splendid day. One of our battle planes brought down two of Fritzy's 06 balloons in the early morning. Fritz retaliated by dumping one of ours in the afternoon. Nothing else doing otherwise received parcel from home containing cakes.

The balloons were used by both sides as observation platforms for artillery spotters. The balloons were seen as a major threat by both sides and as soon as one was spotted going up, aircraft rushed to shoot it down, the hapless observers hoping they could get into the air, spot some targets and call in artillery on their air to ground field telephones. Once the artillery was ranged on target the balloon descended quickly, the men trying to get to ground before they were shot down. If enemy aircraft arrived before the balloon was down the observers used parachutes to bail out.

The sight of the balloons being shot down by the Royal Flying Corps and German aircraft must have been spectacular, hardly a day when 'nothing was doing'. Angus's comments reveal how commonplace such things had become to him, and to all front line soldiers like him.

In the lines the construction of overhead cover continued daily, protection from both weather and enemy projectiles.

2 October
We have been running all day constructing a dugout during the afternoon. Had a tramp for rations at 8.00pm. There are rumours of an early relief going around. Received a Scotsman fired 200 rounds.

3 October
Working on 7.5 dugouts all afternoon. It is still raining; we were shelled a bit about 1.00pm. The Huns sent a mine over at 6.00pm, no one killed but it shook us up a bit. Fired 200 rounds, we get relieved tomorrow.

The relief did indeed take place next day.

4 October
Rotten day. We were relieved by the 106th Company at 12.00pm. I had a tramp to HQ at 6.30pm. with an ammunition box. Returned at 7.00pm and marched to Ypres where we entrained for Poperinge. Arrived in billets at 5.00am and then went wandering around the town for three hours.

5 October
Had breakfast at 9.00am then inspection at 12. OC has told us we are going to a new sector for a few days. I expect it will be the Somme. Very quiet night, no cash or fags. All the boys are on the rocks.

Poperinge had limited entertainment possibilities, but without money even they were out of a soldier's reach. It must have been a boring night in for the troops, with no means to visit the bars or supplement their rations. Luckily there was a pay parade the next day, giving the machine gunners a chance to go out on the town.

6 October
Cleaning guns etc all forenoon. Received letters from home and George. Drew 20 francs pay and had a night out in Poperinge, it's a decent sized town.

The machine gunners had little time to enjoy themselves; they were moving to a new sector. There was only one area where fighting was going on and the 29th Division had now received replacements for their losses of 1st July; the division was seen as fit and rested and ready to rejoin the fight. As he filled his kitbag and webbing Private Mackay knew well where he was going.

7 October
Packed our stuff and marched to Proven station [Proven village is about 6 kilometres north of Poperinge] where entrained at 10pm, destination unknown. We all have an idea that we are going to land somewhere around the Somme. It is a rough journey with plenty of bumps.

The journey south to the Somme through the lush green landscape of France must have made a welcome change from the destruction of the front line. Only the movement of troops up to the lines would have betrayed the fact that there was a war on at all.

8 October
Sunday, had a glimpse of the sea at day break. We arrived at Amiens at 11am where we got out and after hasty food we proceeded to Corbie, fifteen miles away. We arrived in Corbie at 10.00pm, the fifteen miles having turned into twenty [actual distance is 12 miles].

When the machine gunners left the railway station at Longueau near Amiens, they moved out of the city and headed east towards the front lines and the sound of guns. As they marched past the red-bricked houses of Amiens they would have seen the thirteenth-century cathedral of Notre Dame, which looms over the city, the largest Gothic building in France.

Their route out of Amiens was probably along the roman road, leading northeast towards Albert and the Somme battlefield. The road to Albert was the main supply route to the fighting raging at the front and they would have been only one of many units heading that way. In the village of Point-Noyelles the machine gunners would have turned right and down into their new billets around the village of Corbie.

Corbie straddles the river Somme, and in 1916 it was a small village of no tactical importance except as a rest area for troops. The market village was and still is dominated by the huge church of St Pierre; its huge double tower was badly damaged in 1918 during German attacks but the village suffered no damage. The 4th Worcesters' regimental diary states: 'the 88th Brigade had found excellent billets.'

The Army Graves Registration Service set up its headquarters in Corbie and was responsible for the creation of war graves behind the lines, as well as cataloguing the dead and missing. After the First World War it became the Imperial War Graves Commission, the forerunner of today's Commonwealth War Graves Commission, responsible for the upkeep and maintenance of war graves and battlefield memorials around the world.

As the machine gunners settled in around Corbie, they would not have known that Battle of the Somme was coming to an end. The Allies and the Germans had suffered terribly, and the armies could not sustain the losses they were taking. The British New Army had been destroyed and the German Army had lost its finest troops.

By 1 October the British were attacking the Le Transloy Ridge, 4.5 miles short of the town of Bapaume, the main British objective on 1 July. The British Fourth Army had moved slowly and painfully forward but the attack nearly burned out; only more horrendous losses on the Roman road to Bapaume would call an end to the attack.

The 12th Division relieved the 21st Division and then attacked the enemy in Gird Trench, assisted by an artillery bombardment and burning oil fired into the German trenches at zero hour. Once the oil had done its work, the New Zealand Division captured Gird Trench, the junction of Goose Alley and the eastern end of Circus Trench. The 2nd Otago Battalion took its objective and a strongpoint called the Circus; the battalion then reached the Le Bargue road and formed a line with the 2nd Wellingtons before a link up was achieved with the 47th (London) Division.

The 47th Division, on the New Zealanders' left flank, attacked the village of Eaucourt L'Abbaye with the 141st (London) Brigade, who were attacking with tanks. The 1/19th London Battalion was pinned down on the right flank of this attack by machine-gun fire; the tanks then moved up from the Flers line and helped the Londoners move forward. The attack took Eaucourt L'Abbaye before linking up with the New Zealanders on the Le Barque road; the two tanks that had assisted the attack were ditched in the Flers line west of the village.

All along this front, assaults were being made by the 50th (Northumbrian) Division, the regular 23rd Division and the Canadian Corps. These were all moving forwards towards the Butte de Warlencourt, a pimple of land dominating this part of the line.

The Canadians were fighting west of the Roman road north of Courcelette, along Dyke Road and towards Regina Trench. Canadian troops were known as tough fighters and had been involved in combat on the Somme since August, taking part in the fighting at Martinpuich, the Faben Graben and Mouquet Farm. In September they had moved forward and attacked the enemy-held Sudbury and Kenora Trenches before moving on and capturing Regina Trench. However these attacks could not be sustained due to heavy losses and the Canadians had to withdraw.

On 7 October the Canadians resumed their attacks on Regina Trench in the face of heavy German artillery fire and heavy rain. The Canadians took the trench and those on the Le Sars line from Dyke Road to some 400 yards from the Quadrilateral.

The attack was now bogging down as the autumn rains began to fall, turning the battlefield into a morass of mud further churned up by the shellfire from the guns of both sides. It would have been a miserable existence living on the line; fresh troops were needed to carry the battle forward and the 88th Brigade machine gunners were to be an important part of a new push.

In Corbie the machine gunners did not know that they were leaving the 29th Division to take part in this new attack. They were to support an assault on Gueudecourt by the 12th Division. But for now they settled into their new billets.

11

The Fighting at Gueudecourt

9 October
Had breakfast at 9.00am, this is a pretty rotten billet about 12 miles from the line
[actual distance 19 miles]. I expect we will be well into it in a couple days. What a
game? We then paraded at 11.00pm and marched to Longueval.

Movement into the front lines was through the ruins of the French town of
Albert and then out onto the Somme battlefield. As they arrived in Pommiers
Redoubt near the destroyed village of Longueval, the machine gunners would
have seen the remains of Delville Wood off to their right, flattened in the fighting
in July as the South Africans took the area with terrible losses. But they would
however have had little time to sightsee before marching off to find shelter, in
an attempt to get into position before daybreak, hiding from the enemy artillery
spotters until they could move forward.

While waiting in Longueval for the order to move, Private Mackay used the
time to write in his diary.

10 October
We arrived behind the line at 4.00am and had some tea. At 4.30pm we marched to
Flers [2 miles] and then to Gueudecourt [1.5 miles]; we were under shellfire all the
way. Several chaps were wounded.

The road from Longueval to Gueudecourt was fairly flat and a virtually straight
line facing into the German lines, therefore easily observed. It was regularly
shelled by the Germans in an attempt to disrupt the re-supply of the British front.
Moving up that road must have been a nightmare and 'several chaps wounded'
was a light price to pay.

Once they had arrived in the village of Gueudecourt the machine gunners would have had to find cover in the ruins from the incessant German artillery fire. Gueudecourt would have been teeming with 12th Division soldiers waiting for the attack to begin; the 12th (Eastern) Division consisted of the following units and battalions:

12th (Eastern) Division

35th Brigade
7th Norfolks
7th Suffolks
9th Essex
5th Royal Berkshires

36th Brigade
8th Royal Fusiliers
9th Royal Fusiliers
7th Royal Sussex
11th Middlesex

37th Brigade
6th Queens
6th Buffs
7th East Sussex
6th Royal West Kents

Pioneers
5th Northampton

Private Mackay and his comrades in the 88th Brigade Machine Gun Company were in support of the 88th Brigade units attached to the 12th Division for this attack, four companies from the Royal Newfoundland Regiment and four companies of the 1st Essex Regiment. The machine gunners were to fire in support of the Canadians and the regulars of the Essex.

By nightfall on 10 October 1916 the Newfoundlanders were manning 450 yards of front line trench, on the northern edge of village. The 1st Essex were on the Newfoundlanders left flank, ready to move forward in support of the Canadian attack when it came.

As he waited in the scarred ruins of the French village Angus Mackay wrote in his diary,

11 October
Had a sleep in a German dugout all day. Short of rations and no water as we cannot move during the day, it is damn hot. But I know Fritz is getting worse than we are.

It was hot in Gueudecourt from the enemy shellfire falling on the village, not from the weather, which was 61 degrees Fahrenheit, the weather being dull with light rain. The enemy artillery spotters would have seen the build up in troops and knew an attack was coming; the artillery fire was then used to disrupt the attack and destroy the lines of communication to the rear.

At 2.05pm on 12 October the attack went in on the enemy lines, with all four Newfoundlander companies advancing in line with the Essex in support on their left. The soldiers advanced behind a creeping barrage, keeping so close to the slow moving shellfire that a number of men became casualties from flying shrapnel from the exploding artillery rounds.

The German defenders had no chance to leave their trenches before the 88th Brigade battalions were in amongst them. Bitter hand-to-hand fighting took place as the defenders stormed from their dugouts, to find their enemies already in their lines and with rifle butt and bayonet the Canadians and the British drove them out.

By 2.30pm, 20 minutes into the attack, the enemy Hilt Trench was taken and the 88th Brigade commanders were preparing to move on and attack a new location in Grease Trench further along the Beaulencourt road. However, heavy enemy machine-gun fire from the front and right flank forced the attackers back into Hilt Trench; the Germans then counter-attacked and pushed the 1st Essex back to Gueudecourt.

The Newfoundlanders flank was now exposed but Canadian bombers cleared a vacant section of Hilt Trench, doubling the battalion's front. The men then began to dig into the chalk in the trench with their entrenching tools, constructing a new fire step and parapet from the German trench; the line could then be consolidated into a new front line. The 88th Brigade's machine gunners covered the Newfoundlanders as they advanced into Hilt Trench.

12 October
Had a tramp to HQ for rations, I was out in the open so it was quite exciting. We took our guns out in to shell holes and covered NFLD [Newfoundlanders] advance at 3.30pm. Got our gun knocked out and my mate and 2 others were outed for 3hrs.

Their gun had been hit by retaliatory gunfire from German artillery positions as the Germans tried to break up the British attack and organise a counter-attack. As the machine gunners tried to recover from the explosion that had knocked them out, the Germans launched their counter-attack; the Newfoundlanders with Lewis gun and rifle fire drove them off with heavy losses.

The 12th Division attack had been a success; further attempts to push the line forward by the 35th Brigade (7th Suffolks and 7th Norfolks), encountered uncut wire near Bayonet Trench. These battalions were then forced to shelter in shell holes until dark and then fall back into the newly established line.

The enemy then launched further attacks that night, but the stubborn Canadian defenders drove these off until their relief arrived. As the Canadians were relieved by the 3rd Division's 8th Brigade they knew that they had avenged their losses at Beaumont-Hamel on 1 July. They had held the line for 55 hours and sustained 239 casualties of whom 120 were killed or would die of their wounds, but they were one of only a few units who took and held their objective that day. Today a bronze caribou memorial erected by the Canadian government stands in a small battlefield park on the site of Rainbow Trench. The remains of this trench can be seen around the memorial located in this lonely corner of the battlefield.

On other parts of the front, heavy fighting took place in Hazy Trench as the Royal Warwicks tried to make contact with French units on their flanks. Further attacks on Rainy and Dewdrop Trenches at Lesbœufs by the Royal Irish Fusiliers made little headway.

On the 12th Division's right flank the 6th Division attacked Misty and Cloudy Trenches but failed to take Mild Trench. The sunken road at Beaulencourt was taken by bombing parties from the 14th Durham Light Infantry; the 9th (Scottish) Division also attacked the Butte of Warlencourt at this time, suffering heavy losses.

The 88th Brigade machine gunners had suffered badly under the artillery fire, and returned to safer positions behind the lines.

13 October
Came down to HQ with two of our guns which had been knocked out. Awful shellfire, several more of our chaps wounded. We remain at HQ but are stilly shaky on our pins. Sent Postcards to Home and John.

One man was killed in the action, Private W.T. Muir 20683, 88th Company Machine Gun Corps, ex-Royal Scots. He is buried in Dartmoor Cemetery, Becordel-Becourt Somme, Plot II Grave D65.

As the machine gunners rested and recovered from this near miss on their HQ position, the attacks continued. On 14 October the 2nd Seaforth Highlanders from the 10th Brigade, 4th Division launched a surprise attack on Rainy Trench and gun pits south of Dewdrop Trench. They went in at 6.30pm, charging into the enemy lines at 6.38pm, when the German sentries fired a red flare and spotted the Highlanders crawling towards their positions. The attack, led by Captain Woods, took the German positions before being joined by other parties of Seaforths. As the Highlanders entered the enemy trench it was full of German infantry who soon disappeared into deep dugouts; the Scotsmen then remained in the enemy positions for 20 minutes, bombing the dugouts and causing mayhem.

Portions of enemy trenches were then held by the Highlanders for the next 5 hours, until they received orders to retire to their old positions. The Seaforths took heavy losses during this attack with 16 men killed and 53 wounded, Captain Wood being one of them. He made it back to his battalion lines and was later awarded the Military Cross for his gallantry during the action.

Further attacks continued to make headway with the South African's 3rd Battalion seizing Pimple and Snag Trench. The 39th Division also attacked and successfully took the Schwaben Redoubt, near Thiepval, driving the German infantry from this formidable objective.

The confusion of war had posted the machine gunners missing from the line.

14 October

I think we are both reported as wounded as our gun is out of action, but we are alright again. Germans counterattacking last night and were washed out. Our Sergeant and No3 are wounded, the Sgt died later on. The German prisoners say they are fed up. No wonder its pure hell around here. Wrote to George.

Both sides were suffering in the front line trenches as the casualties mounted. Adding to the hell of artillery fire and the bullet the Germans used flamethrowers to attack the Schwaben Redoubt in three separate counter-attacks on 15 October, which were repulsed with heavy loss of life.

As the attacks continued the British troops could see the results of their efforts.

15 October

Wrote to George and A Burr, shelling still going on. There are German prisoners coming in, so I think we might be winning. Lay about all day. Ground around getting heavily shelled, our section is back in support. Good, as they have had an awful time of it. There are several aerial duels going on.

The new line was now being consolidated and reinforcements from the 63rd (Royal Naval) Division took over the Schwaben Redoubt on 16 October. The 63rd was made up of sailors of the fleet and had served in Gallipoli with the 29th Division. This consolidation of the line was taking place in bright sunlight, but a hard frost was on the ground and the British generals knew that harsh winter weather would bring the Somme offensive to an end. One more push was needed, the high ground north of Thiepval and Beaumont-Hamel had to be taken before the attack could cease.

Heavy rain began to fall, over 3mm on Sunday 15 October, 3mm on the 17th and 4mm on the 18th. The battlefield became flooded, turning shell holes into water traps in which men could drown, and turning the already muddy ground into a marshland. Trenches had to be constantly shored up as they crumbled in from the weight of the rain and the vibrations of shellfire, and the men lived in a permanent state of dampness.

16 October

We are still in the same place getting shells galore. I have received letters from home and M.S. Heard we are to get relieved on the 10. Roll on. Our guns are giving Fritz hell all along the lines. Our machine guns are mounted for Anti Aircraft.

There was little actual fighting going on, as units planned and manoeuvred for the next part of the attack. Some units were being replaced by fresh divisions: the 63rd (Royal Navy) Division replaced the 39th Division north of the river Ancre and the 116th Brigade of the 39th Division took over from the 118th Division in the Schwaben Redoubt.

During the lull in the fighting, Private Mackay returned to the scene of his narrow escape from shellfire at Gueudecourt.

17 October

Had a walk to the line and search for our kit, no sign of it. Damn hot corner this, there are shells falling like rain. There are about six tanks all lying about knocked out.

Their kit had probably been destroyed by shellfire or perhaps scavenged by a unit moving into the line; soldiers were constantly on the look out for equipment laying about which they could use. The machine gunners however would have to explain the loss to their battalion quartermaster, and the latter would have to hear a good reason for the loss before he would hand out replacement gear.

The weather was becoming increasingly wintry; frost settled on the lines at night and it rained by day.

18 October

Stood to at 3.00am. Terrific bombardment going on. Worcs [4th Battalion Worcester Regiment] and Hants [2nd Battalion Hampshire Regiment] supported by our guns attacked the ridge and a lot of enemy prisoners. Beastly weather.

As the 88th Brigade continued to attack Grease Trench northwest of Gueudecourt, alongside the 12th Division's 9th Essex 35th Brigade, the 4th Division attacked Frosty, Hazy, Rainy and Dewdrop Trenches west of the village of Lesbœufs. This attack by the 4th Division took the gun pits in front of Hazy Trench but had to pull back. The 1st Lancashires were then held up by machine-gun fire as they assaulted Dewdrop Trench.

The Worcesters' and Hampshires' attack on Grease Trench was successful; support was then given to an attack by the 9th Norfolks (6th Division) into and beyond the Gueudecourt to Beaulencourt road. The Worcesters then blocked Hilt Trench to protect the flank; the 9th Essex continued the attack making little progress into Bayonet Trench, before they were bombed back by the enemy from the flanks.

All along the line, attacks by the 30th Division and the 9th (Scottish) Division were closing into the enemy lines, bombers forcing their way forward into deadly German machine-gun fire. Two tanks sent to assist the attack broke down as they came through Flers; one of these eventually reached the British front line at 8.00am, but the second did not make it as it was bogged down in heavy mud.

In the Butte de Warlencourt area the 9th Scottish discharged smoke bombs and lachrymatory (tear gas) bombs onto the enemy lines, which kept the enemy fire low. The 5th Cameron Highlanders captured an enemy trench near the Le Bargue road; they were then sent reinforcements from the 30th Division. That afternoon an enemy counter-attack gained a foothold in this trench but was pushed out by the British before dark.

Further attacks in this area by the 1st South African Regiment pushed the enemy from Snag Trench; however heavy machine-gun fire from the Butte inflicted grave losses on the regiment. Only a small group of South Africans held Snag Trench and they were soon attacked from the flanks; the Germans now only held 100 yards of this trench on either side of an area they called 'The Nose'.

19 October

We have relieved No4 gun in the captured trench last night. It is a hell of a day of rain. No shelling going on. The Germans are moving and lying about in our trench, it is impossible to get them away as snipers are so bad. We caught a German 10-man patrol against the line and wiped them out. Expect we will be relieved tomorrow, good job as our gun is out of action.

The constant relief of the line continued, with new or rested troops replacing the war weary men. It was a hazardous time for the troops; enemy artillery observers could see that the relief was taking place and called down heavy shelling on the support lines and communication trenches. No relief could be made without losses, but soldiers coming out of the lines knew that they were heading for billets behind the lines, billets where they would get hot food, rest and clean clothing, safe from shell and machine-gun fire.

As the relief came into the line and took up the machine gunners' positions the fighting continued, even as the relief took place.

20 October

87th Brigade are relieving the battalions in the line. I am feeling deadbeat. I knocked out a party of Huns at about 5.30pm as they tried to bomb us. Our relief eventually turned up at 4.00am.

The German patrol had tried to catch the machine gunners unaware just after last light, attacking in an effort to cause maximum casualties and chaos in the British line by the destruction of a machine gun and its crew.

Once the relief was complete the 88th Brigade machine gunners began to make their way back through the communication trench to the rear. They would travelled through a scene of carnage, as the battlefield was not secure and the grave digging units would not have yet set about their work. The area would have been strewn with bodies in various stages of decomposition.

As he made his way back through this wasteland Private Mackay observed:

21 October
We left our trench and went back over the open as the communication trench was muddy and full of the dead. We were snapped at most of the way but no one was hit. I suppose Fritzy was too cold to aim correctly. We were given tea and rum at HQ and marched to a rest camp behind Longueval. Received parcels from John and Mrs Burr containing candle and cigs. What a godsend.

The machine gunners returned to the place they had arrived at on 10 October, eleven days of action ago. They tramped their way from Guedecourt, through Flers and passed the remnants of Delville Wood. As they marched down the road they would have passed other units heading for the line, many of them dead men walking. The would have seen the great British Army logistics machine at work, thousands of lorries, mules and horses at work unloading the railway carriages stocked with rations, petrol, shells and bullets, feeding the insatiable needs of the front line.

As the 88th Brigade arrived in Longueval, severe fighting was taking place in and around the Schwaben Redoubt nearby, with the Germans counter-attacking in two places. This attack was driven back by the 117th Brigade, 39th Division with bombing teams from the 17th King's Royal Rifles and the 14th Hampshires (116th Brigade), clearing the redoubt from the two entry points.

Further attacks on Stuff Redoubt and the enemy positions in and around the Pope's Nose were also carried out and gained some ground. The 4th Canadian Division took more ground when they attacked Regina Trench, north of Courcelette and then east to the Pys road. Defensive flanks were positioned forward of Regina Trench and repulsed three enemy counter-attacks that afternoon, before consolidating the line into the next day.

New gains were made by the 18th Division on the Courcelette and Grandcourt road with bombing fights lasting for some time, but this was soon overcome. The 25th Division then extended the line, but came under British barrage and suffered some losses due to being too close to the artillery fire. A number of enemy dugouts were then cleared along Stump Road Trench but again the British counter barrage hindered these operations, causing some more casualties.

The weather was now bitterly cold and Private Mackay and his colleagues were feeling the effects of the wintry snap.

22 October
Wrote to Bob, home and John. We have lay about all day, but got blankets last night. This is heaven after the line. The Division on our right got thrown back last night so our old line will be shot.

By the morning of 23 October the fighting was very confused, flowing back and forward over the battleground. Some units were being pushed back, but as soon as they lost a piece of ground a counter-attack was launched to try and win it back. To the right of Longueval the 8th Division held the line between Gueudecourt and Lesbœufs, with the 23rd, 24th and 25th Brigades holding the front line against fierce German counter-attacks.

On the right were the 23rd Brigade's regular army battalions, 2nd Scottish Rifles and 2nd Middlesex who attacked Zenith Trench; the Scottish Rifles then pushed on 200 yards beyond Orion Trench but were pushed back. Attacks by the 25th Brigade failed to take the north end of Zenith Trench; the 2nd Lincolns were stopped by brisk enemy fire, with only a few isolated posts taken and held by the 2nd Rifle Brigade.

The 24th Brigade then strengthened the flanks and repulsed enemy bombing attacks; further attacks were hampered by heavy rain and machine-gun fire. The line was held but at a serious cost, the gains made could not be exploited and required reinforcements to move on. The Canadians and the ANZACs moved up to the line to give fresh impetus to the attack.

At Longueval the machine gunners were not getting much rest; a breakthrough by the enemy looked possible around the 8th Division's positions and the 88th Brigade were stood to, in case they were required as reinforcements. As his unit prepared for action Private Mackay wrote:

23 October
Cleaned our guns during the forenoon. We have been ordered to get ready for the line at once; I expect we will go back in tomorrow. I am on guard at 5.00pm, damn rot. Received Press and Journal *and a* Scotsman *from Jock.*

Guard duty was essential but never popular; it involved standing in the open or manning a trench to ensure the safety of the guard's comrades sleeping in the billets behind him. Alongside the boredom of picket duty, came the responsibility of checking the passes of personnel passing through the unit's billet area; it was not unusual for Germans to infiltrate the line dressed in captured khaki serge. One can find many reports in the war diaries of the time of unknown soldiers being challenged by sentries, only to run off before their identity could be established. Any German captured while dressed in an Allied uniform faced execution by firing squad as a spy.

24 October
Still on guard and fed up. It has been raining all day and all movement was cancelled on account of the weather, the mud is something awful. Received parcel containing a writing pad from home. Wrote to Sandy and M.S. Came off guard at 5.00pm, just ready for a kip down.

The Battle of the Somme was coming to a close, the fighting petering out as the weather worsened and the rain turned the battlefield into a quagmire. The British Army was struggling to bring forward the supplies needed to maintain the momentum of their attacks, and only on the left flank were any preparations being made around Beaumont-Hamel to continue the advance.

Canadian troops from the 44th Battalion, 10th Canadian Brigade attempted to extend Regina Trench to Farmer Road on 25 October. This action west of the village of le Sars was unsuccessful and the Canadians suffered heavy losses from German machine-gun fire on their right flank. The appalling weather was also a factor, as the Canadians' advance was bogged down by the clinging mud, their rifles and machine-guns made useless and leaving the men with only their bayonets, entrenching tools and knives to fight with.

Behind the lines, troop movements were cancelled because of the bad weather.

25 October
Wrote to Hugh. We are still in camp and it's raining steadily. Movement still cancelled. The camp is one mass of mud. Roll on a new sector, this lot is no good.

The Germans tried to take advantage of the chaos and launched a surprise attack on Stuff Trench at 5.00am on 26 October, despite the severe weather,. This attack was successfully driven back by the 7th East Lancashires from the 56th Brigade 19th (Western) Division, supported by a heavy artillery barrage.

In camp behind the line the machine gunners were trying to maintain their equipment in working order.

26 October
Cleaning our guns in the forenoon. Drew a shirt and a box of socks. We are preparing for movement which is still cancelled due to the weather.

The heavens opened the next day as 8mm of rain fell on the battlefield.

27 October
Still hanging round doing nothing practical. The Hants and the Worcs have gone back into the line. I expect we will have another go soon. Received Scotsman *from Jock. It is raining cats and dogs through our camp.*

Even in the heavy rain the British High Command pressed for the planned attacks to go on. Many of the generals had only a notional idea of the horrendous conditions in which their men lived. Soldiers today are in continual contact with their commanders and can keep them appraised of such things, but during the First World War only intermittent field telephones, poor heavy radio equipment and runners kept the attacking formations in touch with their rear headquarters.

On 28 October the 33rd Division captured Rainy and Dewdrop Trenches to east of Lesbœufs; however the lead formations of 1st Middlesex and 4th King's (98th Brigade) were bombed out of Dewdrop at 9.30am. The fighting around the eastern edge of the Somme battlefield was beginning to come to an end; the units involved were spent and those attacks taking place were just the consolidation of these new positions.

On the western edge of the battleground, Beaumont-Hamel was still in German hands. Even after the terrible loss of life there on 1 July, no advance had been made. The ground was a mess of shell holes and dead bodies, some still hanging on the wire from the futile attempts to take the enemy lines on that fateful day, the corpses of the British and Canadian soldiers mowed down by German machine-gun bullets laid out in the lines where they had fallen.

Plans were being made to take this area north of the river Ancre, consolidating the line there and up towards Serre and Gommecourt. The Germans had a good view into the Allied flank from Beaumont-Hamel and up towards the British trenches at Thiepval. The line had to be straightened before the Battle of the Somme could end.

The softening up of Beaumont-Hamel had already began as the Special Brigade Royal Engineers made a gas attack on Beaumont-Hamel during daylight on 28 October. The Engineers fired 1,126 lachrymatory (tear gas) shells into the village from 4-inch Stokes mortars, irritating the eyes, nose and mouth of the German defenders, making them incapable of fighting. In the night 135 40lb phosgene (gas) shells were fired into the village and the German positions around Y Ravine. This sulphur-based gas affected the lungs and airways of those caught in its deadly cloudy, causing them to drown in their own mucus as their lungs filled with liquid.

Special Battalions of Gas deploying Royal Engineers had been practising their deadly trade since the Battle of Loos in September 1915. By the autumn of 1916, this new weapon of war had become a fact of life in the trenches. Even when soldiers were able to don their gas masks and capes in time, they were hampered by the heavy equipment that limited their fighting abilities. As these attacks were taking place the entire area was raided and aggressively patrolled, keeping the enemy alert and unable to notice the preparations being made for a larger attack.

As the gas attacks were being made on Beaumont-Hamel in preparation for the push, other units were consolidated their positions on the line. On 29 October the 33rd Division's 19th Brigade tried to take Boritska Trench near Lesbœufs, but were stopped by machine-gun fire. The 17th Division relieved the 8th Division east of Gueudecourt, whilst the 39th Division attacked enemy trenches around the Pope's Nose in severe weather; these conditions eventually stopped the attack.

On Monday 30 October the ANZACs relieved the centre of the Fourth Army front on the Somme battlefield, with the 1st Australian Division relieving the 29th Division. The 5th Australian Division relieved the 50th Division around le Sars, allowing the British to pull back to the rear areas.

As he was being relieved Private Mackay wrote in his diary

28 October
In same old camp however we are going back for a rest soon, roll on.

The following day the Australians arrived.

29 October
Loaded our guns etc on to limbers during the forenoon. ANZACS have arrived to relieve us. Weather rotten. We move tomorrow.

As the Australians entered the lines and replaced the 29th Division that night, the British troops pulled out and began to move back to the rear areas. The divisional transport filled the road, interspersed by the infantry battalions marching to the rear, horse drawn transport and lorries pulling the artillery and ammunition out of the line.

German gunners were aware of this changeover of units in the lines and shelled the roads in the rear; crossroads were targeted in the hope of causing maximum confusion and casualties. The move was difficult; the soldiers trudged along in the mud through the torrential rain, carrying all their equipment and wearing soaking wet, mud caked uniforms.

Once he had reached the rear area Private Mackay wrote in his diary,

30 October
Had a march to a camp four miles away. It is raining steadily all the time and very cold.

He was on the move again the next day.

31 October
Got a motor ride to Ville-Sous-Corbie about eight miles away. The roads are in awful state with mud two feet deep and packed with traffic.

The vehicles being moved up to the front were to reinforce the line and move supplies up to consolidate and stabilise the gains made. Fresh troops were also moved in to replace the exhausted men in the combat area. Other fresh troops were moved into the support trenches behind Beaumont-Hamel: Scottish Highlanders from 51st (Highland) Division, sailor infantry from the 63rd (Naval) Division and West Country men from the 19th (Western) Division prepared to attack the bulge in the German lines. Behind the lines the machine gunners made the best of their break from the fighting.

1 November
Drew 25 francs pay. Doing nothing much, this is a pretty decent village. There is a big Y.M.C.A. and good beer a pleasant change.

The YMCA had gone out to France to offer comforts to the troops by opening tearooms and clubs behind the lines. As the machine gunners relaxed, the build up at Beaumont-Hamel continued. On 1 November the 33rd Division attacked the enemy near Le Transloy; this attack was made alongside a French assault but failed because of heavy machine-gun fire, mud and the general exhausted condition of the troops.

2 November
Parade for cleaning our guns, then drill etc. Received letters from John. Our officer has left and joined another Company.

Along the front lines the 17th Division launched a series of surprise strikes with a party of men from the 7th Border Regiment, taking Zenith Trench. The 7th Lincolns then repulsed an enemy counter-attack on 3 November; bombers from the 7th Green Howards also cleared pockets of German resistance from Zenith Trench. On 4 November the 98th Brigade (33rd Division) failed to take the ridge east of Dewdrop Trench before being relieved.

In their village behind the lines the routine of military life continued for the machine gunners.

3 November
Same parades. I am mess orderly for the day, wrote to John with a photo of my section.

The following day an improvement in the weather seemed to indicate a return to the lines.

4 November
Received Scotsman *and* Peoples Journal *from Jock. The weather is better and rumour says we are here for a week or so. I expect we will go back for another scrap then. Hope my luck still holds good. Had a bath at 3.00pm.*

On the line near Lesbœufs the 33rd Division attacked the enemy at 11.10am on 5 November, and the 2nd Worcesters (100th Brigade) took Boritska and Mirage Trenches. The Worcesters then linked up with the 16th King's Royal Rifles, who had already taken Hazy Trench. A push was then made forward up the Lesbœufs to Le Transloy road, but it took little ground because of failures by the 7th East Yorkshires and 7th Green Howards to make any headway, especially on the right.

In the 29th Division's old positions the 1st Australian Division attacked a salient north of Gueudecourt in the pouring rain. At zero hour (12.30am) the 3rd Battalion sent bombers into the German lines and had some success. Follow up attacks failed and the troops withdrew. Further attacks by the 7th (Australian) Brigade entered the enemy lines at several points but were withdrawn at dusk.

On the Ancre heights the 50th Division attack got off to a bad start when the attacking formations had to physically pull men clear from the mud before the attack could begin. Once the attack was underway the British infantry were repulsed by machine-gun fire in front of the German trenches and were gradually forced to pull back throughout the day. However, the 1st/9th Durham Light Infantry managed to break through two lines of German trenches to establish a presence on the Bapaume Road; these posts failed to hold on and at 10.00pm fell back until all the Durhams were back in their old lines by midnight.

Behind the lines Private Mackay wrote in his diary:

5 November
I attended Kirk at 11.00am. I am feeling pretty rotten. It is raining again, what a country!

12

The Battle of the Ancre

The Battle of the Somme was coming to an end, but there was one more attack to be made at Beaumont-Hamel in order to straighten the bulge in the line and neutralise the strong German defences. Allied troops were moved into place despite the horrendous weather, and in fact the conditions helped to hide the build up. As the line was consolidated and fresh troops moved into the front lines positions to prepare for the attack, garrison life behind the lines continued for the 88th Brigade and its machine gunners.

6 November
Had a general inspection by Brigadier Caley. He intended to give a speech but the rain came on, thank goodness. Received a parcel and a letter from Mrs Burr.

There was little movement in the front lines during this time because of the heavy mud, except for those units transferring from Albert to Beaumont-Hamel for the attack and the supply trains bringing ammunition, shells, rations, fuel, and trench stores such as fresh wood for dugouts, barbed wire, shovels, picks and water. Infantry battalions were in position behind the lines, with the 51st (Highland) Division camped around Mailly-Mallet wood and the village of Forceville.

As the rain poured down, the infantry battalions supplied working parties to the line and practised their role in the forthcoming attack. The 5th Seaforth Highlanders (152nd Brigade) was a typical battle-hardened battalion of the 51st Division, with a strength of 35 officers and 852 other ranks.

7 November
It is raining pretty heavily. No parades. There is a rumour we are getting paid but it did not come off. There was a concert at 8.00pm but it was a rotten affair.

Fighting units were often paid late, and even then they were only given a small allowance to buy the basics and fund a few drinks in local bars and cafes. It was not seen to be proper for armed British soldiers to be drunk in the rear areas, and regimental and company sergeant majors patrolled to ensure that the Military Police kept a tight rein on the men.

The machine gunners eventually heard about the fighting at Gueudecourt on 5 November.

8 November
We parade and clean guns etc, then paid 15 francs in the forenoon. It is a decent day. We have heard the Anzacs lost some trenches and got cut up. Damn dull place just like a cemetery.

The next day the military authorities looked for any breakdown in discipline following the issue of pay.

9 November
The C.O. has had a parade to see how many were drunk in the company. Nothing doing, mounted our guns for anti-aircraft during the afternoon.

Machine guns all along the front had been set up in the anti-aircraft role in case the Germans sent over spotter planes to spy on the British lines. The attack at Beaumont-Hamel had to come as a surprise, so any German aircraft had to be shot down before it could report what it had seen. In fact Angus saw no enemy planes as the weather was too poor for flying.

10 November
Nothing came over. I have received letter from George. Had a bath in the afternoon, relieved by next team at 4.00pm. Rumour is we go to Combles.

The next day the routine continued for the 88th Brigade; however Private Mackay begins to feel the strain of the last few months:

11 November
Wrote to George and Mrs Burr. Received letters from, John, Bob, and M.S. Had a parade at 9.30am, gas drills and stoppages etc. I am feeling damn rotten, never been fit since that 5.9 [shell] blew us up.

There were explosions at 5.00am on 11 November over at Beaumont-Hamel, as the softening up of the German lines began and the No.2 Special Battalion Royal Engineers fired 180 lachrymatory 4-inch mortars shells into the village. This was then followed at 3.30pm by 47 gas drums fired into the village and 39 into Y

Ravine, that kept the German defenders in their gas masks and protective capes all day exhausting them further. Over at Regina Trench, supplementary attacks all along the German line made by the Canadian 4th Division kept the enemy on their toes.

As the attacking troops moved up to their assault lines on 12 November, east of Beaumont-Hamel the 88th Brigade machine gunners were still in their rest billets, receiving lectures and mail. One of Private Mackay's parcels contained a gift worth a fortune to a soldier off the line.

12 November
Received a parcel from John and 300 cigs from Bob. Wrote John, William, Bob and M.S. Went to a service in the YMCA hut at 11.00am and got a lecture on tin hats. More frightfulness.

The frightfulness was about to begin at Beaumont-Hamel once more, as the Battle of the Ancre – the name given to the attack of 13 November 1916 – was about to start. The attack formations were helped as they moved up to the start line by thick fog descending over the battlefield. As the 44,000 attacking infantry moved into the front lines they found them to be in a terrible state; some units actually moved into no man's land to find cover. The experienced Highlanders of the 51st (Highland) Division knew that the shorter distance they had to cover when the barrage ceased, the better for them.

At zero hour (5.45am) the Allied troops went over the top, just as a mine exploded on Hawthorn Ridge (right of Y Ravine) to advance on an 8000-yard front. The attack was held up in the centre by heavy machine-gun fire and uncut wire and could not keep up with the creeping barrage. The fog also caused problems for the attackers, splitting the units up into smaller parties as men lost contact with each other, but it also provided good cover. On the 51st Highland Division's front some Germans had no idea they were under attack until the kilted attackers jumped into the trench beside them. The 51st (nicknamed 'Harper's Duds' after their commander Major General G.M. Harper and their HD shoulder patch) quickly stormed the 250 yards from their front lines into Y Ravine. Their attack was a complete success, as they captured the enemy lines and their objective of Beaumont-Hamel.

The 152nd and 153rd Brigade assaulted the deep fold in the ground at Y Ravine; the going was very difficult, the terrain was littered with the dead left from the attack of 1 July, as well as abandoned equipment. Fierce hand-to-hand fighting took place in Y Ravine as the 6th Black Watch and 7th Gordon Highlanders tried to force their way through at bayonet point; at one stage 100 men were pinned down by heavy fire. Men from the 7th Black Watch managed to move forward through heavy mud and got into Y Ravine, re-supplying the units pinned down there with hand grenades and ammunition so the attack could continue.

When the mine at Hawthorn Ridge exploded at zero hour it destroyed six enemy dugouts and buried 300 Germans (most) alive. The 5th Seaforths swarmed into the smouldering crater to take the German first line. The men of the 5th Seaforths then carried on over the hill and into what remained of the village of Beaumont-Hamel. As they did so, some of the men became bogged down waist deep in a sea of mud, easy targets for machine-gun fire.

The 6th Seaforths were quickly moved forward to come to the assistance of their sister battalion and with the help of the bombing platoons and Lewis gunners, the bogged down 5th Battalion moved on. The two battalions carried the fight into the second line and on to the third before two enemy machine-gun posts held them up. However those were soon dealt with.

The Highland Division had taken its objective, the impregnable village of Beaumont-Hamel, along with several thousand Germans prisoners against all the odds; they now began to consolidate the ground taken. The attack was continued on 14 November but no further gains were made, with the 1st/7th Argyll and Sutherland Highlanders getting as far forward as Munich Trench. A total lack of communication between the gun batteries and the front lines saw the Argylls so heavily shelled by their own British heavy batteries that they were forced to pull back. The Argylls had advanced too far beyond the artillery observers and stumbled into predetermined plotted artillery strikes.

The 51st (Highland) Division dug in their new positions beyond Beaumont-Hamel and improved their new line until they were withdrawn to Mailly Mallet Wood. Heavy casualties occurred during the two days of the attack on Y Ravine and Beaumont-Hamel, with 45 per cent of the 51st (Highland) reported as being killed, wounded or taken prisoner.

Today the Newfoundland Memorial Park stands on the battlefield, the trenches left exactly as they were at the time of the fighting. It remembers the dead of 13 November, and also the 710 men from the Newfoundland Regiment killed or wounded as they crossed no man's land on 1 July 1916. At the bottom end of the park above Y Ravine stands the 51st (Highland) Division Memorial, a bronze statue of a kilted soldier facing the German lines. An inscription on the base of the memorial says in Gaelic '*La A Bhlairs Math Na Cairndean*' (on the day of battle friends are good).

51st Highland Division (13 November 1916)

GIC Major-General G.M. Harper

152nd Brigade
1st/5th Seaforths
1st/6th Seaforths

1st/6th Gordons
1st/8th Argylls

153rd Brigade
1st/6th Black Watch
1st /7th Black Watch
1st/5th Gordons
1st/7th Gordons

154th Brigade
1st/9th Royal Scots
1st/4th Seaforths
1st7th Argylls

Pioneers
1st/8th Royal Scots

On the 51st (Highland) Division's right flank the 63rd (Naval) Division attacked south of Beaumont-Hamel along the valley of the river Ancre, from the villages of Mesnil and Hamel towards Beaucourt. The division had been formed at the outbreak of war, from a surplus of some 20–30,000 men in the Royal Navy Reserves for whom there were no jobs on ships. The Royal Marine Brigade was formed at the outbreak of war and was moved to Ostende on 27 August 1914, although it returned four days later. On 20 September it arrived at Dunkirk with orders to assist in the defence of Antwerp. The 63rd (originally titled the Royal Naval Division) also moved to Dunkirk on 5 October 1914. It had been formed in England in September 1914. At this stage, it had no artillery, field ambulances, divisional supplies or engineers in its ranks. In the haste to organise and move the units to Belgium, 80 per cent went to war without even basic equipment such as packs, mess tins or water bottles. No khaki uniforms were issued. The two naval brigades were armed with ancient charger-loading rifles, and these were only issued to the inexperienced naval ratings three days before embarking for Europe.

Royal Naval Division units that withdrew from Antwerp returned to England, arriving home on 11 October 1914. Approximately 1500 troops of the 1st Royal Naval Brigade crossed the Dutch frontier and were interned in the Netherlands. After a lengthy period of refit and training (scattered in various locations, and still short of many of the units that ordinarily made up the establishment of a division), the Royal Naval Division moved to Egypt, preparatory to the Gallipoli campaign.

By the end of the Division's part in the Gallipoli campaign, very few men with sea service remained. The division transferred from the authority of the Admiralty to the War Office on 29 April 1916, and was re-designated the 63rd (Naval) Division on 19 July 1916. It had already moved to France, arriving in

Marseilles between 12 and 23 May 1916, after which it remained on the Western Front for the remainder of the war. By the time of the Battle of Ancre, the 63rd was a battle-hardened unit.

The men of the 63rd's naval and marine battalions charged forward into the German trenches that November morning, trenches which bordered the river Ancre below. Again the mist helped the attacking infantry to gain access to the almost impregnable German lines, with the 189th Brigade leading with the Hood and Hawke Battalions in the front, Drake and Nelson Battalions following up in the rear. The sailors initially met heavy machine-gun fire, but the enemy front line was soon occupied and all objectives were secure by 6.45am with over 400 prisoners taken from dugouts on the line of advance.

One company of the Honourable Artillery (190th Brigade) – artillery by name but serving as infantry – secured dugouts on the right of the attack by the river-bank, whilst on the left flank of the 63rd Division the 1st Marine Light Infantry managed to link up with the 51st Division. The link up between the two divisions occurred near the base of Y Ravine and the enemy-held lines in Station Trench.

63rd Royal Naval Division

GIC General Sir A. Paris (wounded)

188th Brigade
1st Battalion Royal Marine Light Infantry
2nd Battalion Royal Marine Light Infantry
Howe Battalion
Anson Battalion

189th Brigade
Drake Battalion
Nelson Battalion
Hawke Battalion
Hood Battalion

190th Brigade
1st Honourable Artillery Company
7th Royal Fusiliers
4th Bedfords
10th Royal Dublin Fusiliers

Pioneers
14th Worcesters

Bombing attacks then continued at 6.30am with the 188th and 190th continuing to lead the advance; by 7.40am the Honourable Artillery Company had began to dig in along the German reserve trench and consolidate the gains made. However, fierce fighting hampered the gains made and held up any further advance by the 190th Brigade even though some units did make it up to the Beaumont-Hamel ridge and continued the fight up there.

By 7.45am the forward units of the 63rd (Naval) Division had reached the edge of the village of Beaucourt, meeting with little or no enemy resistance. This attack was halted by heavy enemy artillery fire and men from Hood, Drake and the Honourable Artillery Company were forced to withdraw and dig in. That afternoon these advance elements made contact with the 1st Battalion Cambridge Regiment (39th Division), on the opposite side of the Ancre, near a mill, and received supplies of grenades.

By nightfall the 188th Brigade had linked up with the right flank of the Highlanders in the German support trench, outflanking some German units in their front line. Reinforcements from the 111th and the 190th Brigade then came up into the front line positions and extended the positions taken into an area called Redoubt Alley.

The planned attacks were coming to an end and the 51st (Highland) Division and 63rd (Naval) Divisions were consolidating their grip on the enemy lines at Beaumont-Hamel. An attack by the 2nd Division north of Beaumont-Hamel had smashed the enemy trenches on the Redan Ridge, taking the enemy positions called the Quadrilateral. At Serre the 3rd Division's attack came to an end in waist deep mud that sapped the strength of the attacking infantry. Some of the formations did manage to get into the enemy lines but the assault was futile and all further actions were cancelled.

Behind the lines the 88th Brigade's machine gunners were oblivious to the desperate fighting going on at Beaumont-Hamel:

14 November
I am mess orderly for the day. We have handed our caps into the stores so I expect we will be off into the line soon. We then cleaned our guns, etc. I have received a parcel from home containing socks, towel, soap and some scones.

Mess orderly duties included washing utensils and the 'Dixies' in which meals were transported, not to mentioning the infamous 'spud bashing' – peeling potatoes. Other types of orderlies cleaned latrines, disposed of rubbish, helped the Army Service Corps bake bread or unload stores, and worked in the officers' or sergeants' mess.

In the front line positions the fighting was still going on as Australians from the 2nd Australian Division attacked German positions to the east of the Bapaume Road; they were stopped by heavy machine-gun fire from a German position called the 'Maze'. Further attacks on enemy positions in the Gird network of trenches were severely hampered by machine-gun fire from Butte Trench near the Butte de Warlencourt; this fire apparently destroyed an attack by the 1st/7th Northumberlands who were not heard from after that.

The 1st/7th Argylls pushed two companies into the south end of Munich Trench. By 7.30am the south end was taken and within the next hour the entire trench line had fallen to the Highlanders. At 11.00am British artillery shelled these newly captured positions forcing the Jocks to take shelter in shell holes at the rear. Over the remainder of the day the Highland Division consolidated its positions around Beaumont-Hamel, sending bombing parties from the 1st/9th Royal Scots into enemy positions. As darkness fell the Division's pioneers from the 2nd/2nd Highland Field Company and the 1st/8th Royal Scots dug a new trench called New Munich. Meanwhile the Germans evacuated Munich Trench line.

To the north of Beaumont-Hamel the 2nd Infantry Division swept through the German front lines and attacked enemy positions in Munich Trench south of Serre. Some of the 2nd Division units advancing across no man's land became lost in the mist and were badly cut up by a haphazard enemy barrage.

Units of the 99th Brigade (22nd Royal Fusiliers, 22nd Royal Fusiliers, 1st Royal Berkshire's and 1st King's Royal Rifles) then entered the 51st Division's line and advanced, entering Leave Avenue Trench north of Beaucourt. Realising their error and unable to hold this ground the 1st King's Rifles withdrew into Sunken Wagon Road, north of Beaumont-Hamel; however the 1st Berkshires' arrival in Munich Trench helped consolidate the line.

Bitter hand-to-hand fighting then took place, becoming confused as some German defenders surrendered whilst others fought on. At the top of Sunken Wagon Road the British regulars overran Lager Alley communication trench and then on to extend their hold on ground in Serre Trench. Troops in Serre Trench however were forced back in to the Sunken Wagon Road later in the morning, joining support troops from the 23rd Royal Fusiliers moving up to reinforce them.

On the 2nd Division's left flank the British laid a heavy barrage that stopped the build up of a German counter-attack from Serre. Enemy positions in the Quadrilateral (which had destroyed the 4th Division's attack on 1 July) were also overran by the 22nd Royal Fusiliers as this battalion moved into Lager Alley Trench. They then dug a trench to the Cat Street Tunnel.

Thinking that Munich Trench was clear of enemy troops and under British control, the 11th Royal Warwick' and 6th Bedfords attacked Frankfort Trench (just beyond Munich Trench) at 2.45pm. As these battalions moved forward they came under heavy machine-gun fire from Munich Trench and were forced to fall back into the Wagon Road, where they became mixed up with the various units already sheltering there.

These attacks were taking ground at Beaumont-Hamel but only trench by trench; losses were heavy as the British troops push forward beyond the village. Soldiers cleared the enemy trenches with bombs and bayonets, lobbing hand grenades into the German dugouts as they passed by. Hearing the cries of their comrades in other dugouts, many Germans left their own hiding places and surrendered.

On Wednesday 15 November 1916 the 88th Brigade machine gunners were on the move again:

15 November
Packed up and marched off at 9.00am F.M.O. Camped at Meulte, for the night, in tents about 6 miles away expect we will reach the line by the 17. Very cold.

The village of Meulte is south of Albert on the road towards Bray-sur-Somme and Peronne, and was one of the major jumping off points for the attack on 1 July. Close to the village at La Boisselle is the largest crater on the Somme battlefield. The 'Lochnagar' crater was formed when 28 tons (60,000lbs) of the explosive ammonal was set off under the German lines, two minutes before zero hour on that day. British tunnellers had placed the explosives in two chambers under the enemy front line; as the British artillery barrage ceased and the attacking British formations climbed out of their trenches and began to cross no man's land, the explosives were detonated. Leading units of the 2nd and 3rd Tyneside Scottish, the 10th Lincolns (Grimsby Chums) and 11th Suffolks took some casualties from the concussion of the blast and falling debris, but did initially take all their objectives that day.

The machine gunners began their move back into the support line trenches.

16 November
We got our guns ready for the line and marched off at 10am, we reached Ginchy at 3.00pm. We then started for reserve trenches where we settled down for the night about 3000 yards from the line. Bags of shells coming over, it's very cold. Two men wounded going up. We have relieved the 24th Company, 8th Division. This is a hot corner.

The Germans counter-attacked at 3.00pm on the 16th and retook Gird Trench; this assault was launched after a heavy artillery bombardment. The British and Australians holding Gird were forced back into their start positions in the front line trenches.

British troops who were still managing to hold new positions worked to consolidate them, straightening the British line and shoring up the battered trenches. Along the front from Serre in the north to Montauban in the south, reinforcement and replacement of the front line units continued under cover of darkness. Once relieved, the war weary troops trudged to the rear, passing destroyed villages, burned forests and thousands of white crosses where their comrades had fallen.

Once in the rear they were assigned billets in cellars, tents, Nissan or wooden huts where they could rest and dry their kit then clean their weapons and equipment. They had to be brought back up to fighting readiness as soon as possible, in preparation for the next battle that would surely come.

Meanwhile their replacements in the line would have spent their time re-digging and shoring up trenches, digging dug outs for shelter and repairing the damage done by shellfire. The trench line had to be made habitable for the coming winter; this meant the provision of latrines, communication trenches to the support trenches and the reinforcement of parapets and firing step, which now faced the enemy. As this work went on the Germans continued to shell the British line to try and disrupt the work. Both sides also aggressively patrolled no man's land searching for prisoners or causing a general nuisance.

In the line near Ginchy the 88th Brigade machine gunners were busy re-supplying the lines at dusk.

17 November
Received Scotsman *and a letter from John. Had a struggle with rations over shell holes and barbed wire in the dark, then got washed out of our dugout when we got back. Very funny to read about but I am damn well fed up. One of our chaps killed last night. Hun attacked on our left.*

18 November
Got a fire going and got our breakfast after some cursing all around. Rain snow and frost mixed up rather unpleasant. Hear we go up to the line in a couple of days. Leave is cancelled so that is one bright spot. Mud up to the neck. This country is not worth fighting for.

Morale was low, but could be improved by the issue of new equipment. As General Haig declared the Battle of the Somme to be over, Angus Mackay wrote in his diary:

19 November
Some muddy conditions. Sent postcard to John. Wrote to John. Had a tramp to HQ, got gum boots. Bags of shells as per usual. Some close shaves.

Gum boots were issued in an attempt to limit the number of cases of trench foot. Nothing could protect the soldiers from the shellfire though, a hail of steel falling from the sky like lethal rain. The barrage was constant, as artillery batteries tried to disrupt their enemy's plans, forcing soldiers underground, into cover and cause as many casualties as possible. These casualties further drained manpower resources as wounded men were carried to the rear by stretcher parties, often made up of front line troops rather than dedicated medical personnel.

The artillery took its toll on the 88th Brigade's machine gunners as it did everywhere else on the Western Front.

20 November

Our next gun got five men killed by one shell. Gillingham, Clayden, Scott, Little and Brown, all good lads and been with us since we left Suez. Received letter from home. We go into 1st Line tomorrow morning. Better weather in last 24hrs.

These five soldiers were killed outright in the explosion. Today they lie together close to where they fell at Guards Cemetery, Lesbœufs, Somme, Plot VII, Graves B1 through to 5B.

F.M. Brown
Private
9390
88th Battalion, Machine Gun Corps
Son of Martin Brown, of 72, Highfield Seamer Rd., Scarborough

James Clayden
Private
21434
88th Battalion, Machine Gun Corps (Infantry)
Formerly Essex Regiment
Husband of Evelyn Clayden, Tofield, Alberta, Canada

W.G. Gillingham MM
Corporal
21502
88th Battalion, Machine Gun Corps

G. Little
Private
21443
88th Battalion, Machine Gun Corps
Son of Robert and Elizabeth Little, of 65, Prittlewell St., Southend-on-Sea, Essex

Andrew Blake Scott
Private
20689
88th Battalion, Machine Gun Corps
Son of Mr and Mrs James A. Scott, of 1, Drum Terrace, Edinburgh

These five men were only a few of the 419,654 British and Commonwealth casualties of the Battle of the Somme, all to gain an area 6 miles by 20 miles. Over 600,000 Germans were killed and wounded defending this ground.

There was no time for Angus to grieve for his fallen comrades.

21 November

Packed up at 5.00am and proceeded to the line. We arrived about 7.00am, bags of shells coming over but we got there all right. Our position is in a broken trench just behind the firing line. Shells are falling all around us but none in our home yet.

The machine gunners had moved forward about 2500 yards to a position where they could lay down supporting fire for troops in the front lines. Angus does not mention the hard work involved in moving the Vickers guns, tripods, ammunition and his section's personal equipment forward through the communication trenches and into their new positions, but it would have been heavy work. Once in position the guns would need to be mounted, dug in, test fired and camouflaged, a task made harder by the muddy ground. The heavy German shelling continued.

22 November

We had a pretty tough time of it during the night. I thought Fritzy was coming over. He must have had the wind up as we had a heavy barrage for most of the night. However no one hurt so far and we get relieved tomorrow morning if all goes well.

23 November

Hell of a time of it last night shells like rain for six hours. One of Fritz's aeroplanes brought down beside us. We were relieved at 7.00am and got orders to depart to HQ for leave. Best news I've heard for sometime. Drew 50 Francs pay then got to Albert by limber.

13

Leave and the New Year

Angus's road home to his family in Scullomie was a long one; it was not just the 1000 or so miles of distance, but the fact that it was his first homecoming in over two years. He was a veteran soldier, he had seen action and he would have been changed by his experiences. He would also be returning to a family in mourning; one of his brothers was dead.

He would find Great Britain a different place; attitudes had hardened as a result of the long casualty lists since 1914. Thousands of epithets and pictures of the dead and missing appeared daily in newspapers across the country. Women manned the arms and munitions factories, worked in steel factories, drove buses and trams, filling in for the men at the front. This freedom gave women independence for the first time, releasing them from their traditional roles of wife and mother. Many men disliked this but the female workers were vital to the war effort.

But first he had to get out of France. He and his fellows were in Albert, once a small rural town, but by November 1916 it was badly damaged and home to thousands of Allied soldiers living in its bombed out houses and cellars. The civilian population had gone, leaving their homes and the huge church in the centre of the town with its damaged golden dome roof and the basilica with the effigy of the Virgin Mary, which leant at a right angle as a result of shellfire. It was said that when this effigy fell into the street below the war would end; it fell in the summer of 1918, a few months before the Armistice.

Albert today with its rural French houses, pretty cafés, shops and rebuilt church, stands in total contrast to the Albert of 1916. A visit to the museum built under the church allows one to gaze into the resurrected bunkers, with dummy soldiers and weapons standing guard. A glimpse into the tunnels reveals telephone lines and cables.

In November 1916, Angus was only concerned about his leave, while around him the guns roared and khaki clad soldiers continued to move into the line.

24 November

Hung around Albert station until 4.00am then got into cattle trucks and got to Amiens at 10.00am. It was rough travelling. I was damn glad when we got to Havre [Le Havre] at 12.00pm. No boat tonight so we had a kip in some sheds.

The journey crammed into cattle trucks would not have been a comfortable one as the train jostled through the darkened French countryside, and the move to Le Havre from Amiens would have been slow. After their night in the sheds the machine gunners headed for the ship that would take them across the English Channel.

25 November

Paraded at 3.00pm and marched to harbour. I got an extra 2 days so that's so much to the good. We had some tea at the YMCA and got on board at 6.00pm. Boat set off at 6.30pm.

The extra two days were travelling time because of the distance Angus had to travel from the south coast of England to the Highlands of Scotland, the entire length of the United Kingdom. He does not say where he landed on his return to Blighty but his journey to Scullomie would have involved travelling by train through England into Scotland, changing train at Edinburgh or Glasgow then travelling on to Inverness, before catching a train to the village of Lairg in the Highlands.

Once he left the train at Lairg the last leg of his journey through 38 miles of barren countryside must have seemed an eternity. At his journey's end he would have seen the Kyle of Tongue, with the village of Tongue nestling beneath Ben Loyal with the Munro Ben Hope way in the distance. He must have gotten a great welcome from his parents and friends. No doubt the whiskey flowed.

Unfortunately Angus made no entries in his diaries for the duration of his leave; his thoughts and fears can only be guessed at. He must have made a great impression on his family, coming home in his front line uniform, carrying his kit including rifle and bayonet. No doubt he told many tales of his exploits in Gallipoli, Suez and at the Somme.

4 December

I left Scullomie at 5.30am and got on the mail car for Lairg where we arrived at 11am. About 4 inches of snow. Robbie [his older brother] and D Mackay came to Lairg station. Had a good dram there. Arrived in Leith at about 9.30pm and met John [his brother in the Leith Police] and J. Paxton. Had a night in 61 Restalrig Road [John's house] damn pity it was not a week.

The following day he went out visiting around Leith.

5 December

Got up at 8.00am and had a general visit all over along with John. I saw Diane and Harriet and also visited my old boss. To my sorrow I had to terminate my spells in Leith at 10.20pm when I get on board and proceeded to London en-route for the war. W Mowat, McGourley, Paxton, Alex and John were at the station.

His brother's house at 61 Restalrig Road is not there today, demolished to make way for a block of flats, although number 63 still stands. Angus no doubt would have had many a dram with the friends, work colleagues and mates he visited that day and it was probably with a heavy heart he caught the night train from Waverley Station, heading for London and back to the war.

The night train arrived in London at 7.30am the following day:

6 December

Arrived at King's Cross at 7.30am, had dinner and breakfast all in one and then wandered over London in buses. I was so lost that all my grand intentions of visiting Jack and Hugh Munro had a flight. We eventually got to Waterloo and dumped our kit in the Union Jack Club about 12.00pm. Then we had spell of bar drinking etc until 2.30am when we got our kit and a present of socks, scarf etc and got on board a train for Southampton where we arrived at 5.30pm. Went straight on board ship.

The Union Jack Club was a privately run transit camp near Waterloo station, complete with dormitories and storage areas for kit. To Angus and his friends, London must have seemed a huge and exciting place full of the hustle and bustle of life. Even though it was less than 100 miles from the front, London was far removed from the fighting; only the Zeppelin attacks later on would bring the war home to the civilians.

The UJC is still a British forces hotel today, providing accommodation for soldiers as they travel through London en route to their units around the world. Unlike when Angus stayed there, it now has both male and female accommodation, as well as a family section.

Angus's train to the troop ship would have been packed with soldiers returning to the front from leave, newly trained recruits heading into the lines to replace the losses of the Somme, and men who had been sent home to recuperate from wounds and were now pronounced fit enough to fight. The crossing from Southampton would have been uneventful, the troopship guarded against submarines by destroyers of the Royal Navy.

7 December

I awakened about 8.00am and found we had arrived in Havre [Le Havre]. We marched to a rest camp and got some Biscuits and Bully. Think of it after ten days of high feeding. It is a rough breaking in.

8 December
Got turned out at 4.30am and marched to the docks where we got on trucks. We started off at 8.00am Very slow travelling but we don't worry going this way.

9 December
Arrived at railhead near Carnoy at 4.30am. No sign of R.T.O. [Rail Transport Officer]. So we had a kip down until 9.00am. Then we started off after a few hours tramping in the mud found our transport lines. Here we found our Company had gone to the Ville eight miles away for a rest. Anyway we trekked again until we reached Ville about 1.00pm and found our section in a café killing time.

The 88th Brigade machine gunners were still on the Somme; there is no settlement called Ville in the region, however the French for town is 'Ville' so the machine gunners were presumably in a place christened 'Ville' by the soldiers. The café they visited would have done a brisk trade with the soldiers, selling them wine and the soldier's favourite meal of egg and chips.

The routine of military life had changed little whilst Angus had been away, the usual round of mail and poor food.

10 December
Nothing much doing. We are billeted in a loft. I got a parcel from home, Stevenson, and Mrs Burr, also a Scotsman *and a* Journal *from Jock. Wrote to John, home and George.*

His family at home had not forgotten him and his mail began to flow again; the food parcels were a welcome supplement to Army rations, and newspapers kept Angus up to date with current affairs and the life he had left back home. They would also have kept him appraised of the casualty lists from the Somme; many of the names would have been known to him.

11 December
On guard all day. Rum was issued to cheer us up at 5.00pm. I came off guard at 7.00pm.

12 December
Cleaned guns in the morning. Nothing doing owing to the rain, very cold. We expect to shift tomorrow. Back for a rest. Wrote to Bob Stevenson. Sent postcard to Ritchie and Paxton.

The 29th Division badly needed a rest in order to receive new drafts of men and refit with new equipment. Rumours of an imminent move persisted.

13 December
Wrote to Sandy. There is nothing doing today. Rations are very bad. Bully and biscuits for breakfast, dinner and tea. Rumour says we go to Amiens for six weeks rest. Roll on. Pretty decent weather though.

The city of Amiens, about 20 miles behind the lines from Albert, was the rear base area for the British in the Somme region. Supplies from the channel ports arrived there by rail through Abbeville before being transported into the lines by the men of the Army Service Corps. The road from Amiens to Albert was the main artery feeding the front. All around Amiens were large rest camps where the men could recover. Other units were billeted in the French villages behind the lines.

The rumours of a move had been true.

14 December
Same damn rations. We were paraded at 11.30am and marched to Buire where we entrained for Hangest. We are carrying 2 days worth of Bully and Biscuits. Arrived in Hangest at 6.00pm. Had a march to a village two kilos where we spent the night in a barn.

The empty buildings where the soldiers were billeted had been vacated by civilians who had moved out of the battle area. All along the front, men turned empty French villages into their new homes, the unit billeting officers chalking unit names on house doors and barn walls.

The machine gunners' new billets were northwest of Amiens along the river Somme, on one of the main supply routes to the coast. The barn Angus mentions could have been in any number of villages around the modern French village of Hangest sur Somme; the closest village today is Bourdon, north across the river.

The next day they were on the move again.

15 December
Rations ditto. We paraded at 11.20pm and had a march to Moullins Vidame about 14 kilos away. We arrived at about 3.30pm. Billeted in a tumbledown barn. Received parcel from M.S. containing cakes, cigs, socks and a [writing] pad.

They had moved south into the countryside west of Amiens, travelling a route through the villages of Soues, le Mesge, Riencourt and Oissy on their way to Moullins. The village where they stayed is today called Moullins-Dreuil rather than Moullins-Vidame as in the diary entry. The diary clearly shows the efficiency of the British Army mail system, which delivered Private Mackay's parcel to his new 'tumbledown' billet on the day of his move.

16 December
Had a go at orderly buff for breakfast but I was put on guard at 11.00am as the guard on duty was not up to the mark. Received letters from K. McLeod. Cold and wet sort of climate.

Angus gives no indication of why the man he relived from guard duty was not up to the mark; he may have been unwell or simply dog tired from days in the line. Even 30 miles behind the lines guard duty was still important; enemy spies were believed to be everywhere and units were responsible for their own security both in and out of the lines. Sentries also acted as guides to visiting dignitaries and as fire pickets.

17 December
Received letter from home, Bob [his brother Robert], Stevenson, M.S [Murdo Sutherland], Turner [Private S.B. Turner Machine Gun Corps, Base Depot S/18 APO, BEF] and William [his brother in Edinburgh]. Wrote to K McLeod, William and Turner. Nothing much doing, dodged church parade.

18 December
Wrote to W. Mowat and M.S. Parade at 7.30am for physical jerks. Mounted guard for the rest of the day. There is nothing much doing. Very dull place to spend Xmas and New Year. Wrote Don and David Mackenzie.

The chill of winter was penetrating Private Mackay's bones, but at least he had shelter; the men at the front had only the star filled skies and a covering of snow.

19 December
Had a standard test during the forenoon, passed alright. Damn cold job. Received letter from George. Roll on pay day we are all broke.

Payday was not far away; this was a chance to buy some extras.

20 December
Wrote to John. Drew the handsome sum of 10 Francs. Just enough to buy a packet of Woodbines.

The soldiers were bored and whenever soldiers are bored the cards come out to pass the evenings.

21 December
Lost the damn lot at Pontoon. Usual parades, miserable weather.

All along the British lines the soldiers huddled over their braziers to keep warm. Not much fighting was going on, but patrols still probed in no man's land and artillery and machine fire was laid on the enemy trenches to keep the sentries' heads down and limit the movement of patrols. There was no Christmas truce on the Western Front in 1916 as there had been in 1914; too many had died for there to be any inclination to fraternise amongst the soldiers.

Behind the lines the routine was tedious; after the hell and thrill of battle, experienced soldiers did not take garrison life seriously.

22 December
Very cold. Physical jerks again before breakfast. Very dull time.

Even mail from home couldn't raise a smile.

23 December
Received Press and Journal *and* Scotsman *a consolation prize.*

Christmas in France away from his loved ones in Scullomie and Edinburgh was laying heavily on Angus's mind.

24 December
I'm still going on as usual. It's rotten weather, very wet and very cold. If France has been like this all the time it accounts for the inhabitants sore deals. This climate would make a brass monkey grow whiskers.

Even Christmas Day failed to raise spirits as no celebration was laid on.

25 December
Xmas day. Some Xmas, cold tea and bacon for breakfast. Stew for dinner and damn poverty for tea. Roll on the end of the war. Not even a P.C. to light up the gloom.

There was hope for Private Mackay on Boxing Day, as mail from home reminded him he had not been forgotten, but he did pull a duty.

26 December
Orderly buff for the day. Splendid day, I got a pair of socks, some cigs as a Xmas present. Also got a letter from Bob, who is in Edinburgh, I hope he is having a good time.

There was still no let up in duties behind the lines; the guard was still posted but the smartest man could be excused, the 'stickman'. Private Mackay achieved the coveted 'stickman' status.

27 December
Received letter from home. Paraded for guard at 8.00am and got the stick. Received letters from John and Home.

Training continued in preparation for fresh offensives in the New Year. It also served to occupy the men, as there was little to distract them in the rest camps apart from the odd French café or Salvation Army hut providing glasses of *vin blanc* and cups of decent coffee.

28 December
Usual routine, wet and miserable. Gun cleaning etc…

Eventually the weather improved enough to allow the machine gunners to take their Vickers guns out onto the range.

29 December
Went to the range just outside town for some practice. Guns were going at 600 [rounds] a minute. Pretty decent score at 400 yards.

Things were looking up as the New Year approached.

30 December
Usual parades. Received letter from Kate Macleod and a parcel containing brandy from Reid. New Year is going to be brighter than Xmas, anyhow roll on Hogmanay night.

The year of 1916 was drawing to a close; Private Angus Mackay had been through some of the worst fighting of the war so far. He had come through the carnage of the Somme unscathed, although there had been a few close calls. Unlike almost 20,000 of his comrades he had survived the bloody 1 July. Over a million British, Commonwealth, French and German troops had died on the Somme battlefield.

Considerations of what the New Year might hold were far from his mind; rather he was concerned with thoughts of his friends from Scullomie and Tongue serving in the British Army around the world.

31 December
Received letter from Turner also Scotsman from Jock. I won 3 francs at pontoon. Bright little gathering in café to celebrate the occasion. Nothing like the old times in Scullomie. Where are all the boys tonight?

Many of his friends had been killed in action; of the 75 men from Tongue serving in the forces, 15 came from Scullomie. Most of the men were in the British Army on the Western Front serving in the infantry, mainly the Seaforth Highlanders, the local regiment at that time. Others were serving in the support units of the Royal Engineers, Royal Artillery, motor transport units and the newly formed Tank Corps in the front line. Some of the men were in the Royal Naval Reserve on board Royal Navy ships.

On that night Angus's diary entry includes a poem.

Awake, for morning in the bowl of night,
Has flung the stone that puts the star to flight,
And Lo the hunter of the east is caught,
The sultans currents in a blaze of lights.

Omar Khayam

The New Year brought renewed hope for peace and a conclusion to the war, as a memo entry states:

We have spent Xmas and New Year at in Mollens ViDame. I hope the next will be a brighter place. So roll on the end.

There was no holiday to observe the New Year and there appears to have been no celebrations held by the machine gunners.

1 January
Had a spell on the ranges with our guns. Our gun team holds the record for shooting so far. Cleaned guns after we came back. Otherwise it's a very dull day. Roll on pay day.

2 January
We had a route march. Just a pleasant stroll around the neighbouring villages. Good weather. I expect we will have a go somewhere on the Somme soon. This is too good to last.

3 January
Had forenoon on ranges. Snap shooting, also some sniping.

'Snap shooting' was firing at targets of opportunity, such as individuals moving in the open. Training continued for the men; they had to be ready for the spring and summer offensives.

4 January
Brigade manoeuvres about 8 kilometres away, very cold day. Came back about 2.00pm and got the magnificent sum of 10 francs. Some pay.

There appeared to be little to spend money on in the area.

5 January
Usual parades going on. Very dull time. Roll on when we shift. Received letter from John also a Scotsman.

6 January
Got of paraded our Coy on parade attack drill. So I got a day in. Got a Peoples' Journal from John. Heard we go to Carpice for a week then over the top near our old home, pretty decent weather but a damn dull place.

Private Mackay makes no reference as to why he got off the Company parade; maybe he was ill or excused duties. The following day he and his unit were on the move again.

7 January
Got a parcel from Mrs Burr containing cakes etc. Marched to the next village. Our team and Essex met in the Brigade cup-tie. Result Essex 2 MGC 0. Rotten day, nothing due.

The machine gunners were heading back to the front, moving from village to village eastwards towards the Somme battlefield. The mail followed them as they trained, carried out fatigues or supplied working parties to the Royal Engineer units who were repairing the roads that fed the front lines.

8 January
Wrote to John and Bob. On fatigues along with the froggies [French soldiers]. We are road mending at Chsey about 5 kilometres away. Received a parcel from home containing cake. Wet day.

9 January
Wrote home. Orderly buff for the day so I was excused all parades. We shift from here on 11th January so I expect another scrap before long.

Angus Mackay was an old hand by now and his predictions were correct.

10 January
We are trotting around all day loading limbers etc. Getting ready for the move. Rotten weather. However I expect the trenches were much worse.

His thoughts were of his fellow soldiers suffering in the unprotected trenches at the front; at least he and his comrades had tents to shelter in. The 88th Brigade was on the move again, back to the line despite the weather.

11 January

Rotten weather. Paraded at 9.00am F.M.O. and marched to Airaines about 11 kilometres away. We entrained at 2.00pm and arrived at Corbie about 7.30pm where we got billeted for the night.

The machine gunners had travelled about 45 kilometres to the east of Amiens, and were back in the Somme just behind the town of Albert. The village of Corbie was beside the river Somme in a low valley; the village would have been surrounded by the tented encampments of the British Army.

12 January

Nothing doing except gun cleaning at 1.00pm. Corbie is a decent sized town. But as we all stony [broke] that does not help much. Very wet today.

As the wait continued the soldiers filled the time reading and writing letters.

13 January

Received letter from Bob. Gun cleaning again during the forenoon. We got a bath at 2.30pm, a regular cat wash. Wrote to George after tea. It's very cold and muggy weather it must be rotten in the trenches. Still in Corbie but rumour says we shift in a few days for the trenches and then over the top. Something to look forward to.

Preparation for the return to the line were well advanced.

14 January

Went to the Kirk at 9.30pm. Received PJ and a Dispatch from Jock, wrote to George. Snow falling most of the day. Our limbers are loaded up and ready.

15 January

We paraded at 11.00am for CO's inspection. Getting everything ready for the off tomorrow. Very dull time as the funds of our section would hardly run to a packet of Woodbines.

14

A Frozen Winter

The move back to the front was an easy one as the 88th Brigade machine gunners got a lift. It made a change from marching.

16 January
Paraded at 9.00am and boarded Lorries. We had a voyage to Mansel Camp about 20 miles away where we got into tents for the night, it was damn cold.

The weather was bad; snow and freezing weather was making life even more difficult for the soldiers living under canvas in their bell tents. A number of innovations were tried during the war to help the men survive the rigours of winter.

17 January
We turned out at 7.00am in about 4 inches of snow. Rubbed whale oil into our feet to prevent frostbite, it's badly needed as tents are not bon in this climate. We are about 6 kilos from Combles. Next stop?

They were now back on the Somme battlefield to the southeast of Longueval, near their old positions; it was ground familiar to the 29th Division, the site where they had fought during the Somme offensive. The billets behind the lines now housed the troops garrisoning the front line for the winter.

18 January
Wrote to K Macleod, TB Turner. Nothing doing except cleaning up. We have been shifted to a camp about 300 yds away at 1.00pm. Good huts, best billets we have struck yet.

The huts would have been an improvement on the tents but it was still hard to continue the routine in the bitterly cold weather.

19 January
Turned out at 7.30am for drill. Had frost all night made it damn hard to get away from the blankets. Got 10 francs pay. Scotsman *from Jock. Expect we go into the line on the 21 January.*

The British military tried out various methods of protecting the soldiers against the cold weather. The old saying says goes that 'an army marches on its stomach,' but it is also true that a soldier with bad feet is of little use.

20 January
Wrote home. Drill at 7.30am followed by whale oil application to prevent frostbite. Hut inspection at 11.00am. Still keeping very cold but healthy. Time hangs rather heavy, nothing more than cards to pass it away and to make matters worse letters are few and far between. Received P.J. and a Despatch from John.

The days passed slowly, filled with the routine of semi-garrison life behind the lines. Only the mail and small luxuries from home broke the tedium.

21 January
I am orderly buff for the day. Received a letter from John and a parcel from the Duchess of Sutherland's fund. Killing time playing brag [card game]. Very frosty weather but healthy enough.

Back in Britain, local organisations were set up to gather money and goods for the troops. Women knitted socks, balaclavas and scarves which were then sent out to France. The Duchess of Sutherland, whose home was in Dunrobin Castle in Golspie, gave her name to one of these collections. The parcels were welcomed by the men, not only for the items they contained but also because they showed that they had not been forgotten by the people at home.

22 January
Wrote to John usual parades. Keeping rather chilly, we all look like sweeps, as our hut has no exit for smoke. We shift to the line tomorrow.

Soldiers would put up with a smoky billet rather than be cold; anything was better than that. The First World War soldier had none of the comforts of the modern day soldier, no thermal clothing, no sleeping bags or insulated combat boots.

The move back into the line was on again.

23 January
Paraded at 10am and marched to Guillemont where we went into dugouts for the night, half of our team went into line, we relieve them on Thursday.

Guillemont, just east of Longueval, was just behind the British lines on the Somme. The line had been consolidated towards the town of Combles and on south towards the French lines south of the river Somme towards Peronne and Saint Quentin. The machine gunners were to hold the line in support of the infantry, providing covering fire for trench raids and large scale attacks.

24 January
Felt rather shaky last night couldn't get warm, no wonder I awoke at 3.00am and found a row of icicles hanging around my lip. Rumour is we are in for a scrap.

As the move back into the line proceeded, the day would have been spent readying the guns and ancillary equipment. As he prepared to return to the hell of the line, Private Mackay's thoughts turned to his own precarious existence.

25 January
We got out of kip at 9.00pm. We go into the line tonight. Again we venture into the region where the game of life and death is played as frequently as pitch and toss was played along the shore of Leith.

The machine gunners knew that they might not survive the journey into the line, and once there they would be at the mercy of shrapnel and the sniper's bullet. It was a game of chance with poor odds.

The journey from Guillemont to the front line trench at Combles was only 3 kilometres and would have been made at dusk, the sky illuminated by Very flares and the flash of guns. The reserve and communication trenches ran parallel to the road which is still there today. The heavy mud meant that the machine gunners had to balance on the duckboards that lined the trenches.

26 January
Got into our trench in front of Combles about 6.00pm after a very exciting journey along duckboards over the open all the way. A very cold all night. Rum ration went quick. We fired 500 rounds to stop the gun from freezing. We made tea from ice broken from shell holes. There are 3 lines of trenches.

The temperature of the water in the cooling jacket of their Vickers gun was dropping as it lay on the parapet, so intermittent burst of fire would have been fired to stop it from freezing. As dawn broke an early morning call came from the Germans.

27 January

Shells started going over like a swarm of angry bees at 5.30am. 87th Brigade attacked a bridge on our left. We fired about 500 rounds at nothing in particular. Fritzy has got very angry and has been leading us a hell of a life ever since. However we get relieved tonight if we are lucky. Still very cold, it's freezing hard. We got relieved at 08.30am just as Fritzy started a counter attack; shells were falling all around us as we trekked back to reserve. We got to our G.P. at 12.00pm.

Angus's stint in the line was over for now. After 24 hours under shellfire a spell in the reserve trench would have been a welcome respite.

28 January

Read a letter from Bob containing 10 shillings and a paper from John. Turned out of our kip at 9.00pm and carried rations to the next gun. Then the old brazier came into play and with melted ice we had tea and bacon, we are soon getting our feet in. Shelling is still rather heavy.

29 January

Received a letter from Hugh, Sandy and Bert Turner. I had a decent sleep last night. Our gun is in a sunken road halfway between Morval and Les Bouefs. So we get any amount of old iron thrown at us. We get relieved tonight. Got to Guillemont safely at 7.00pm.

The British front line was in a good position, with good arcs of fire over no man's land and the enemy lines beyond. Once they had been relieved, the machine gunners made their way back through the communication trenches 3 kilometres to the rear. They then bedded down in bunkers.

30 January

Had a good night in dugout. Electric light and wire beds. Wrote to Bob, Hugh, home, J. Reid and Bert Turner. Had a walk to the YMCA about 4 miles away and got some smokes. It's a cold day, snowing. We are pinching wood.

The bare earth walls of the bunkers would have been shored up with timber or corrugated iron sheets to provide some insulation, but the men still froze. Every scrap of wood was collected for firewood to be burnt in braziers or stoves taken from bombed out French houses. Eventually men began to succumb to the cold.

31 January

Paraded at 3.00pm and had a trek to the trenches in front of Morval where we relived the 87th Brigade. Decent dugout but it is damn cold. My mate Gordon went into dock with frostbite.

The front line was quiet as both sides suffered in the depth of winter.

1 February

Got out of kip at 11.00am. Rather a job parting with the blankets in this weather. However Fritzy is rather decent this spell. Wrote to John and Sandy. Wish some letters would turn up. Relief due on 9 February.

2 February

Received letters from home and K Macleod. Sat up all last night keeping the home fire burning, it was too damn cold to sleep. Wrote home and K Macleod. We got ready for a stint, but it did not come off.

The British continued to probe the enemy line with patrols and trench raids, giving the Germans little opportunity to dig in. The Allied generals could not let the enemy construct deep dugouts as it risked making any future attack as disastrous as that of 1 July 1916. Aggressive tactics and pre-emptive strikes were the only way to win the war.

All around them the machine gunners they could see the build up and consolidations continue.

3 February

Tanks are moving around so I expect there is dirty work going on. We have been relieved by No4 team and I expect we will now get nights kip. The cold is so intense that it is impossible to keep the guns from freezing. I had to heat it over the fire three times last night, and then it froze again in 10 minutes. Received Scotsman *from John. Strafe going on over on our left.*

In the days before anti-freeze, keeping the Vickers at the right temperature was a difficult task. Frost caused the gun to jam, leaving the machine gunners at the mercy of a German raid.

The tanks Angus saw then appear to have gone into action.

4 February

Had our breakfast at 11.00am. Our chaps captured 100 men and 3 guns last night near Gueudecourt. Still keeping damn cold. We were relived by No4 section at 9.00am and went into reserve.

The strafe on the left – mentioned in the entry for 3 February – was support fire for a trench raid on the enemy lines, and the tanks Angus saw would have given support. The trench raid would have been carried out with a box barrage around it and the machine strafe was used to stop enemy reinforcements rushing into the front lines.

Things were on the up for Private Mackay and his fellow machine gunners.

5 February

Got our breakfast at the usual hour, 12 noon. We have a splendid little dugout, fireplace, chimney which is complete luxury on the Somme. Received a parcel containing a pipe and a Press and Journal from Jock.

As they sat in their warm dugout that night the machine gunners did not know that the British High Command was preparing for the Battle of Arras, in which the 88th Brigade and its machine gunners would fight its most desperate battle yet.

The war was now in its third year, and across Europe young men from many nations faced each other in trenches. On the Western Front, troops from France, Britain, Belgium, Portugal, Africa, India, Australia, Canada, New Zealand and other Commonwealth countries opposed the Germans and Austrians from Ypres in the north to the Swiss frontier in the south. On the Eastern Front the Germans fought the huge but poorly equipped Russian Army; in Mesopotamia and over the Sinai Desert in Palestine the British, supported by the Commonwealth, faced the Turkish forces of Atta Turk. There was even fighting in the horn of Africa as the Germans battled the British, French and Belgians to retain its colony in East Africa.

Thousands of young men lay buried in makeshift cemeteries or on the battlefield where they had fallen; many more had simply disappeared, drowned in the mud or vaporised by shellfire. Those still living hoped that this would be war's final year, that they would survive to go home to their families and live out their lives to die as old men, survivors of the 'war to end all wars'. Little did they know that 1917 would bring no respite, but rather fresh offensives and new weapons as the British tried to push the Germans back to the Hindenburg Line.

The Hindenburg Line was an immense defensive system built by the Germans after the Battle of the Somme, as the British consolidated their gains. Between October 1916 and the beginning of February 1917, construction was carried out using French and Russian slave labour; the end result was a line of heavy fortifications stretching almost 100 miles from Lens, near Arras, to the river Aisne near Soisson.

This line, masterminded by Generals Paul von Hindenburg and Erich Luddendorf, would allow the Germans to withdraw and shorten their front by 30 miles, allowing the release of thirteen divisions into reserve. These reserve forces could be rushed into other parts of the line to bolster the defences in case of another British offensive.

As the Germans prepared to retire from the Somme it was still bitterly cold.

6 February

Quiet day, had breakfast a bit earlier nearly got frozen before I got the old fire going. There are very few shells today. We get relieved tomorrow for another short rest. We had some revolver practice.

It was quiet because the Germans were preparing to move into their new positions; not much re-supply of the German artillery lines would have taken place, giving the British some respite from the incessant shelling of their positions.

The revolver practice would have been a welcome break. The Webley Mark VI revolver was the service pistol during the First World War; it weighed 2.4lbs loaded and had a 6-round cylinder for the .455 rounds. It had an effective range of 50 yards and was issued to machine-gun crews as a personal weapon; it was a hardy piece of equipment and proved to be very efficient in the mud of the trenches. It was also issued as a side arm to officers, trench raiding parties and tank crews, and used extensively by the Royal Navy and Royal Flying Corps.

The 88th Brigade was finally relieved in the reserve trenches just behind the line, when a fresh unit was moved up.

7 February

Got relieved by the 69th Coy at about 6.00pm. We soon beat it to HQ where after slowly freezing to death for three hours we got into trucks and bumped our way to Mansell Camp. Stew and bed in tents at 2.00am.

Relief had come from the 69th Brigade of the 23rd Division, made up of infantry pals battalions from Yorkshire. The Brigade consisted of the 11th Battalion West Yorkshires, the 8th (Service) Battalion Yorkshires, the 9th (Service) Battalion Yorkshires, the 10th Battalion Duke of Wellington's, the 69th Machine Gun Company and the 69th Trench Mortar Company.

The 88th Brigade was pulled out of the line back to Mansell Camp; the machine gunners travelled back to their HQ and then 12 kilometres to the camp. Mansell was a comfortable haven for the soldiers, having tents, showers and field kitchens, situated not far from Mansell Copse at Mametz. Mametz had been badly damaged on 1 July when it was attacked by the 7th Division with great success.

However, Mansell Camp was not to be the machine gunners' home for long, as they were sent further into the rear.

8 February

Turned out at 7.30am for fatigues. Some cursing going on. It is cold enough to freeze a brass monkey. There is intense artillery fire going on somewhere. Got into Lorries at 3.30am and had a ride to Coisy 18 miles away, we arrived at 7.30pm. Very cold run.

The machine gunners had moved further back to the small village of Coisy north of Amiens, an uncomfortable journey in open trucks. Coisy was a typical rural hamlet taken over by the British Army; soldiers would have been billeted in houses, barns or under canvas in bell tents. This far behind the lines, French peasants were still able to tend their crops, and supplemented their income by selling eggs and other produce to British soldiers weary of bully beef.

9 February
Decent billets but rather airy. Got a wash at 10.00am and then cleaned our guns for inspection. Got a fire going and felt more at home. Received a Scotsman *from Jock also a letter from home and John.*

Even after a rapid move, the Army Postal Service knew where the 88th Brigade was, a testament to how important the British High Command thought the post was to morale.

10 February
Paraded at 9.00am for gun cleaning, some job this after 16 days in the trenches. Passed the remainder of the day at pontoon, I'm 15 francs out. Hell of a rest place this one, bar, shop and coffee house and you have to get up damn early to get a look in. No blighty, fags or baccy to be got within five miles. Roll on the end of the war.

Cigarettes and pipe tobacco were important to the soldiers and became a sort of unofficial currency. Health ramifications notwithstanding, there was nothing like a smoke to calm the nerves in times of crisis.

11 February
Received letter from D M Gordon also a parcel containing shirts and pants from John. I was cleaned out at pontoon. Church parade held at 11.00am, I was damn glad when the padre ceased fire as we were nearly frozen. Wrote to John, home and D.M Gordon.

12 February
Exercise at 7.30am and then usual gun cleaning parades until 12.30pm. Rotten feeding this time out it was greasy stew every day and no pay yet. A damn rotten hole this is.

Up on the front lines the Germans' preparations to move back to the Hindenburg Line were well underway, a withdrawal that the British High Command were totally unaware of. The Germans also planned to lay waste to the ground they were about to retire over: wells were to be poisoned, trees felled to block roads and all bridges were to be blown in an effort to delay the inevitable Allied pursuit.

In the transit camp the British soldiers of the 29th Division knew little of this; however a rumour of a move back to the front was in the air.

13 February
I am orderly buff for the day. Usual parades and pontoon to fill in the time. Received a Scotsman *from John. Rumour we shift on Saturday or Sunday.*

Life in camp rarely seemed to hold much appeal for Angus Mackay, especially when he had to carry out 'orderly buff' or company runner duties. Despite the dangers and hardships he seems to have preferred life in the line. His diary shows that he just wanted to get on and finish the war.

14 February
Usual parades, we got paid 10 francs. Damn poor pay for this job. Roll on the finish; I would like a decent scrap to finish it for good and all.

15 February
We are still going on as per usual sloping arms etc. I have received letter from Jock also a Press and Journal, we are still playing pontoon, and I am winning so far.

Training continued, and for once Angus considered it time well spent.

16 February
I have been appointed Range Finder. We had a very interesting lecture from the CO during the forenoon. Then a kit inspection etc, we are still playing pontoon winning some this time. A thaw has set in, some mud around.

The role of range finder entailed target acquisition for the man actually firing the Vickers, through range distance calculations and accurate target identification. It was a position of some responsibility and the range finder was accountable to the gun crew commander, as accurate range, distance and identification was essential in a fire fight.

The rumoured move appeared to be about to take place.

17 February
It is a holiday as we expect to shift tomorrow ready for another scrap. It is still thawing, mud, mud and more mud. Cold weather is better than this damn sludge. Had a good night, blew some of my pontoon winnings. We move at 9.00am back to Mansell Camp by motor lorries. It's not much better there than Coisy.

As they prepared to leave for the line the situation changed, a case of what soldiers call 'hurry up and wait'.

18 February
Got out of kip early and packed up only to hear that the movement was cancelled. There was some cursing, believe me. Thaw really setting in, some mud.

The move eventually took place the next day. As he travelled with his unit, Private Mackay saw his experience as a soldier finally recognised.

19 February
Got notice to pack up and march to Lavieville [approximately 25 kilometres away] where we arrived at 5.30pm. It has come out on orders I am now acting Lance Corporal, I expect I will need to attend the machine-gun school at Comurs near Étaples, for a course of M.G. instruction.

Angus had made the rank of Lance Corporal, the hardest rank to reach in the British Army and the easiest to lose. His professionalism as a soldier had been recognised and he had obviously proved himself on his range finder course.

20 February
It is raining cats and dogs. We are paraded at 9.00am and marched to Mansel Camp where we arrive at 4.00pm. I am dog tired and no billets. We had a shake down in a YMCA hut.

The machine gunners returned to Mametz; the 15-kilometre march from Lavieville had taken them most of the day in the heavy rain. The journey over the rain soaked, lunar landscape of the Somme must have been difficult.

They did not get much chance to rest at Mansell Camp before they headed back into the line.

21 February
We paraded at 2.00pm and marched to the front line trenches at Sorely. Hell of a thick mud up to the knees and bags of shells knocking around. Settled down about 9.30pm.

After a rough ride the 88th Brigade was back at the front, an even more unpleasant place than usual as the thaw increased the volume of glutinous mud.

22 February
Received letter from home and K McLeod. It is impossible to sleep as mud is up to my knees and no dug out. Four days here will make us grow whiskers.

They were in the line near Longueval; the diary specifically names 'Sorley' but today there is no settlement of that name in the area. The village may have been destroyed or perhaps Sorley was the name of a trench system or defensive position.

Only a tot of rum was able to keep up the men's spirits up.

23 February
I had a sleep leaning against the trench, so I awakened feeling fit for the rum issue. We got a fire going after some cursing and growling. The guns are very busy today, mud, mud and more mud.

Thanks to his promotion Angus was able to leave the mud and head behind the lines.

24 February
Got a chance to slip out to HQ at Harwood near Combles for the purpose of instruction. Had kip. Artillery very busy, there is a rumour of a scrap by 27.

As the enemy withdrew from their trenches and fell back towards the Hindenburg Line, Acting Lance Corporal Angus Mackay fell out from his trench and proceeded back behind the lines to attend his first British Army training course since he had joined up. He was bound for a training school near the infamous 'Bull Ring' training base at Étaples, south of Boulogne in northern France, for instruction in the technicalities of machine-gun warfare, even though he had been fighting for the past two years. With his experience of Gallipoli and the Somme he could probably teach his trainers a thing or two about the Vickers machine gun.

15

Training at Étaples

The war would have felt very far away to Angus Mackay during the next two weeks; he did not know about the German retreat taking place towards the Hindenburg Line or that Britain's Russian allies would soon withdraw from the conflict following the first of a series of revolutions. This withdrawal was too late for the millions of Russians who had already died on the Eastern Front.

25 February
Marched off at 9.00am and marched to railhead at Plateau, arrived there at 1.00pm. We got into trucks at 6.00pm and got underway at 8.00pm.

The journey to Amiens was made in the dark through the rear of the British lines, over the Somme battlefield and through the destroyed town of Albert. It would have been an uncomfortable move from Combles to Albert, but beyond Albert the countryside was undamaged by war, making the 46-kilometre journey rather scenic.

On their arrival in Amiens, Angus and the other soldiers heading for the machine-gun course had a break in their journey.

26 February
Monday, arrived at Amiens at 7.00am, had about 4hrs in station and managed to get some grub. Got into train at 12.00pm and reached the school at 6.00pm. Seems a decent place.

The journey from Amiens to Étaples would have been a surreal one for a combat soldier, travelling through 110 kilometres (65 miles) of rolling French farmland, untouched by war. The machine-gun school was at Camiers, north of Étaples (or as the soldiers knew it 'Eat Apples'). It was at a main base depot with admin blocks, stores, workshops and tented accommodation for the pupils.

The area today is known as the Le Blanc de Lornel, and the ranges were nearby to the east of the present day Insitute Albert Calmette. Other ranges were at St Cecile Sur Plage.

Machine-gun crews who came to the machine-gun school were in close proximity to the Bull Ring base camp, a brutal retraining ground where soldiers returning from regular or convalescence leave were toughened up before they returned to the front lines. It was not unusual to see 20,000 men being drilled at one time, and the instructors were notorious for their brutal regime. They wore thick yellow bands on their sleeves to donate their teacher status, earning them the nickname 'canaries', as they had the reputation of never having been at the front. In September 1917 the camp's troops mutinied in response to their bad treatment; a somewhat fictionalised version of the event was the subject of a 1978 book *The Monocled Mutineer* and a 1986 BBC television series of the same name.

Luckily the students at the Camiers machine-gun school had no dealings with the canaries in the Bull Ring.

27 February
Tuesday, wrote to Donald and John. Breakfast at 7.30am, parade at 9.00pm. We had a general description of the Vickers gun, a mount gun drill. Clothing inspection and mechanism after dinner, finished at 4.00pm. We have time to spare but I think it will be interesting.

As a ex-TA soldier Angus would not have been used to the day in day out routine of a training camp; his basic training had taken place in a drill hut in Edinburgh over a couple of nights a week or on the weekends, and he had really learnt most of his skills at the front. However, it did not take him long to get into the routine, as each day blurred into the next.

28 February
Breakfast 7.30am, parade at 08.30am. Lecture on gun drill then knocked off for dinner at 1.00pm. Another lecture and more gun drill until 4.15pm. Gun gun all day, some school this.

1 March
Thursday, paraded at 7.30am for breakfast, usual gun drills and lectures until 4.15pm. Received letter from M.S. Splendid YMCA on camp also a good canteen. The camp is just outside Étaples Station, on a sea beach. Pity it's on the wrong side of the channel.

2 March
Usual parades. Range cards and range finding. Splendid weather. Aeroplanes provide bags of amusement as they practise attack here during the day. Passed the remainder of the day playing draughts and Bagatelle in the YMCA.

The machine-gun crews were learning about the complexity of range finding and range distance using a range card, a sketch of the assigned sector the crew would have to cover with their gun. The cards helped in the planning of controlled fire and acquiring targets in poor visibility, and the range finder in each crew would draw his own, continually reassessing the sector and updating the card as necessary to include new targets and changes in topography. The cards were also valuable when the crews were relieved, as they could be handed over to help the new men orientate themselves in an unfamiliar sector.

Training continued even at the weekend.

3 March

Parade is at 8.30am, damn rotten job this getting out of kip at 6.30am. Washing is to damn cold to be pleasant. However I am learning things about scientific murder that I did not know before. The majority of our instructors have never been in the firing line and they have the cheek to tell us all about the Vickers Gun. Our class finishes on the 16 March. Papers say our Brigade captured a piece of trench near Sailly.

The instructors were not held in high regard; some of them were senior non-commissioned officers who been wounded at the front and were unfit for further fighting, but others had held the cushy training jobs since the outbreak of war and had never seen active service.

4 March

Church parade at 9.30am. Rest of day nothing doing, I was appointed mess orderly for tomorrow. Had a quiet day reading in the YMCA and swotting up on the mechanism. I never thought my old gun had so many screws about it.

This was clearly the first time Lance Corporal Mackay had read about his gun in a technical manual, having spent two years learning about its more practical side. Now he was learning about the gun's construction and what made it work, how to repair it if it failed and how to use it to more deadly effect.

The weather was not particularly suitable for much outdoor training, and the machine gunners underwent a mixture of outdoor practical and indoor classroom theory.

5 March

Stuck my head out of the tent flap and found we had a couple of inches of snow for a change. Usual parades and lectures on scientific murder. Wrote home and to KB McLeod.

Lectures on killing were not popular; the machine gunners knew their gun was not an ornament, that it had been built for a specific reason.

6 March
Usual parades very cold. We had to keep in the hut as it is impossible to stand outside
due to the sandstorms.

Heavy winds battered the French coast, blowing sand inland from the sea making
life around Étaples very uncomfortable for the soldiers.

7 March
Broke as per usual. Snow most of the day. Damn cold day school this, sand and snow
storms all mixed up.

The next day Angus received terrible news from his brothers in Edinburgh:

8 March
Received a letter from John and Bob. Poor Don gone under on 23 February. He was killed in
action at ELARISH. May God help the old folks to bear it and roll on the trenches again.

His brother Donald had been killed in action in Palestine; the last time Angus saw
him was on Lemnos on 21 December 1915, during the Gallipoli evacuation. On
21 December 1916 the British had captured El Arish, from where they hoped
they could both protect Egypt and threaten the Turks in Palestine. Despite the
objections of their German chief-of-staff, Kress von Kressenstein, the Turks had
left two detachments in Egypt, one of which was captured on 23 December at
Maghaba.

This only left a 2000-strong Turkish force at Rafa, 25 miles east of El Arish
(now on the border between the Gaza Strip and Egypt). This was made up of two
battalions from the 31st Regiment and a battery of mountain guns, defending
a strong position at El Magruntein, to the southwest of Rafa. The position was
made up of three groups of defensive works, backed up by a central redoubt on a
hill; the position was surrounded by a cleared area nearly 2000 yards wide.

The British dispatched a mobile column under Lieutenant General Philip
Chetwode to attack Rafa, consisting of three of the four brigades of the Anzac
Mounted Division, the 5th Mounted Brigade (Yeomanry), the Camel Brigade
and No. 7 Light Car Patrol (made up of six Ford cars each armed with a
machine gun).

The column left El Arish late on 8 January 1917, and after a night march
they surrounded the Turkish position at El Magruntein at dawn on 9 January.
Chetwode's cavalry force was not well suited to the job of storming a strong
infantry position, and no progress was made during the morning or most of the
afternoon. Between 3.00pm and 4.00pm news reached Chetwode that Turkish
reinforcements were moving towards Rafa, and at 4.30pm, having made no
progress, Chetwode ordered a withdrawal.

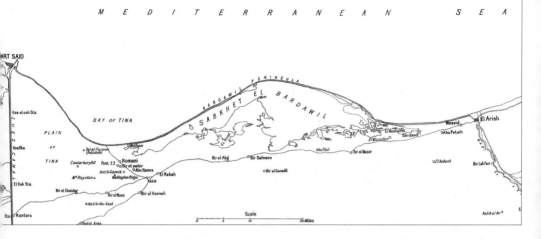

Just as Chetwode issued this order, the situation changed dramatically. The New Zealand Mounted Brigade captured the central redoubt after a bayonet charge. Soon after this the Camel Corps captured one of the three groups of defensive works. Chetwode immediately cancelled the order to withdraw, and the remaining two defensive positions were soon captured.

The Battle of Rafa cost the British 71 dead and 415 wounded, while the Turks lost 200 dead, 168 wounded and 1434 captured. With the British positions at El Arish now secure, attention turned towards a possible invasion of Palestine. The War Cabinet decided to postpone any invasion until late in 1917, after the planned spring offensive on the Western Front. Despite this policy, the British commander in Egypt, General Murray, decided to make an attempt to capture Gaza, to clear the way for the main invasion. Two attempts would be made during the spring of 1917 in March and then in April, and both would end with Turkish victories

Cavalry patrols kept the country up to and beyond Rafa continuously under observation; steps were also taken to bring in the local Bedouin tribesmen on the Allies' side. On 23 February, information was received that the Turkish-held town of Khan Yunus had been evacuated, and the New Zealand Mounted Rifles carried out a reconnaissance. They arrived at dawn to find the position strongly held; after manoeuvring the enemy out of his front line of defence and taking some prisoners, they withdrew without difficulty. Trooper Donald Mackay was killed in action during a cavalry charge, along with 33 others from the Wellington Mounted Rifle Regiment; he is buried in Plot C, Grave 90, Dier El Belah Military Cemetery, Palestine.

Continuous pressure encouraged the enemy to withdraw their garrison from Khan Yunus, and on 28 February 1917 the cavalry of the Egyptian Expeditionary Force entered the town, while the Turks withdrew to Gaza and Beersheba. The

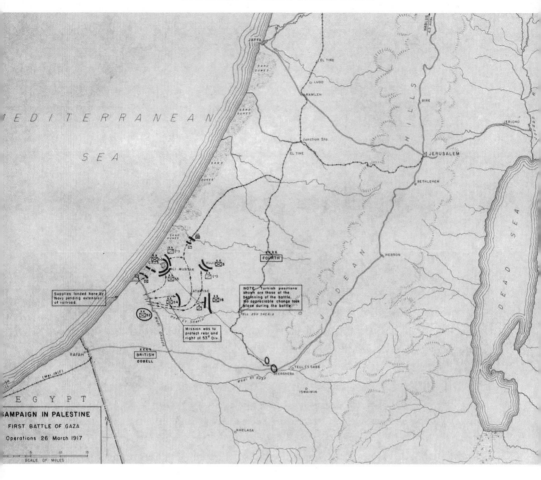

British railway was pushed forward to Deir el Belah, which became the railhead in April 1917, and an aerodrome and camps were established there.

The cemetery in which Donald was buried was begun towards the end of March 1917 and remained in use until March 1919. Most of the burials were made either from field ambulances from March to June 1917, or from the 53rd, 54th, 66th and 74th Casualty Clearing Stations and the 69th General Hospital from April 1917 until the Armistice with Turkey. Many bodies were disinterred from the surrounding areas, such as Khan Yunus, and transferred to the cemetery after the peace. It now holds the remains of 724 Commonwealth soldiers and ten men of other nationalities.

In his diary Lance Corporal Mackay did not dwell on his brother's death:

9 March
Had some practice on the beach swing traverse etc. It's very cold snowing still. Bad job this as it's always gives the Huns a spell. Got 10 francs, wish the course was finished.

Even if he did not reveal his own feelings, he did wonder how his parents were coping with this second loss.

10 March
Had a few hours on the beach doing stoppages and light tripod drills. Lecture by CO. Evidently they are preparing for open warfare. Received a letter from home with a note at the end from Bob telling of Don's death on 23 February. Poor mother she must feel it and the old boy also although he never says much. Concert in YMCA.

At least the machine gun course was proceeding well.

11 March
Attended church parade in YMCA at 7.45pm. It has been a splendid day of sunshine. This is the only idle day we get. The course finishes on Friday then mud once more.

Thoughts of the trenches were not far from the soldiers' minds. On the Somme the 29th Division were being relieved by the Guards Division, a process which had begun on 4 March and would be complete by the 20th.

Elsewhere in the world, US President Woodrow Wilson decreed that all merchant ships sailing in waters where German submarines were active should be armed. Russia would soon sue for peace with Germany, but the US – a much more powerful supporter of the British and Allied cause – would soon enter the war.

12 March 1917
Wrote home. Physical jerks for half an hour and usual parades afterwards. It has been foggy most of the day. Have not seen any papers but heard that our company had been badly cut up.

This diary entry seems to refer to a trench raid by the 29th Division's 86th Brigade who had attacked the German lines on 1 and 2 March. This raid – supported by the Newfoundlanders from the 88th Brigade – sustained substantial casualties of 19 officers and 363 other ranks. The Allied troops captured the village of Saillisel, east of Lesbœufs, killing many of its German defenders and taking 2 officers and 71 other ranks prisoner. The raid also consolidated the line and the gains made during the Somme fighting.

Lance Corporal Mackay had little time to consider his unit's losses as he took over as gun firer for the day.

13 March
I am gun Number 1 for the day. Usual parades. It is a misty day so we did not get any range practice in. Had a lecture on open warfare, which is expected very soon. It will be a bit of a change.

On the gun the duties were allocated as follows:

No. 1	carried the tripod and fired the gun
No. 2	carried the gun and fed the ammunition
Nos. 3 and 4	carried the spare ammunition and water
No. 5	section runner
No. 6	range taker

Thus far the war had been mostly conducted from trenches and in the narrow confines of no man's land; however the British commanders dearly wanted to break through the German lines into the country beyond, in order to fight a more fluid battle. Open warfare would mean the freedom to move through the countryside with tanks and cavalry, outflanking the enemy, rolling over defensive lines from the rear. In the event it was not until 1918 that the British, French and Commonwealth troops would be able to develop a truly modern fighting structure. However, the machine-gun crews practised hard for this innovative type of warfare, in the hope that they would have a chance to use their new skills.

14 March
Usual parades and practice at range with light tripod; it was a rotten show. Had our usual concert in YMCA and a rifle inspection.

The light tripod had been invented for open warfare to allow the weapon to be moved and set up more quickly. Mounted on a light tripod, the Vickers gun mounted came into action in 25 seconds, whereas it took 50 seconds on the Mk4 large tripod.

15 March
We paraded amongst the sand dunes and did attack practice with small arms. It was interesting but we have seen the real stuff too often to get excited. Spendid weather.

Time passed quickly as training filled the machine gunners' days, and the course was soon over.

16 March
Parades until 2.00pm then we marched off at 5.00pm and camped in Étaples for night. No damn rations and lousy blankets.

They were going back to war, rejoining the 29th Division to prepare for the new offensive, one which, it was hoped, would end the conflict or at least the stalemate of trench warfare. As Lance Corporal Mackay left the machine-gun school at Étaples, his Division was in the process of pulling back from the Somme and heading for rest camps around the French village of Cavilion.

Cavilion is 18 kilometres west of Amiens, 67 kilometres from the lines at Morval, where Lance Corporal Mackay had left his unit two weeks before. The 88th Brigade were now en route for their old billlets at Molliens Viedame. The machine gunners would rejoin their units as they fell back from the front to rest, recover and re-equip for the Spring offensive.

As he made his way back to his unit, Angus described his journey:

17 March
Paraded at 6.30am and marched to the station where we entrained at 10.00am. We travel via Amiens and Corbie. We arrive at Meault about 15 kilometres from the line at 5.00pm. Got some tea when we rejoined our company and I have recived a parcel from Mrs Burr. We are billeted in tin huts, bags of mud.

The journey by train from Étaples station would have been a slow one; the 103 kilometres to Amien would have been the fastest part of the journey. Moving the 20 kilometres to Corbie, then on to the village of Meault was probably done by truck. Meault – the small village four kilometres south of Albert – was the 88th Brigade's rallying point as it came out of the front lines and all the Brigade's infantry battalions, artillery, engineers and supply columns staged there as they moved out of the lines. The military police would have marshalled all the units and their equipment into billets or tented encampments to prepare for a move further back.

As he settled back into his unit Angus wrote,

18 March
We have been loading limbers since 9.00am Expect to begin training soon. Received mail from K Mcleod. Spent most of the day scrubbing up our equipment. What a hell of a life this is.

He was right; they were moving back to begin training for a new offensive north of the Somme around the French town of Arras. The Battle of Arras would see some of the fiercest fighting as the British put into practice the lessons learnt from the Somme – mass infantry attacks supported by tanks, and the creeping artillery barrage – in an attempt to break through the German lines.

The 29th Division was on the move north to join the battle.

19 March
Breakfast is at 5.00am. Entrained at Edge Hill about 4km away and proceeded to Airaines via Corbie and Amiens. Marched from Airaines to Mollens Vidame where we settled down in the old bilets at 3.30pm. Wrote home and to K Mcleod.

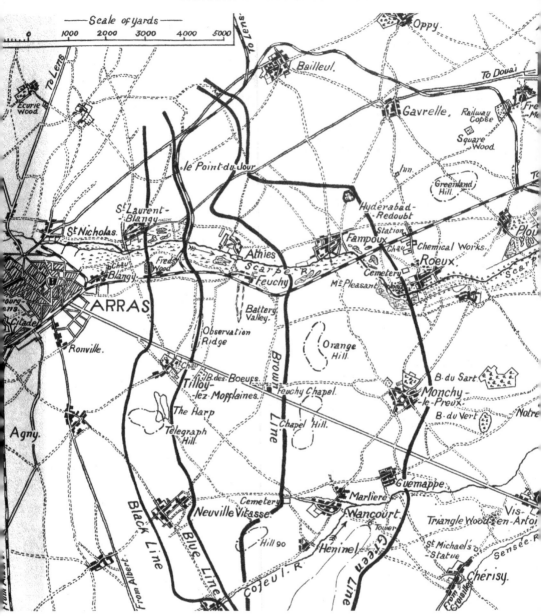

Edge Hill was a local railway station on the narrow gauge railway line leading back from the front to the supply depots in the rear. The Brigade's journey of ten hours covered a distance of 65 kilometres, so it was a slow journey for the soldiers.

On arrival at his old billets, the soldiers appear to be keen to get back to the fighting and Angus Mackay's training and experience was finally recognised.

20 March

May I get 1000 of the guns. Wrote John. I have been promoted to paid Lance Corporal. Inspections etc going on, it's a kind of a rotten billet this is a collection of draughts and waterspouts. Rumour says we are in for a long spell of training in open warfare.

The training began in earnest the next day.

21 March

Had a route march but had to turn back owing to snowstorms. Bully and biscuits going strong, we are all stony broke. I have been promoted to full corporal in tonight's orders. I am orderly corporal.

The newly promoted Corporal Mackay now had the rank of section commander and gun team commander. The rank of corporal is the lowest in the British Army which has any real command and control responsibility, as the NCO is given control of his own troops, while being subordinate to the troop or platoon sergeant.

The rank also carried more duties and an additional role in the daily routine of the soldiers' lives, as Angus discovered.

22 March

I am Orderly Corporal for the day. Paraded the sick. Feels sort of strange to be shoved up all the way at once. Received a parcel from Bob with a 10 shilling postal order in it. George [brother in the 83rd Siege Battery of the Royal Garrison Artillery] has won the D.C.M. on 10 February, good lad.

George Mackay had been awarded the Distinguished Conduct Medal, which was given to NCOs and other ranks for acts of heroism on the field of battle. The following citation appeared in the *London Gazette* in April 1917.

> 28242 Gunner G. McKay, R.G.A.
> For conspicuous gallantry and devotion to duty. He displayed great courage and initiative in laying a wire to the enemy's front line under very heavy fire. He set a splendid example throughout the operations.

It was an ongoing battle behind the lines to keep the men clean, fit and ready for action; dirty, louse ridden men did not have good morale and did not fight well.

23 March

We were paraded at 9.00am for baths. Rotten weather at 40 degrees below zero and muddy. I declined the pleasure and came away as clean as ever. F.M.O. immediately afterwards. Wrote to John and got 20 francs pay at a shouting parade.

The shouting parade was the unit pay parade. Prior to receiving their pay, soldiers had to march up to the paymaster's table and shout their name and regimental number before being handed what they were due and signing for it.

24 March

Usual parades. Taking cover etc. Had a rotten time in billets, it's raining steadily. If it does not stop shortly lifeboats will be needed. Had a spell at pontoon. I hear we are moving to Belgium soon.

The rumours were only partly true; as the 29th Division trained (unknowingly) for the Battle of Arras, other units were moving north into Belgium, in preparation for what would become known as the Third Battle of Ypres.

As the 88th Brigade's machine gunners waited to move on they tried to keep themselves busy; if they did not then the British Army did.

25 March

Church parade at 9.00am, nothing much doing except pontoon for the remainder of the day. Very cold weather.

26 March

Monday we have had a Divisional scheme, 88th Brigade defending, 86th and 87th attacking, we wiped them out or would have in actual warfare. Received letter from home and a P.J.

27 March

I am orderly corporal for the day, carried out sick parade, etc. Still snowing. My section is on the range. Clothing inspection at 2.00pm. Usual fried egg and chips for tea. No letters.

Things were hotting up as the training became more intense and realistic.

28 March

Parade at 9.00am Getting our guns cleaned. Had a show in the afternoon doing overhead fire over advancing infantry. It was a great success; our guns fired 10,000 rounds.

The training was almost over and the move north to Arras was about to begin.

29 March

We were paraded at 9.45am and marched to La Chaussee Trancourt 2 kilos we have decent billets for the night. On the move again tomorrow. Destination unknown so far but I expect we go north.

16

The Battle of Arras and the Last Entry

The British Army was on the move towards the French town of Arras. The British Commander General Haig had decided to attack the Germans there and attempt to take the high ground dominating the British, the salient which had developed between Arras south to the river Ancre on the Somme. The attack had been planned for the summer months but after the Russian military collapse following the February Revolution (which took place in March in the Gregorian calendar) the assault at Arras was to be launched early.

Attacking British divisions faced six German divisions ensconced in heavily defended positions, concrete and steel bunkers, deep trench lines with machine-gun posts behind 100-yard deep belts of barbed wire. The British generals hoped to break through the enemy lines into the open ground beyond, and then use their cavalry divisions in support to exploit the infantry gains and rout the enemy.

The 29th Division's 88th Brigade moved slowly north from the Somme.

30 March
Paraded at 10.00am. Our Brigade is in C & R. We had a short trek to Vignacourt about 7 kilos, where we got into billets. Decent sized place. Received a parcel and some socks from Sandy, also a letter from home.

31 March
Paraded at 9.00am. Cleaning guns and inspection until 12.00pm. Received letters from John and Bob also a PJ with George's photo in it, also received an Evening News. Expect we will shift tomorrow. I drew 15 francs at 3.00pm. Sent P.C. to John and home. Rotten weather it's very wet and cold. Roads too muddy to make our tour pleasant.

The daily regional Highland newspaper, the *Press and Journal*, had published a photograph and an article to celebrate Angus's brother George's medal award. It made a change from the growing casualty lists and photographs of the fallen.

Angus was right about the shift; as an NCO, Corporal Mackay moved as part of his unit's advance party. He moved to his new location by a rather novel form of transport.

1 April
Got up at 5.00am and cycled to Beauval, advance party for billeting purposes. It was damn heavy going, 20 kilos. Company arrived at 2.30pm. Received letter from D. Gordon. It's wet.

The advance party moved at the head of the unit to set up the new billets, and as an NCO Angus had to find shelter for his men in houses, cellars, barns or under canvas. This was only temporary accommodation, and the next day they were on the move again.

2 April
Paraded at 8.15pm and marched to Mondicourt. Arrived at 1.00pm. Just got into huts when snow storms began. Received letter from home. Wrote to DKM. This is a rotten village.

Around Arras, preparations for the forthcoming battle were well underway. Narrow gauge railways had been laid to bring ammunition, men and supplies into the lines, new roads were built, existing roads were improved, water supply lines were laid and a vast network of underground tunnels and shelters were dug under the town and out towards the front lines. These tunnels would eventually have electric lighting and tramways, and would shelter three divisions (over 50,000 men) from the German observers' view; the build up had to be kept as secret as possible. It had been going on since the end of the Battle of the Somme, and air operations were conducted by the Royal Flying Corps from early March. In early April the RFC knocked out over 40 enemy aircraft and British losses were also heavy, but they knew that they had to dominate the sky over Arras so that their airmen could spot enemy artillery. British artillery had been bombarding the German lines on a daily basis for months in an effort to cut the enemy wire, interrupt the lines of communication and supply, and wear the men down.

3 April
Wrote John and home. Paraded at 9.00am for gun cleaning, then gas drill at 11.00am. The ground is covered with snow. This village takes first prize for mud and filth, beats the Somme. We are making for Arras.

Angus soon realised that they were heading for another offensive on as grand a scale at that of the Battle of the Somme.

4 April

Loading and unloading, it looks like we are in for another 1 July stunt. Open warfare is expected roll on. Received letter from K Mcleod and papers from M.S. cleaning limbers at 5.00pm.

The British generals hoped that the Battle of Arras would be a totally different kind of operation to the Somme, with greater cooperation between the infantry and artillery, and the barrages strictly controlled by forward observers and aircraft. The rank and file knew that for all the strategic improvements, they still ran the risk of being cannon fodder.

The machine gunners were soon on the move north once more.

5 April

Splendid day. Employed during the morning cleaning out our billets and packing up. We then had a march past and an inspection from the C.O. Paraded at 2.00pm and marched to Le Souich, 8 kilos and billeted for the night.

The distance marched was actually just over 11 kilometres; they were now 36 kilometres west of Arras, and would have been able to hear the crash of artillery in the distance. All around them other units were heading in the same direction; many were already just behind the lines, ready to move through the network of tunnels into the front lines in Arras itself, in order to attack the German lines at zero hour on 9 April.

Amongst the units moving towards Arras were thousands of Scotsmen from the 9th (Scottish) Division, 15th (Scottish) Division and the 51st (Highland) Division; today the Battle of Arras is sometimes referred as the 'battle of the Scottish battalions'. The units included the Argylls, the Gordon Highlanders, the Seaforth Highlanders, the Black Watch, the Cameron Highlanders, the Cameronians (The Scottish Rifles), the Royal Scots, the Royal Scots Fusiliers, the Highland Light Infantry and the King's Own Scottish Borderers.

Routine duties continued for Corporal Mackay as he approached the battle.

6 April

We are still at Le Souich. I am the orderly corporal for the day. My section is employed washing limbers. Damn rot. They have bags of oil for limbers here, when we go into the line we cannot get any. Red tape.

The final preparations were almost complete and Angus was philosophical about his situation.

7 April

12 men from our company are being left behind in case we get wiped out. So things are looking up. We can look forward to a rather interesting time in the vicinity of Arras. I hope we don't come up against a brick wall like 1 July. Anyhow if it comes to the worst this is a poor life. We paraded at 11.45am and marched to Coullement about 10 kilos. Damn rotten place and no cash or fags. Roll on.

Before an attack 10 per cent of each unit was left behind in case the 90 per cent who went into battle were wiped out. This nucleus was then used as a base to rebuild the unit, with the addition of new recruits, battlefield replacements and volunteers.

Corporal Mackay knew the fight was coming and that it was coming soon.

8 April

Received letter from Hugh, who is in Cannanare. Cleaned guns and limbers during the morning. Big numbers of cavalry passing through us going towards Arras. Wrote Bob and K Mcleod. Smash expected near Arras.

At zero hour (4.45am) on 9 April 1917, General Allenby's Third Army attacked Vimy Ridge to the north of Arras. The attack was well planned and rehearsed; Canadian engineering units had dug huge tunnels some nearly six miles long, tall and wide enough for the heavily loaded soldiers to move forward to the front lines, and whole battalions of men slept in massive underground chambers, sheltered from enemy shelling.

British and Canadian Artillery units fired 1,135,000 shells (50,000 tons), onto Vimy Ridge before the attack, and attacking waves of troops left their trenches following closely behind the creeping barrage. The British infantry had been trained to stay close to the barrage so that the German defenders had no time to man machine guns.

South of Vimy Ridge the 51st (Highland) Division attacked German trenches east of Roclincourt behind a creeping barrage; with the 6th Battalion Seaforth Highlanders in the lead, the Division attacked three lines of enemy trenches before finally taking the third line trench (known as the Black Line Trench). The 6th Battalion, Gordon Highlanders were on their right flank and the 9th Battalion, Royal Scots from the 154th Brigade were on their left. As the artillery barrage moved, the Highlanders rushed forward and stood on the enemy parapet shooting the German soldiers as they came out of their dugouts. According to the battalion's war diary: 'this was a very effective way to deal with defending troops, most of the enemy dead were found shot in the head as the battlefield was cleared.' The first line of enemy trenches was soon taken with few 6th Battalion casualties; on the flank however a number of enemy soldiers managed to reach shell holes and began sniping at the advancing Gordon Highlanders. By 7.00am the objective was secure, but the Highlanders had taken heavy casualties.

In the centre of the attack the 9th (Scottish) Division attacked from the suburbs of Arras at dawn; waves of infantry left the houses and cellars they had sheltered in overnight and charged into the enemy lines. The German first line trench (the Brown Line) was their first objective; once this was taken the 4th Infantry Division moved through the 9th Division, assaulting the village of Fampoux.

The attack was an outstanding success; a creeping barrage helped the attacking waves cross no man's land and quickly overwhelm the German defenders in the first line trenches. The attackers quickly moved along the ridge above the river Scarpe taking the German trenches one by one; any German soldiers not killed were taken prisoner and sent to the rear. The enemy artillery positions at Battery Valley on Observation Ridge were abandoned by their crews; as they saw the Highlanders charge towards them with fixed bayonets, the Germans began to fall back. The 2nd Battalion Seaforth Highlanders had moved up behind the 9th (Scottish) Division; their war diary notes that they stood by a road 'watching batches of between 50 and 100 prisoners being marched to the rear by cavalry escorts.'

The enemy was now completed disorganised and their line had been breached; however no follow up operations could be mounted due a lack of reserves. The cavalry were too far away to be brought forward and even though the way was open right through to the German Headquarters at the village of Monchy-le Preux, no follow up attacks were made.

By nightfall, significant gains had been made: 13,000 prisoners had been taken, along with 31 heavy artillery pieces, 130 field guns and 334 trench mortars and machine guns, dealing the enemy a logistical blow. Only in the south – where British and Australian forces were frustrated by the strong flexible defence put up by the Germans – was only minimal ground taken. The British then began to consolidate their gains under a heavy downfall of sleet and snow. However, although the opening phase of the battle was generally successful in achieving its aims, it had resulted in relatively large numbers of British and Canadian casualties.

The British generals now knew they had to move forward fresh troops and exploit the gains made by attacking formations. As his unit waited to move forward Corporal Angus Mackay was becoming aware of the stunning open hours of the attack.

9 April

We are still in the same place. Usual parades. Drew 15 francs pay. I have heard we have captured 3000 huns near Arras. Damn rotten weather. No letters turning up.

As dawn broke on 10 April 1917, Canadian forces pushed on and finally took Vimy Ridge after stiff resistance from the Germans defenders, who had been told to hold it at all costs. The Canadians had 10,602 men wounded during the attack and 3598 killed. The Germans took over 20,000 casualties.

South of Arras, further consolidation was taking place as the British strength-ened their lines and reinforced their gains down towards the river Scarpe and up to the western edge of the village of Monchy le Preux. Meanwhile the 88th Brigade began to move towards the front lines in preparation to join in the fight.

10 April
Paraded at 9.00am, and marched to Gouyena [Gouy-en-Artois] about 11 kilos [actually 19 kilometres]. It's a rotten road and snowing most of the time. We have passed several buses full of wounded Germans. We have settled down in huts for the night 12 kilos from Arras.

The roads were in a poor state due to heavy traffic moving into the line, the problem compounded by the bad weather. Pioneer battalions and the Chinese workers of the Labour Corps worked round the clock to carry out repairs; many of the Chinese labourers now lie buried in France, thousands of miles from home, having been killed by shell fire and gas attacks while carrying out their tasks.

The news of the scale of the successes at Arras began to filter down to the machine gunners, and they could see that the enemy was being beaten back.

11 April
Parade at 9.00am. Gun cleaning it is very cold. There are thousands of German prisoners passing us all morning. It must have been a real push this time. Heavy fall of snow during the afternoon. Damn hard luck.

The German prisoners were being taken to the PoW camps to the rear of Arras. According to the Geneva Convention, which the countries on both sides were signatories to, sick and wounded military personnel had to be cared for, regardless of nationality. The Convention also recognised the neutrality of medical person-nel, hospitals and ambulances identified by the emblem of a red cross on a white background. Soldiers taken prisoner could expect to be treated humanely, with dignity and to be fed and sheltered by their captors. They were also allowed to keep their gas masks in case they were caught up in a gas attack.

The sight of the defeated prisoners being marched to the rear would have raised the morale of the men of the 29th Division as they waited to move forward.

12 April
We paraded at 7.00am and marched to Arras where we arrived at 2.00pm. Hard graft and damn poor grub. No billets on arrival.

The 29th Division deployed from Arras to join VI Corps; on 12 April the Division's brigades entered the lines with the 88th Brigade relieving the 12th Division, taking over the line close to Monchy-le-Preux during the night and into the early morning of 13 April. The 87th Brigade took over the line on the 88th Brigade's right flank, occupying the ground down to the river Cojeul. These two brigades now dominated the ground around the village of Monchy-le-Preux. The 29th Divisional Headquarters was in the Petite Palace Chateau in Arras with the 86th Brigade in reserve.

The 1st Battalion Essex Regiment's 88th Brigade's (not Angus's 88th) war diary describes that day.

Thu., Apr 12, 1917

The Battalion marched from billets at FOSSEUX to ARRAS [about 10 miles] and on arrival was at once ordered to proceed with the remainder of the 88th Brigade to relieve the 37th Brigade near MONCHY-LE-PREUX. The Battalion arrived at ARRAS at 3pm and left to carry out the relief 4 miles off at 6.30 p.m. Owing to intense congestion on the road and other delays the relief was not completed until 3.00am on 13.

Prior to leaving ARRAS orders had been issued for an attack on the German line in company with the 1st NFLD to be made on the 13 at an hour to be notified later.

The attack was to be made from an Assembly trench which was to be dug on the night of the 12/13 by 2nd Hants, 4th Worcs were in support to the attack.

Owing to the late hour at which the Brigade relief was completed & consequent impossibility of making adequate preparation for the attack the operation was postponed.

At daylight therefore on the 13th the Brigade was situated as shown in the attached map.

At 11 a.m. orders were received to make the attack at 2.00pm These orders also were cancelled a few minutes before Zero.

During the night 13/14 the 2nd Hants dug the required assembly trench and operation orders were issued to the Battalion. by Lt. Col. Halaham. App. B.

At 5.30 a.m. on 14th the barrage fell and the battalion left the trench & carried out the assault.

In spite of a certain weakness of the barrage the objective was gained and by 6.30 a.m. all companies had reported that they were busy digging in.

In the mean time 'X' Coy detailed to form a flank guard to the thence attacking Coys had at once come in contact with the enemy.

Therefore acting under Capt. Foster's orders No. 5 Platoon got into shell holes at about 0 1b 8.1 and opened fire. No. 8 Platoon being checked by machine-gun fire from ARROW COPSE No 7 was directed to outflank this copse with the result that No 8 could again get forward , capturing the 2 machine guns & driving the enemy out of the copse. The small wood at O 2a 7.5 was also in hostile occupation but was cleared by Lewis Guns & Rifle Grenades. The Company then moved forward to the N. end of the copses where all platoons came under fire from a line of hidden machine guns. The company now began to form the chain of strong points as detailed in operation orders.

From this point no further definitive news could be gathered as to the fate of this company. A few men eventually rejoined the battalion & from their statements it is certain that all Platoons their proper positions where they were at once attacked by very superior German forces & were finally overwhelmed in these positions at a time between 6.30 and 7.30 a.m.

The main attack by the remaining 3 Companies having reached their objective by 6.30 a.m. started to dig in and reports were sent back to Battalion Headquarters that large forces of the enemy could be seen in the BOIS du SART & the BOIS des AUBE PINES and that all covering parties were sent forward were at once coming under heavy machine gun & rifle fire.

It became apparent rapidly to the Coy commanders that an immediate counter attack was being prepared and this also was reported to Battalion Headquarters. These reports were confirmed by two Company commanders in person returning wounded from the main attack (Capt Tomlinson Capt Caroline).

Steps had already been taken to get the Artillery on to the points where the enemy was reported to be massing but owing to the destruction of the wires by shell fire it was an hour before the guns opened fire.

By 7.30 a.m the counter attack had fully developed in all its strength of at least 9 battalions. The weight of the attack seams to have come from the N. East & thus fell on 'X' Coy. This Coy in spite of a stout resistance was gradually overwhelmed. Vide app. C.

From 7.30 onwards no reports, messages or wounded men arrived at Battalion Headquarters or the Aid Post it is therefore apparent that 'X' Coy having been overrun the hostile forces got between MONCHY & the attacking Companies of the Essex & NLFD. No men have returned from these Companies.

As soon as it became clear that MONCHY itself was being attacked patrols were put out from Headquarters party to hold street barricades in MONCHY. No German succeeded in entering MONCHY. It must be remembered that during all this time the town was under an intense enemy barrage thus rendering it almost impossible to reinforce or support the two Battalions & making the work of the respective Hqrs parties extremely arduous.

Except for a certain amount of support from the 4th Worcester & 2dn Hants they fought on alone & these two battalions broke up a German attack designed not to drive them back but to retake MONCHY itself.

Appendix C. contains a copy of the Special Order issued by the G.O.C. 88th Bde.

Of the Officers who went into action the following is killed: 2/Lt. L. Cousins.

The following are wounded: - Captains R.E.G. Caroline, J. Tomlinson, Lieutenant. W.J. Taylor, R. Eastwood. 2/Lt's H. Ockendon, S. Andrew, F.W. Barker.

The following are missing: - Capt H.J.B. Foster, Lieutenant C.R. Brown, 2/Lts A.L. Piper, S.N.R. Eyre, C.H. Feline H.R. Newth, P.W. Coombs, L.F. Portway; G.W. Turk.

Total casualties 17 officers & 644 OR. out of a strength of 31 officers & 892 O.R.

Sun., Apr 15, 1917.

The remnants of the Battalion were now withdrawn & went to billets in ARRAS.

To the right of the Essex, the Newfoundland Regiment advanced at 05.30am on the morning of 14 April 1917. Under the cover of a creeping barrage they entered into the enemy-held salient to the east of the village of Monchy-le-Preux. This was the first time that the Allies encountered the German's new tactics of flexible defence. During the Battle of the Somme the German defenders had been ordered to stand fast, then to counter-attack to recapture territory as soon as it was lost. This tactic had led to casualty figures almost as high as those suffered by the Allied assailants. The new German tactic was a front line that would be allowed to give under pressure, backed up by reinforcements waiting to counter-attack in the rear.

The 88th Brigade was attacking on a two-battalion front behind this barrage, with the Newfoundlanders – commanded by Lieutenant-Colonel James Forbes-Robertson – on the right, with the 1st Battalion Essex Regiment on the left. The Newfoundlanders and Essex were attacking enemy positions in an area of the front known at the time as Infantry Hill. Having reached their objective the attacking units found themselves pinned down by a counter-attack by the 3rd Bavarian Regiment, launched from a wood east of Monchy, called Bois du Sort. The Essex Regiment took part of their objective but the Newfoundlanders were being badly mauled by machine-gun fire.

The gallant Newfoundlanders pressed on against the German battalions that were swiftly deployed in a counter-attack. Soon the Newfoundlanders found that they were being attacked from three sides, and by 10.00am their commanding officer was told that there was not a single unwounded Newfoundlander east of Monchy.

As the Germans surged forward, the only troops available to prevent the Germans from taking the village completely were those manning the Battalion Headquarters – about 20 men. Of these, only ten managed to avoid the German bombardment and took up positions to defend the village.

For the next four hours these ten men and a machine gun, under command of Forbes-Robertson – were all that stood between the Germans and Monchy-le-Preux, a pivotal position on the Arras battlefield. From the edge of the village the Newfoundlanders kept up their fire against 200 to 300 Germans until they were finally relieved. Their effective fire tricked the Germans into thinking that they

were up against a much superior British force, and they were not able to successfully mount an attack on the village. On the night of 15 April the 86th Brigade
of the Essex Regiment came out of reserve and relieved the 88th Brigade around
Arras, allowing the battered survivors to withdraw and recover from their ordeal.

Today in Monchy-le-Preux a Caribou memorial mounted on top of an old
German pillbox faces towards Infantry Hill to commemorate the losses of that
day and the handful of men who fought off a massive German counter-attack.
29th Division total losses were 45 officers and 1227 other ranks. A total of 166
Newfoundlanders were killed with a further 141 wounded and 153 captured. Essex
losses were 17 officers and 585 other ranks; 475 were declared as missing in action.

Corporal Angus Mackay was severely wounded as he fought with the
88th Brigade Machine Gun Company alongside the Essex Regiment and
Newfoundlanders that day. He was taken prisoner by the Germans and after he
had received first aid at a field hospital he was transferred to a German military
hospital in Darmstadt, Germany. His parents back home in Scullomie were initially informed in April that he was missing in action; however he was able to
write to them from hospital to say that he was wounded.

On 5 May 1917 Corporal Angus Mackay died from his wounds. He was buried
with full military honours by his captors. At the end of the war his body was
moved to Niederzwehren Cemetery, 10 kilometres south of Kassel in northern
Germany. The Germans began the cemetery in 1915 for the burial of prisoners of
war who died at the local camp. During the war almost 3000 Allied soldiers and
civilians – including French, Russian and Commonwealth – were buried there.
In 1922–23 it was decided that the graves of Commonwealth servicemen should
be brought together in four permanent cemeteries. Niederzwehren was one of
those chosen and in the following four years, more than 1500 bodies were transferred from 190 burial grounds in Baden, Bavaria, Hanover, Hesse and Saxony.
There are now 1796 First World War servicemen buried or commemorated in
the Commonwealth plot at Niederzwehren. This total includes special memorials
to thirteen casualties buried in other cemeteries in Germany whose graves could
not be found. Corporal Angus Mackay, Machine Gun Corps is buried in Plot 1,
Row B, Grave 12.

At the end of the First World War his name was placed on the war memorial
in Tongue alongside those of his brothers, Donald and Magnus, and 18 other
men from the village and surrounding area. Built by Mr Brock of the Inland
Revenue with public donations, and taken to the site by Mr Mitchell from
Ribigill, the Tongue War Memorial was unveiled on Saturday 8 October 1921
by Mr Alexander Mackay who had lost three sons, and Mrs Robert Mackay and
Mrs Burr who had both lost two, in the presence of the Duke of Sutherland. Mr
William Matheson and the Reverend Lundie led the service; psalms were sung
and prayers were said for those who did not return home. The proceedings were
brought to a close with the singing of the National Anthem.

After the Second World War another name was added to Tongue War Memorial; Flight Sargeant Alex Mackay RAF was killed on a Halifax bomber raid in 1944 over France. Alex Mackay was Angus Mackay's nephew, the son of Angus's brother John.

Corporal Mackay's war was over. He had paid the ultimate sacrifice as one of 158,660 casualties of the Battle of Arras, having survived the horrors of Gallipoli, the war of attrition on the Ypres Salient and the Battle of the Somme. He was only one casualty of the 702,410 British combatants killed between 1914 and 1918, and one of the 5,704,400 men and women who served in the British Army during the First World War.

The war rumbled on as he was interred. The 29th Division continued to battle the Germans for possession of Monchy-le-Preux, and the Battle of Arras ended in stalemate around Guemappe, Blangy and in the chemical factory at Rouex. Success at Messines ridge in June 1917 led to a new hell at Ypres on 31 July, when men of the British and Commonwealth armies died in their thousands in the rain soaked quagmire of the battle around Passchendaele, at which Britain lost 240,000 men for no military gain. The 29th Division was also to the fore of the attack when tanks were used at the Battle of Cambrai on 20 November 1917, when 45,000 men died as the breakthrough the British generals hoped for eluded them. The gains made by the tanks were lost in the German counter-attacks launched within a week of the British success.

In early 1918, with Russia out of the war, the Germans moved divisions from the Eastern Front to the Western Front and on 21 March 1918 they launched Operation *Michael* against the British lines on the 1916 Somme battlefield. The German attack was launched at 4.30am with 4,000 guns firing a heavy barrage on the British front line. Five hours after the bombardment, enemy 'storm trooper' battalions hit the British lines like a battering ram, attempting to force a way through. During the first day of the offensive it looked like they might succeed, as the Germans broke through the thinly held line and into the British rear area. The Fifth Army suffered a disaster and had to retire; whole regiments of British soldiers disappeared as the storm troopers attacked using new tactics where they bypassed strongly held positions.

British losses on the first day were 38,500 men, of whom 7500 were killed; Fifth Army alone lost 382 guns, and it was only the arrival of French support troops that stopped the retreat. The German High Command made some serious mistakes however, which robbed them of success. Their units had no armoured cars, no motorised machine gunners or cavalry available to pursue the retreating British troops, so the advance had to proceed at infantry pace. The storm troopers soon began to take heavy losses as the British defence stiffened, casualties the German High Command could not replace with fresh troops.

The British Army fought with its 'back to the wall' and the soldiers were soon exhausted by the heavy enemy attacks; some parts of the line were only held by scratch units of cooks, drivers and other non-combatants. Most of them had joined the army never expecting to meet the enemy with a fixed bayonet.

The German onslaught was held but the British had lost ground – over 40 miles in 16 days. With the German guns in range of Amiens they were finally stopped at Villers Brettoneux and Hamel. The Germans had lost 348,000 of their finest storm troopers, casualty levels that they could not maintain.

A further German attack was made on 9 April 1918 – codenamed *George* – launched in the Flanders area at Neuve Chappelle against a weak Portuguese Division. It had penetrated three miles into the British lines by noon and by the following day the Germans had captured another 24 miles, causing General Haig to issue his most famous order of the First World War.

> There is no other course open to us but to fight it out. Every position must be held to the last man: there must be no retirement. With our backs to the wall and believing in the justice of our cause each one of us must fight on to the end.

The Germans could no longer sustain the two offensives, *Michael* and *George*; they had taken heavy losses and had few reserves to replace them, and were running low on supplies. *Michael* and *George* were combined into one offensive code-named *Georgette*, which continued until the end of April; it cost Germany dear, 348,300 men against Allied losses of 351,793. These were losses the Allies could take but the Germans – at the end of long supply lines – could not.

The Germans then launched a further attack on the French on the Chemin de Dames Ridge, reaching the river Marne on 3 June 1918 and threatening to attack Paris. The French Army counter-attacked alongside US troops. Allied armies soon stemmed the German advance but with heavy loss of life. However German losses were heavier and discipline amongst the German troops soon began to break down. In Soisson, German storm troopers found the vast French wine cellars too tempting and were often to be found lying drunk in the streets. German officers found their units stopping in the face of light Allied resistance, and in some places officers lost control of their units due to drunkenness.

On the afternoon of 6 June 1918 the Allies counter-attacked, the Americans taking part in their first battle at Chateau Thierry, and finally the German attacks were stopped. The American Marines took heavy losses, and at Belleau Wood the 4th Marine Brigade alone lost 5711 casualties. However, the road to Paris had been closed to the Germans.

On 15 July 1918, 52 German Division attacked to the east and west of Reims, but the French had been warned by a German deserter a few days beforehand. The man had demanded he be allowed to keep his gas mask when he was taken prisoner, raising the suspicions of his captors. Under interrogation he told them about the upcoming attack, allowing the French time to pull back from their front line trenches just out of range of the German guns. When the Germans attacked they found the trenches empty except for isolated suicidal French machine gunners who cut swathes in the ranks of the advancing storm trooper battalions. The French then counter-attacked, driving the enemy back with heavy loss of life; it was the beginning of the end for Germany.

The final days of the First World War began with an attack by French and US divisions, as the new Allied Supreme Commander – the French General Foch – launched the Second Battle of the Marne on 18 July 1918. The assault in the Champagne region of the front was made with the support of tanks and French cavalry reserves, and was successful in making the Germans withdraw gradually.

On 8 August the British Army under General Haig and the 1st French Army attacked to the south of the 1916 Somme battlefield. This attack – aided by 500 tanks and 800 aircraft – was made on a misty morning and took the Germans completely by surprise; 30,000 prisoners were taken and 400 guns captured. The official German account states, 'this was the greatest defeat the German army suffered.' A further attack on 21 August along the Albert to Bapaume road took 34,000 prisoners in two weeks of fighting; at last the Allies could smell victory.

As attacks were mounted all along the German line, signs of the collapse became obvious. However, German artillery and machine gunners still put up a stiff defence and caused heavy Allied casualties. On 28 September the British attacked the Hindenburg Line and took more ground in one day than they had taken in three long months in 1917; a Fourth Army attack was also a complete success. The British had learned the tactics of modern warfare and were putting the hard lessons of the previous years to the test.

The German High Command were taking unacceptable losses for no end and decided to sue for an armistice; however there would be six more weeks of heavy fighting before the guns fell silent. Six weeks of stiff resistance put up by brave, stubborn German infantry who slowed but failed to stop the final Allied offensives.

On 11 November 1918 at 11.00am the guns final stopped; even on that final day the fighting continued up until the very last moment. Millions had died, their bodies scattered along the front lines of France, Russia, Gallipoli, Italy, Mesopotamia, the Sinai Desert, Palestine and many other places around the world. The stalemate of trench warfare on the Western Front had used up the youth of France, Germany, Great Britain and her Commonwealth; no breakthrough was ever made by either side. It is a matter of record that the survivors of the original BEF from the Battle of Mons in August 1914, found themselves standing very close to those positions they had occupied in 1914 in November 1918. The war ended very close to where it had all begun.

The 29th Division fought throughout the final battles in 1918: the Battle of the Lys at Neuve Chapelle in April, then at Ypres in September. On Armistice Day the 29th Division advanced towards Germany through Belgium; they had advanced 80 kilometres east of Ypres in the final few weeks of the war as they chased the retreating Germans.

When the armistice came into force the Division concentrated around the Belgian towns of Flobecq and Lessines, where they were selected as one of two British divisions to advance into and occupy part of Germany. The march to occupy the German Ruhr began on 18 November, with the Division advancing down two parallel routes in four groups advancing through Belgium and entering Germany at Malmedy. The Division continued until it reached the outskirts of Cologne on 9 December.

The 29th remained as part of the occupation force in the neutral zone around the Ruhr until March 1919, slowly shrinking as men were demobbed and sent home. New battalions of men from Britain replaced the war weary veterans as they went home to their families.

Angus Mackay was one young man from a small village in the Highlands of Scotland who did not survive the horrors of the First World War, like so many other young men from across the world. His diary tells his story and his feelings about what he witnessed and experienced. He left out the dreadfulness of war; however he knew that he was not immune from its pain and the possibility of death.

The final diary entry Angus wrote was actually for 10 August 1917, three months after his death. He clearly had no illusions as to the fragile nature of his own mortality.

10 August
This is my 22nd year. Don't expect I will get to see it. Anyhow I will be damn lucky if I do.

Appendix 1

29th Division
Order of Battle

The 29th Division was formed at Nuneaton, Rugby, Banbury and Stratford between January and March 1915, by bringing together units of the regular army that were on overseas garrison and similar duties around the British Empire. Training and mobilisation took place in the Midlands, in the area Warwick-Nuneaton-Rugby.

86th Brigade

2nd Battalion, the Royal Fusiliers (joined January 1915)
1st Battalion, the Lancashire Fusiliers (joined January 1915)
16th (Service) Battalion (Public Schools), the Middlesex (joined April 1916, disbanded February 1918)
1st Battalion, the Royal Munster Fusiliers (joined January 1915, left April 1916)
1st Battalion, the Royal Dublin Fusiliers (joined December 1914, left October 1917, rejoined April 1918)
1st (Service) Battalion, the Royal Guernsey (joined October 1917, left April 1918)
2/3rd (City of London) Battalion, the London Regiment (joined August 1915, left January 1916)

87th Brigade

2nd Battalion, the South Wales Borderers (joined January 1915)
1st Battalion, the King's Own Scottish Borderers (joined January 1915)
1st Battalion, the Royal Inniskilling Fusiliers (joined January 1915, left February 1918)
1st Battalion, the Border (joined January 1915)

88th Brigade

1/5th Battalion, the Royal Scots (joined March 1915, left July 1916)
4th Battalion, the Worcesters (joined February 1915)
2nd Battalion, the Hampshire (joined February 1915)
1st Battalion, the Essex (joined February 1915, left February 1918)
2nd Battalion, the Leinster (joined April 1918)
st Battalion, the Royal Newfoundland Regiment (joined February 1915, left April 1918)
2/1st (City of London) Battalion, the London Regiment (joined August 1915, left January 1916)

Divisional Troops

1/2nd Battalion, the Monmouthshire (joined as Pioneer Battalion, May 1916)

Engineer Units

2nd (Lowland) Field Company (joined 15 January, left 16 February, subsequently renamed 410th Field Company)
455th Field Company (joined 15 March, renamed from 1st (West Riding) Field Company)
497th Field Company (joined 16 February, renamed from 3rd (Kent) Field Company)
510th Field Company (joined 15 January, renamed from 2nd (London) Field Company)

Appendix 2

29th Division Timeline

16 March 1915
Sailed from Avonmouth, landing in Egypt two weeks later

10 April 1915
Moved to Mudros Island

25 April 1915
Landed on Gallipoli, at Cape Helles

28 April–12 July 1915
Battles for Krithia and the Achi Baba heights
The Division occupied positions on Cape Helles

2 January 1916
Withdrawn from Gallipoli and moved to Egypt

29 March 1916
Landed at Marseilles and proceeded to the Western Front

1 July 1916
Battle of Albert (first phase of the Battle of the Somme 1916)

1–20 October 1916
Battle of Le Transloy (eighth phase of the Battle of the Somme 1916)
(88th Brigade)

9–14 April 1917
First Battle of the Scarpe (first phase of the Arras Offensive)

23–24 April 1917
Second Battle of the Scarpe (second phase of the Arras Offensive)

16–17 August 1917
Battle of Langemarck (second phase of Third Battle of Ypres)

20–25 September 1917
Battle of the Menin Road (third phase of the Third Battle of Ypres)

26 September–3 October 1917
Battle of the Polygon Wood (fourth phase of the Third Battle of Ypres)

4 October 1917
Battle of Broodseinde (fifth phase of the Third Battle of Ypres)

9 October 1917
Battle of Poelcapelle (sixth phase of the Third Battle of Ypres)

20 November–7 December 1917
Battle of Cambrai

9–29 April 1918
Battle of Estaires (first phase of the Battles of the Lys)

10–11 April 1918
Battle of Messines, 1918 (second phase of the Battles of the Lys) (88th Brigade)

12–15 April 1918
Battle of Hazebrouck (third phase of the Battles of the Lys) (less 88th Brigade)

13–15 April 1918
Battle of Bailleul (fourth phase of the Battles of the Lys) (88th Brigade)

17–19 April 1918
The First Battle of Kemmel (fifth phase of the Battles of the Lys) (88th Brigade)

18 August 1918
The Advance in Flanders (took part in the Action of Outtersteene Ridge)

28 September–2 October 1918
Battle of Ypres 1918

14–20 October 1918
Battle of Courtrai

Bibliography

Arthur, Max *The Last Post* (Cassell Military Paperbacks, 2006)

Asworth, Tony *Trench Warfare 1914–1918* (Pan Books, 2000)

Bayne, John *Soldiers of Scotland* (Brassey's UK Ltd, 1999)

Batchelor, Peter F. and Christopher Matson *VCs of the First World War* (The History Press, 2011)

Budge, Ally *Voices in the Wind* (North of Scotland Newspapers, 1996)

Cave, Nigel *Beaumont-Hamel* (Pen and Sword, 2008)

Chorley, W.R. *R.A.F Bomber Command Losses Volume 5 1944* (Midland Publishing, 1997)

Coombs, Rose E. *Before Endeavours Fade* (After the Battle, 2006)

Creighton, Reverend O. *With the 29th Division in Gallipoli* (Naval and Military Press, 1921)

Darman, Peter and Ian Westwell *World War 1 Day by Day* (Grange Books, 2004)

Evans, Martin *The Battles of the Somme* (Weidenfeld and Nicholson, 2005)

Gillon, Captain Stair *The Story of the 29th Division* (Naval and Military Press, 1921)

Giles, John *The Somme Then and Now* (After the Battle, 1986)

_____ *The Western Front Then and Now* (After the Battle, 1992)

_____ *Flanders Then and Now* (After the Battle, 1994)

Gliddon, Gerald *VCs of the 1st World War Arras & Messines* (Sutton Publishing, 1998)

Groom Winston *A Storm in Flanders* (Atlantic Press, 2003)

Hart, Peter *The Somme* (Weidenfeld and Nicholson, 2005)

Henderson, Diana M. *The Highland Soldier* (John Donald Short Run Press, 2004)

Holt, Tonie and Valmai *Battlefields of the First World War A Travellers Guide* (Parkgate Books Ltd, 1998)

Holt, Major and Mrs *Battlefield Guide to the Somme* (Pen and Sword, 2008)

_____ *Battlefield Guide to Ypres* (Pen and Sword, 2008)

Jackson, John *Private 12768-Memoir of a Tommy* (The History Press, 2005)

Laffin, John *A Western Front Companion 1914–1918* (Sutton Publishing, 1994)

Liddle, Peter H. *Voices of War*(Leo Cooper Ltd, 1998)

Luxford Major JH N.Z.M.G.C *With the Machine Gunners* (Naval and Military Press, 1921)

Middlebrook. Mary and Martin *The Somme Battlefields* (Penguin, 1994)

_____ *First Day on the Somme* (Pen and Sword, 2006)

Mileham. Patrick *The Scottish Regiments 1633 to 1996* (Sarpedon, 1996)

McCarthy, James *Somme Day by Day (*London, 1993)

MacDonald, Lyn *1914* (Penguin, 1989)

_____ *1915* (Penguin, 1997)

_____ *1918 To the Last Man* (Penguin, 1997)

_____ *Roses of no man's land* (Penguin, 1997)

_____ *Somme* (Penguin, 1997)

_____ *They called it Passchendaele* (Penguin, 1997)

Persico, Joseph E. *11th Month, 11th Day, 11th Hour (*Hutchinson, 2004)

Pope, Stephen and Elizabeth Anne Wheel *The First World War Dictionary* (St Martin's Press, 1996)

Reed, Paul *Walking the Somme* (Pen and Sword, 1997)

Simkins, Peter *Chronicle of the Great War (Western Front)* (Continental Enterprise Group, 1997)

Steel, Nigel and Peter Hart *Defeat at Gallipoli* (Pan Books, 2002)

Stevenson, David *History of the First World War (*Penguin, 2005)

Warner, Phillip *The Battle of Loos* (Wordsworth Editions, 1994)

Westlake, Ray *British Battalions on the Somme* (Pen and Sword, 1997)

Westlake, Ray *Kitchener's Army* (The History Press, 1993)

Index